MUSEUM RHETORIC

RSA·STR

THE RSA SERIES IN TRANSDISCIPLINARY RHETORIC

The RSA Series in Transdisciplinary Rhetoric is a collaboration with the Rhetoric Society of America to publish innovative and rigorously argued scholarship on the tremendous disciplinary breadth of rhetoric. Books in the series take a variety of approaches, including theoretical, historical, interpretive, critical, or ethnographic, and will examine rhetorical action in a way that appeals, first, to scholars in communication studies and English or writing, and, second, to at least one other discipline or subject area.

Other titles in this series:
Nathan Stormer, *Sign of Pathology: U.S. Medical Rhetoric on Abortion, 1800s–1960s*

Mark Longaker, *Rhetorical Style and Bourgeois Virtue: Capitalism and Civil Society in the British Enlightenment*

Robin E. Jensen, *Infertility: A Rhetorical History*

Steven Mailloux, *Rhetoric's Pragmatism: Essays in Rhetorical Hermeneutics*

M. Elizabeth Weiser

MUSEUM RHETORIC

Building Civic Identity in National Spaces

THE PENNSYLVANIA STATE UNIVERSITY PRESS
UNIVERSITY PARK, PENNSYLVANIA

All photographs in this book appear courtesy of
M. Elizabeth Weiser.

Library of Congress Cataloging-in-Publication Data

Names: Weiser, M. Elizabeth, author.
Title: Museum rhetoric : building civic identity in national
    spaces / M. Elizabeth Weiser.
Other titles: RSA series in transdisciplinary rhetoric.
Description: University Park, Pennsylvania : The Pennsylvania
    State University Press, [2017] | Series: The RSA series in
    transdisciplinary rhetoric | Includes bibliographical
    references and index.
Summary: "Examines the role of museums in promoting
    cultural heritage and national identity, focusing on
    rhetorical understandings of public space and civic
    engagement"—Provided by publisher.
Identifiers: LCCN 2017017647 | ISBN 9780271079035
    (cloth : alk. paper)
Subjects: LCSH: Museums—Social aspects. | National
    museums—Social aspects. | Rhetoric. | Nationalism. |
    Cultural property.
Classification: LCC AM7 . W39354 2017 | DDC 069—dc23
LC record available at https://lccn.loc.gov/2017017647

The Pennsylvania State University Press is a member of the
Association of American University Presses.

It is the policy of The Pennsylvania State University Press to
use acid-free paper. Publications on uncoated stock satisfy the
minimum requirements of American National Standard for
Information Sciences—Permanence of Paper for Printed
Library Material, ANSI Z39.48–1992.

Typeset by COGHILL COMPOSITION COMPANY

Printed and bound by SHERIDAN BOOKS

Composed in ADOBE JENSON PRO, BERLING NOVA SANS PRO

Printed on NATURES NATURAL

Bound in ARRESTOX

To all whose hearts and minds remain
open to the stranger.

Cuando a nosotros nos hablaron de un museo pensamos: "¡Un Museo? ¡Cómo vamos a hacer un Museo?" Nos parecía algo retrógrado, ¡cómo nuestro problema iba a estar en un Museo? . . . Porque para nosotros un Museo era una cosa estática, donde había salas donde se colgaban cosas, . . . dónde hay objetos puestos ahí con una leyendita y punto.

[When they spoke to us about starting a museum, we thought: "A museum? How are we going to create a museum?" It seemed to us a little retrograde: how would our problem be in a museum? . . . Because for us, a museum had been a static thing, where there were rooms where they hung things, . . . where there are objects with a little sign and that's it.]
—Mabel Penette Gutiérrez, president, Relatives of the Disappeared and Detained for Political Reasons, speaking about the proposal for the "Memoria Abierta / Open Memory" Museum

A museum isn't a house. It is an idea in debate.
—Peter Aronsson, coordinator, European National Museums Project

Contents

Illustrations

Acknowledgments

This book could not have been written without the support of my family, Matthew and Sophia Tidwell. Their sacrifice makes their pride in my work particularly mystifying—and endlessly gratifying—to me, and they are both truly a blessing.

For intellectual stimulation and many happy memories, let me particularly thank the magnificent Eunamus team of Bodil Axelsson, Peter Aronsson, Simon Knell, Sheila Watson, and Andy Sawyer.

For providing me with the perfect places to live, deep thanks to Viv Golding and her husband, David, and to Joanna Dahlin and David Torrell and their companionable cat, Kirk. Thanks as well to friends Kosta Economou in Sweden, Gudrun Whitehead in England, Kamil Rozsypal in the Czech Republic, Michele Binstadt in Australia, Jenny Hodbod in Ethiopia, Doug and Laura Rose in Uzbekistan (whose help getting around that beautiful country was so invaluable I can't begin to thank them enough), Alan Cibils and Martha Farmelo in Argentina, Fatma Tanriverdi and Kerem Köksal in Turkey, Katey Borland in Mexico, Young Zhang and Freeman in China, Kris Rutten and Ronald Soetaert in Belgium, and three terrific guides: Chris Green in South Africa, Hani Ahmed in Egypt, and Gashaw Assefa in Ethiopia.

As for scholarly thanks, besides the brilliant members of the Eunamus Project (whether I met you in person or not, your scholarship inspired me), let me tip my hat to the Kenneth Burke Society, the members of ICOFOM, the Inclusive Museum Research Network, the Mershon Center scholars, and the participants in the Rhetoric Society of America's Summer Institute 2015 "War of Words" seminar. I especially thank the various people who so generously read portions of this book over the past few years: Jim Phelan, Nan Johnson, Carolyn Skinner, Ann George, Bodil Axelsson, Amy Shuman, and Robyn Warhol, and the three graduate students I worked with during the course of this project, whose insightful work influenced my own in many ways: Erika Strandjord, Jennifer Herman, and Lauren Obermark. I particularly thank Greg Clark, whose two days of advice and encouragement made for a different and much better book. As I was finishing the manuscript, John Wetzel's keen eye and clever suggestions were invaluable, and Evelyn Antis's help made the task go more quickly. Finally, I am deeply indebted to Kendra Boileau at Penn State Press, the series editors, Michael Bernard-Donals and Leah Ceccarelli, the three anonymous reviewers, and copyeditor Suzanne Wolk, all of whose comments contributed substantially to the final version of the manuscript.

I would never have been able to undertake this project without the generous support of my campus, the Ohio State University at Newark, and particularly its dean and director, William MacDonald, whose financial and intellectual support for my work over the years has been invaluable. The Newark Campus Professional Standards Committee also assisted with several travel grants. On the Columbus campus of Ohio State, the Mershon Center for International Security Studies and the College of Arts and Sciences both provided key fiscal support for my work with the Eunamus Project, and the Department of English generously supported Greg Clark's visit. Finally, let me thank Linköping University and the University of Leicester for their in-kind contributions of workspace and equipment.

I could personally thank the world itself for being peopled with kind, generous, helpful individuals, country after country, year after year. From the stranger in Bangkok who got me and my backpack a ride on the back of the mailman's motorcycle when I showed up lost in her alley, to the Ethiopian Airlines worker who let me sit in the jump seat on the only plane back to Addis Ababa, to the waiter in the closed restaurant in Cuzco who made me coca tea for altitude sickness when I stumbled into his doorway, the kindness of people warms my heart. You are so numerous, and your legacy of humanity far exceeds the scope of this poor project—you have all schooled me in the far greater project of life.

Introduction

We live in a divided world—divided nationally, in our personal relations, even within ourselves—and we rightly seek unity. But while an overemphasis on division leads to alienation, scapegoating, and war, an overemphasis on unity brings hegemony, xenophobia, and the silencing of difference. For nearly two decades, the United States has witnessed the excesses of both impulses—years of war engendering a popular sense that any dissent is traitorous, then years of economic hardship engendering niche populism that resists any unifying motives. Traveling around the world, I saw the same dichotomy writ large across the globe—crackdowns and hegemony in one country, chaos and open warfare in another. I undertook this project thinking of rhetorical theorist Kenneth Burke's contention that the "invitation to rhetoric" lies in transcending the dichotomy: "Put identification and division ambiguously together, so that you cannot know for certain just where one ends and the other begins, and you have the characteristic invitation to rhetoric," he wrote (1950/1969, 25). Rhetorician Christa Olson added more recently, "In identifying with another, we become 'substantially one' rather than 'wholly one' with that other, just as biological offspring both share the body of their mother and yet also remain distinct from it" (2014, 163). Rhetoric is the ambiguous embrace of both identification and division, love and strife between self and other, or, as rhetorician James Kastely notes in a recent article on Burke's *Rhetoric of Motives*: "In a dialectical theory of identification, neither unity nor division precede each other; rather, they exist simultaneously or atemporally, as a pair of mutually implicated terms—they are relational terms who are logically impossible without each other" (2013, 186). Love/unity/identification is of course to be strived for, but without strife/diversity/division we cannot know the Other *as* Other, as someone/some nation with perspectives and passions different from our own, with whom we need to work if we are to approach any kind of substantial oneness.

I was reminded of the dialectic of unity and division one summer day in 2011, while sitting in the airport in Kigali, Rwanda, waiting with people from many nations for a plane to Addis Ababa. We sat in rows, while in front of us on a small television the national anthem of South Sudan played for the first time to the huge crowds gathered there to celebrate their new nation. I thought of Burke's comment that "the future is really disclosed by finding out what people can sing about" (1937/1984, 334–35), and I wondered, as I listened to the united voices singing words I didn't understand, just how those beliefs and values they were singing about would be carried forward. Having just come from the Genocide Memorial Centre in Kigali, it was clear to me that these aesthetic questions of motives were not superfluous ponderings in a pragmatic world but were vital to a meaningful future. Would the nation be able to envision itself as one without sacrificing critical thought to blind nationalism? Would it tell an inclusive story that allowed multiple voices to be heard? Could it use its past to build a future? As I write this now, several years later, South Sudan endures a vicious civil war, the ultimate division, but in some ways this only makes more vital the original question of what motivates a people to become a public, and then to maintain that comity. I am committed to the belief that cultural expressions are a large part of what binds us together as diverse peoples while allowing us the space to debate, forcefully but without force of arms, what that culture looks like. Within the walls of museums, visitors can celebrate unity and ponder diversity and so wade in the dialectical stream of "substantial oneness" rather than stumble on its rival banks of silence or combat.

The Beginning

In 2007, I attended a conference in Prague and visited the old Czech National Museum. A massive stone block darkened with age and soot, its bulk filled the upper side of the long quadrangle that is historic Wenceslas Square, heart of the 1989 Velvet Revolution. The museum is a stunning gilded gem of nineteenth-century architecture inside its capacious entryway and up its red-carpeted stairs. But it was undervisited, and in many of its interior rooms I was alone with the cramped specimen cases, struggling to decipher exhibits from the limited signage, where history seemed to end in about 1000 C.E. History was more apparent outside the building, at the foot of the curving stone stairway leading from the museum down to the square. There, a simple flagstone cross in the pavement

1 | The entrance to the Museum of Communism, Prague.

marks the spot where, in 1969, student Jan Palach set himself on fire to protest the crushing of the Prague Spring. His act was emblematic of Czech despair under Soviet control, his image invoked again and again during the Velvet Revolution. But to learn Palach's story, I needed, instead of the National Museum, to walk several blocks to the other end of the square, turn the corner, and enter a small private museum above a McDonald's—the Museum of Communism, where Palach's story is enshrined with those of many others in the history of twentieth-century Czechoslovakia (see fig. 1).[1]

What is it, I asked myself then, that compels people to tell the stories that embody historical memory? What compels a person, or a nation, to build a museum? By the time I completed this study, almost a decade later, I was asking more questions: How are individuals persuaded by exhibits to unite their identities with the civic identity, and how does that civic identity change when they do so? What do museums as sites of rhetorical persuasion contribute to museum studies? What do museums as sites of engagement with civic history contribute to rhetorical studies? Most important, what does cultural heritage contribute to the world? I found museums playing a critical, celebratory, occasionally prophetic role in public discourse, providing dialectical perspectives on shared pasts and presents, promoting epideictic visions of longed-for futures, warning and commemorating and allowing a busy world the needed space to critically contemplate its changing values.

This book argues for a rhetorical reading of national museums as sites where multiple, intersecting, and at times conflicting acts of identification converge. Out of these acts of identification and division, a sense of the national story is forged and reforged. Specific aspects of national narratives (including *spatial narratives* and what I call *deep narratives*) combine with material artifacts (including my expansion of Burke's *mythic image* into a material realm in which objects are already *constitutive acts*). Together, narrative, space, and object promote aesthetic experiences that allow individuals to identify with collectives. I employ a Burke-flavored theoretical lens to develop a framework for analyzing how national museums use their spaces to promote *antithetical, semiconscious,* and *means-to-an-end identifications* between individuals and their societies, which I illustrate with a wide range of examples. I argue that a greater understanding of how the civic role, the self in society, is mediated in the voluntary but constructed space of a national museum provides us with a motive for a strenuous examination of the ways in which civic identity in modern diverse societies is continually enacted not only on the expected political and media stages but also at the intersection of the real and the aesthetic.

With grants and encouragement from a variety of sources, I began in 2008 to travel to the six inhabited continents, collecting research on museums in twenty-two nations that I chose based on some combination of four criteria:

the geographic variety of their location
the renown of their national museum
the newness of some factor in their story (new nation, newly renovated
   museum)
my familiarity with their particular national story

I traveled to museums in Mexico in 2008; Australia and the United States in 2009; Argentina, Peru, England, and Italy in 2010; South Africa, Rwanda, and Ethiopia in 2011; New Zealand, China, Thailand, Uzbekistan, India, Turkey, Egypt, Germany, Tunisia, Sweden, and England in 2012; and Belgium in 2013. I also spent a semester working with some of the world's experts in museum studies during a sabbatical at Linköping University in Norrköping, Sweden, and the University of Leicester in Leicester, England, as they finished work on the three-year collaborative project European National Museums: Identity Politics, the Uses of the Past and the European Citizen (Eunamus), funded by the European Commission.

The purposeful transdisciplinarity of my project means that I have spent much time reading and speaking with experts outside my chosen field of modern rhetorical theory. I have explored narrative theory, communication studies, history, sociology, psychology, geography, current affairs, and, most extensively, museum studies. Rhetorician Debra Hawhee distinguishes *transdisciplinarity* from *interdisciplinarity* by noting that the former is an "effort to suspend—however temporarily—one's own disciplinary terms and values in favor of a broad, open, multilevel inquiry" (2009, 3), and this has been my aim since the beginning, engaging with colleagues, particularly in museum studies, on their own terms. Even as both rhetoric and museology look to audience awareness and sociopolitical identity formation, there is almost no crossover in their scholarship—most scholars seem unaware of the richness of one another's fields. Thus I frequently find myself explaining to museum studies scholars just what modern rhetorical studies is, while scholarship such as a recent extensive communication studies review that aimed to "situate communicative inquiry within the broader scope of museum studies in order to uncover the distinct contribution of these examinations" (Mancino 2015, 259) mentioned just one museum studies scholar.[2] So much of the work in these fields grows from similar observations, arrives at similar rich insights, and seeks to influence the same displays of public memory, that it is my hope that this book can introduce scholars to one another across disciplinary boundaries.

Museum Rhetoric

This study begins with the premise that history museums are public spaces that depict not what we were but who we are, and that the question of *who we are* is a critical first step in any debate over *what we do now*. Thus studying the rhetoric *in* museums—rhetorical museology—can help us to see how the rhetoric *of* museums—museological rhetoric—shapes public debate about the parameters of national citizenship.[3] The museum's depiction of "who we are" provides an understudied opportunity to expand our understanding of public space, civic engagement, and national identity formation. Examining the rhetoric in/of museums also contributes a theoretical framework to the ongoing debate over the importance of cultural and aesthetic heritage to civil society, which, in the United States at least, is frequently challenged by self-styled pragmatists across the political spectrum. Far from superfluous even in a pragmatic world, museums are primary institutions of the public sphere that demand *critical interpretation* and *identification*—two powerful forces for civic engagement.

What can a *rhetorical museology*—one that examines how individuals are persuaded to unite their identities with the civic identity through object, text, and space—contribute to the social role of museums? A great deal. Interpreting the social world within a rhetorical narrative framework, replete with narrative's markers of temporality and causality and the affective persuasion of materiality, a museum layers onto the social realm a national life story that proposes a flexible unification of diverse pasts. That museum narrative of unified social diversity, in turn, works rhetorically to invite each individual to identify his or her own personal life story with the collective story. This is not merely the psychological identity work that museum studies scholars have examined previously. Instead, rhetorical museology allows us to see historical social narratives and individual identity work as the warp and weft of an interwoven identification process with always evolving communal values invoking memory made manifest in material space. Further, by framing a national story and empowering it with the staged presence of material objects, the national museum works not only on those who visit but on the nation as a whole, as its collections select, reflect, and deflect the story the nation tells itself about itself. This book analyzes examples from around the world of changing nations managing their national collections and narratives, successfully and not, in an effort to change national values. Such a view emphasizes the importance of museums as "cultural glue" for the nation, while they work also to be "cultural goad," moving the nation into the future. A rhetorical museology thus allows museologists to more richly explore the effects of museums on their nations.

A *museological rhetoric*, in turn—analyzing the role of rhetorical museums as sites of civic engagement—contributes an equally great deal to the field of rhetorical studies. The museological perspective on rhetoric focuses attention on the ways in which materiality and narrative intertwine as bodies move through crafted space, inventing modified civic experiences out of aesthetic encounters. Museums' interpreted display of the social world is an ongoing expression of the power of ceremonial epideictic rhetoric (in its visual, spatial, and material as well as textual forms) to reflect and strengthen but also to create communal values from individual affects.[4] A greater understanding of how the civic role is mediated in a national museum provides the field of rhetoric with greater insight into civic identity formation in modern diverse societies where the old forms—a speech or pageant—no longer persuade. Museums are indeed material spaces, but above all they are highly crafted spaces, offering symbolic narratives via words, objects, and architecture that together shape the actions of their nations.[5] A museological approach moves us from fruitless discussion of the "truth" or "bias" of museum exhibits into more useful discussion of how these exhibits craft a version of the past to promote values for the future, and what that means for each visitor. The question is not whether or how museums shape the past story but why they do so in this way at this time, beyond the usual culprits of power and hegemony. As communication scholar Susan Mancino writes, "The history-memory dialectic, public memory inclusive of collective memory and collective remembrance, and the consequences of contemporary museums as sites for visitor interactivity provide three openings from which communication scholars consider the functions and implications of museums" (2015, 262). A museological rhetoric, then, allows rhetoricians to explore more deeply the intertwining effects of public memory and material epideictic rhetoric on their citizens.

I opened this book with the epigraph from Swedish cultural historian Peter Aronsson—"A museum isn't a house. It is an idea in debate"—a line I heard him deliver in Budapest at the final conference of Eunamus, the three-year transnational project he headed. Museums, Aronsson asserted, can be the spaces in which people come together to pause and reflect on their world. This is the contribution of humanities to the political world, to provide a place for "thought moving to action" (2012). The debate needs the house, the material displays that make concrete a people's communally valued heritage. But these materials work together with the narrative to promote identification experiences for individuals who move through crafted spaces and back to the civic community outside the walls, a world of which the museum is also a part.

What Is Rhetoric?

Let me pause to briefly explain the lens through which I examine national museums in this book: rhetoric. In the Western tradition, rhetoric has always been seen as an art of influencing others, from Aristotle's definition in the fourth century b.c.e. as the "ability, in each particular case, to see the available means of persuasion," to Kenneth Burke's more recent notion that it is "the use of language as a symbolic means of inducing cooperation in beings that by nature respond to symbols" (1950/1969, 43). Rhetoricians in the twenty-first century often emphasize the nonlinguistic aspects of these symbolically persuasive moments, and point out that this symbolic action uses us as much as we use it—that is, persuasion is material as well as ideational, and it is unconscious as well as intentional. Whether through hours of reasoned debate or a thirty-second sound bite, a lengthy printed manifesto or a two-hour film, the figure of a swoosh or a bitten apple, rhetoric is the way the world is manipulated around us for the purpose of persuading ourselves and others that something matters and that we should respond to it. Rhetorician Barry Brummett calls it "the social function that influences and manages meaning" (1991, xii).

Rhetoric is concerned with the public sphere, with how individuals interact in social scenes as they forge—in union and in opposition—the imagined community. Rhetoric and sociology, then, have a similar focus on the social, but a different methodology beginning in differing premises. As a field housed partly in English studies, rhetoric reads between the lines of cultural and stylistic manifestations of public life to consider the mechanisms by which popular identity is forged. How does that pageant, song, memorial, website, campaign—or museum—influence our sense of ourselves as beings in community? Rhetoric shares a focus with popular culture studies on the artifacts and experiences of culture all around us that nurture us into being whatever we think of as "ourselves" (Brummett 1991, xix), in much the same way that being immersed in our native language nurtures in us the ability to speak that language fluently and largely unconsciously. As Burke said, we are by nature beings who respond to symbols.

It can seem duplicative to discuss history museums as a topic in rhetoric rather than in history, cultural studies, or even literary criticism. Rhetoric, though, has a unique stance. The editors of the collection *Places of Public Memory* distinguish rhetoric from its sister fields in that it "organizes itself around the relationship of [discourses, events, objects, practices] to ideas about what it means to be 'public'" (Dickinson, Blair, and Ott 2010, 3). A rhetorical lens might consider how the British Museum's stance of "disinterested holder of the world's treasures" shapes and reflects a particular public identity, and then how individual Britons are invited to assume that identity themselves. The mantel of that identity is significantly different from the one shaped and reflected by, say, "America's attic" at the National Museum of American History, or from the sense engendered by entering "the King's treasury" at the Thai National Museum. Each of these perspectives brings forth a different sense of one's role in a society—more or less hierarchical or populist, more or less beholder or beholden—and therefore it engenders a different range of responses as one embraces, modifies, or resists the identity offered.

A Burkean Framework

This process of building an identity that is in dialogue with a created communal identity Kenneth Burke calls *identification*, the major focus of this book. Burke's great contribution to rhetorical theory was the realization that for someone to be persuaded by another (a person or a nation), one needs to identify with that other, finding commonality in "speech, gesture, tonality, order, image, attitude, idea, *identifying* your ways with his" (1950/1969, 55). Burke's six decades of work on the role of symbols in inducing cooperation in beings who identify with one another forms the bedrock of modern American rhetoric, and his theories start from the premise that life and the language we use to describe its experiences are necessarily rich with symbolic significance. He termed this attention to the *craft* of communicating the "socioanagogic" perspective—the ways that "things of the senses are secretly emblematic of motives in the social order, so that all visible, tangible entities become an enigma, and materials become a pageantry" (1953/1968, xv). This perspective examines, as Burke said of Flaubert's novels, "the *verbalization* of experience, the conversion of life into *diction*," in contrast to the purely mimetic "verbalization of *experience*, the conversion of *life* into diction" (1953/1968, 7). In Burke's socioanagogic perspective, the crafted aspect of the real is the focus of study.

This perspective frames the book because I believe that it describes the nature of a museum. All museums—historical, scientific, and artistic—select aspects of the world, turning them into crafted exhibits, turning life into *diction*. These selections, in turn, must necessarily promote certain values and perspectives over others—a process that Burke described on several occasions with the dictum that "vocabularies that will be faithful *reflections* of reality" must develop "vocabularies that are *selections* of reality" that sometimes "function as a *deflection* of reality" (1943b, 27). As people discuss their world, certain points are inevitably highlighted; others are ignored. Of course, this dictum is itself a reduction, since the "reality" being selected, reflected, or deflected exists in a form impossible for humans to truly experience: any description of reality—even to ourselves—necessarily involves the reductive forces of language. Burke eventually summarized this process in his "Definition of Man," noting that one is "separated from his natural condition by instruments of his own making" (1966, 16). Efforts to describe the world inevitably shape that world, which is why, for Burke, language choices are never neutral but are instead symbolic action (1945/1969, 61).

While material studies may argue that it is the de-verbalization of life—the rise of motion over symbolic action—that holds particular interest today, I want to use these material spaces, these museums, to argue for not abandoning the symbolic. The nature of the encounter between visitor and museum display encourages a type of identification between individual and nation that is both semiconscious and purposeful, combining intellectual and affective responses to the national life story, as we shall see.

It is this natural effect of *all* human communication that is heightened in museums, where the vast swath of human and natural history, knowledge, and culture is displayed and interpreted, reduced to particular objects and their meanings that can be narratized, encapsulated, walked through, and somehow absorbed in the space, ideally, of an afternoon. Furthermore, this selected reality can be heightened by the display of particular objects that carry high, even mythic significance for a particular set of visitors—those who identify themselves with the nation being so encapsulated. In short, museums are more than memory sites. They are the only public information institutions that intentionally straddle divides between style and content, intellect and affect, past, present, and future, fiction and nonfiction, rhetoric and dialectic, unity and diversity, permanence and change. The mental and physical attitude that they evoke at their most powerful, embracing ambiguity and open-ended consideration, as I will demonstrate, is in dangerously short supply in other, less aesthetic sectors of the public sphere.

Thus the Burkean framework of this book leads us back to Burke's overarching public interests: the value of ambiguous language in public discourse and its role in cooperation and conflict resolution, identification, and division. As Burke wrote relatively late in life, summing up a lifetime of politico-aesthetic thinking, people inevitably fail "to distinguish clearly enough between things and symbols" (1967, 50) and therefore invest the symbol with monological meaning. "Citizens in a democracy," though, are charged with paying attention to the "ambiguities of identification" that are always inherent in "that tiny first-person plural pronoun, 'we'" (50). To deal with that "we," the narrative of history in any museum may well need a split personality. On the one hand, its series of images encourages individual identification with the national "we." On the other, identification with the ambiguous "we" calls forth a need to present a national myth that is more dialogical, more flexible, and more capable of incorporating fully those ambiguities of the individual subjects making up the "we." This interest in ambiguity I continue in this study, as I investigate ways that museum spaces attempt to persuade toward a communal identity that is ambiguous, embracing multiple perspectives and critical dialogue.

Prior Studies

Museums have no doubt been "studied" since there were first modern museums—we can look back to curator George Brown Goode's *Principles of Museum Administration* at the end of the nineteenth century as an example of a study of the display of collections, their management, and the role of the museum in society—but museum studies as a field is relatively new. The professionalization of museum *staff* on a global level can be marked by such events as the founding in 1946 of the International Council on Museums (ICOM), a branch of UNESCO, and the same global professionalization of museum *studies* can be marked thirty years later with the addition to ICOM of ICOFOM, the International Committee for Museology. ICOFOM uses museologist Georges Henri Rivière's 1981 definition of museology: "an applied science, the science of the museum. Museology studies its history, its role in society, the specific forms of research and physical conservation, activities and dissemination, organization and functioning, new or musealised architecture, sites that have been received or chosen, its typology and its deontology" (quoted in Desvallées and Mairesse 2010, 54). The Anglo-Saxon world favors "museum studies," with its implication of interdisciplinarity, over "museology," and "museum studies" is the term I will use more often here. However, one aspect of "museology" is particularly important to a rhetorical study, and that is its etymological implication that what is studied is not only *museums* but the *museal*, which ICOFOM notes is a term that goes beyond the physical museum to "a viewpoint on reality with regard to the world of heritage (to consider something from the museal angle, for example, means to ask oneself whether it is possible to preserve it for exhibition to the public)" (Desvallées and Mairesse 2010, 43). This book, like museology, looks toward the museum's perspective on the world.

Within the realm of museum studies, meanwhile, I might use museologist Eilean Hooper-Greenhill's 1992 *Museums and the Shaping of Knowledge* as the marker of a turning point toward the current day. A founder of the School of Museum Studies at the University of Leicester, Hooper-Greenhill has produced a body of work on the museum as communication medium rather than repository, which theorized for a global community the educational rather than the curatorial approach, the shift from a focus on objects to one on human interaction. In this early book she begins, "Our perception of the world, we are told, will be different once we know and are familiar with these paintings. . . . But if museums are places in which we may come to know new things, and where our perceptions may radically change, what is the nature of this knowing, and how are these changes brought about? . . . The analysis of the various elements that together make up the 'reality' that we call 'the museum' has barely begun" (1992, 2–3).

Hooper-Greenhill goes on to analyze the history of that museum reality, using as her framework Michel Foucault's classification of three historical "epistemes," or paradigms, that include the Renaissance, characterized by "interpretation and similitude, with things being read for their hidden relationships to each other" (12); the classical, in which "knowing was no longer to consist of drawing things together, but in setting things apart" (15); and the modern, "a new form of knowing, based on the questioning of why things were how they were, [and in which] the activity of knowing was the questioning, the analysis, and the exposition of organic and functional relationships between material things" (18). As an institution born in the Renaissance and grown in the classical era, today's modern museum, therefore, displays its objects in relation to people, not other objects—hence the modern emphasis on storytelling, historical context, and visitor engagement, bringing visitors' stories into contact with the object. As Ann Davis, for many years the president of the International Committee for Museology, notes in a recent article, "many museums today are shifting their focus away from their collections toward their visitors. They aspire to be more democratic, more inclusive, less elitist and more pluralistic. Museum staff recognize, increasingly, that there is not one, true narrative but many stories, sometimes in conflict with each other. Museums are realizing that they must dismantle the barriers to widespread participation in their activities. They must become more community centered" (2016, 91). The new centrality of visitor response is a move toward audience awareness that brings museum studies closer to rhetoric.

Once the focus of study shifted from object per se to the scenic context of object-audience-place, and once reality was, as Hooper-Greenhill's title indicates, "shaped" by museums' display practices, the field of museum studies necessarily turned toward the more people-oriented disciplines of anthropology, sociology, cultural studies, and history for its epistemological frameworks and methodologies. This turn to the humanities and social sciences marks what has become known as the new museology, a scholarly movement that professional history museologist Max Ross succinctly sums up in his article "Interpreting the New Museology" as "a transformation of museums from being exclusive and socially divisive institutions" to institutions whose collections now "represent not just the world views of ruling classes, but also popular culture and the histories of non-elite social strata" (2004, 84–85). The new museum often sees its mission not as the distribution of knowledge but as the production of a sociopolitical effect in its community, and new museologists, in turn, study these effects of museums on the world. The scholars of this new sociocultural and historical museum work, including particularly Knell, Watson, Aronsson, and Kaplan, who examine the implications of national identity; Berger, Lorenz, and Poulot, who consider the role of historical narratives in building this identity; MacLeod and Dudley, who evaluate the space of those retellings and the objects therein; and Falk, Golding, Davis, and Smeds, who look more deeply into the implications for and of their audience, have in turn produced the museological work on national museums with which I interact more thoroughly in later chapters.

Rhetorical scholars will recognize in the epistemic, sociocultural focus of the new museology our field's own slightly earlier development of the new rhetoric, the twentieth century's refashioning of classical rhetorical theory into a flexible, sociolinguistically based analytical tool, or, as I put it in another context, "In the New Rhetoric . . . the Aristotelian belief that 'audiences are moved by means of language' . . . became a tripartite focus on *language* as symbolic action for persuasion that unites divided humans, on *dialogue* as the preeminent means by which persuasion should occur, and on *communally constructed truths* as the aim of dialogue" (George, Weiser, and Zepernick 2013, 8). All three of these foci are on display in the intersections between museums and visitors contemplating past, present, and future in these rhetorical spaces.

With their gaze set firmly on the existential world, rhetoricians, particularly in the United States, have focused the bulk of their historical attention on performances of public citizenship in a variety of public spaces. Communication scholar Gerard Hauser, in his key 1999 monograph *Vernacular Voices: The*

Rhetoric of Publics and Public Spheres, analyzed the ways in which public discourse engenders dialogue in key communal spaces (though not museums), and in an article from the same time ("Aristotle on Epideictic"), he discussed the "portrayal" and "display" of communal values. In his groundbreaking *Rhetorical Landscapes in America* (2004), rhetorician Greg Clark, starting from the premise that "anything that prompts social cooperation by presenting to people symbols of collectivity with which they can each identify themselves is rhetorical" (5), studied natural and constructed landscapes that transform individual experiences into communal ones, thus making a place into a "rhetorical landscape" that contributes to crafting a unified story of nationhood. Museums in this context are grouped with tourist guides, placards, etc., as tools that *prepare* readers for the encounter with the landscape. This focus on the experiential can be seen as well in Clark's later article "Rhetorical Experience and the National Jazz Museum in Harlem," in which, with so much of the Jazz Museum not yet built, the "experiences" are gained from walking Harlem's neighborhoods on a guided tour (2010, 14).

Meanwhile, the burgeoning transdisciplinary field of public memory studies has touched rhetorical studies through researchers such as Bradford Vivian and Anne Demo and their work on remembering and forgetting, and most particularly foundational scholar Carole Blair and her co-authors over the past three decades (Neil Michel, Greg Dickinson, Brian Ott, Marsha Jeppeson, Enrico Pucci). Their work on public monuments in particular forged the link between memory studies and materiality as early as Blair, Jeppeson, and Pucci's 1991 analysis of the Vietnam Memorial, "Public Memorializing in Postmodernity," in which the authors recommended looking at memory sites to move beyond the symbolicity of rhetoric. As Blair notes in a later article, "If rhetoric's materiality is not a function of its symbolic constructions of meaning [but its real physical presence] then we must look elsewhere: we must ask not just what a text means but, more generally, what it does; and we must not understand what it does as adhering strictly to what it was supposed to do. Both these directives open a vast field for us to contemplate" (1999, 23). This "vast field" has been richly mined by a number of U.S. communication scholars over the past two decades in multiple case studies of museums large and small, as rhetoricians have become increasingly interested in the motivational role of memory. Amy K. Levin's collection *Defining Memory* (2007) discusses the localization of memory in small U.S. museums; Dickinson, Blair, and Ott's *Places of Public Memory* (2010) examines the materiality of memory in both museums and memorial sites, and Michael Bernard-Donals's recent *Figures of Memory* (2016) explores the displacement of memory at the U.S. Holocaust Memorial Museum. Cultural critiques abound: Dickinson, Ott, and Aoki's examination of the Buffalo Bill Museum's privileging of masculinity and whiteness; Fried's look at the avoidance of geopolitical responsibility in the Smithsonian's *September 11* exhibit; Poirot and Watson's analysis of the whitewashing of slavery in historical Charleston; my own examination of the "indigenous problem" with the narrative at the National Museum of American History, among others. Like their global colleagues, multiple U.S. scholars have examined the material construction of memory in case studies of such rhetorically charged sites as the National Civil Rights Museum (Atwater and Herndon 2003; Armada 1998), the U.S. Holocaust Memorial Museum (Hasian 2004), the September 11 Memorial and Museum (Paliewicz and Hasian 2016), the Creation Museum (Lynch 2013; Kelly and Hoerl 2012; Scott 2014), and the North Carolina Museum of Art (Zagacki and Gallagher 2009), while Eric Aoki, Greg Dickinson, and Brian Ott have collaborated to push theory forward in their examination of a variety of museums of the West (2006, 2011, 2013).

Communication scholars Kendall Phillips and G. Mitchell Reyes, meanwhile, have expanded this public memory work beyond the United States with their edited collection *Global Memoryscapes* (2011), which joins with European collections such as Aronsson, Amundsen, and Knell's *National Museums: New Studies from around the World* to examine the increasing complexities of framing public memories in a globally diffuse world in which public citizenship is increasingly fluid. David Gruber's article on a politically charged exhibit at the Hong Kong Museum of History continues U.S. communication scholars' work with museums and citizenship.

Citizenship, as communication scholar Ekaterina Haskins notes, is a particular focus of rhetoricians, who "pay special attention to the discursive mechanism by which rituals and artifacts of memory participate in the construction of citizenship as an embodied identity" (2015, 9). This attention to the embodied construction of citizen memories has led Haskins to her recent *Popular Memories* (2015), which examines extramuseal participatory forms of commemoration and their effect on the development of democratic citizenship. She argues from case studies, as does Clark, for the role of popular experiences in promoting communal engagement, although her studies are more fluid, more evocative of change than of permanence. She also argues, as I do here, that more inclusive, dialogical experiences engender greater civic engagement.

Just as rhetoricians have extended their traditional focus on texts into the nonverbal realms of materiality, space, and physicality, so have museum scholars extended their focus on objects into a focus on the object within a spatial and temporal narrative (see especially Suzanne MacLeod's collection *Reshaping Museum Space* of 2005). Similarly, the recent rhetorical focus on the affective experience of bodies in space (most notably in Debra Hawhee's *Moving Bodies* of 2009) is matched by museum studies' theorizing on the affective visitor experience in Davis and Smeds's thought-provoking collection *Visiting the Visitor* (2016).

As is evident from the diverse perspectives of these critiques, as official culture in a museum attempts to engage the populace, it finds itself in increasing conflict with popular cultures and their diverse contentions of whose stories should be depicted and displayed in order to create a "truthful" historical identity—a conflict we shall see arise repeatedly in later chapters. Rhetoricians and museum studies scholars, therefore, might well find common ground in a greater degree of dialogue over the new museological revolution that advocates for museums as places of community engagement and social dialogue. An excellent example of scholarship on this revolution is Viv Golding's *Learning at the Museum Frontiers: Identity, Race, and Power* (2012), in which Golding demonstrates how museums can be a "frontier zone" where diverse groups forge a kaleidoscope of their own histories. Meanwhile, writing studies scholar Chaim Noy's ethnographic examination of visitor books as spaces that "invite and allow visitors to become rhetors and to engage in ritualistic and public modes of writing [to] . . . become participating/contributing members of a community" (2015, 196) and communication scholar Nicole Maurantonio's critique of the same community-building function of visitors' Post-it note responses in a multiperspectival U.S. Civil War Museum (2015, 85) are just two examples of a rhetorical contribution to how that revolution plays out rhetorically in the material (con) texts of the museum setting.

As museologist Sophia Psarra sums up, "Today museums have a different role. . . . The themes of classification on the one hand, and personal or national identity on the other, mark the transformation of museums from universally accepted facts to socially constructed themes and contents, from displaying certainties to shaping individual means and contexts, from science to narrative, and finally from social reform and cultural improvement to the complexity of the visitor's experience" (2005, 81). This new role for the twenty-first-century museum not only influences how the museum presents information to visitors; it also brings the museum into contact with the world. "The trajectory of museum architecture in this transformation has moved from public monument to spatial experience," Psarra notes, "and from forming a social event to shaping national and cultural aspirations" (81). Modern museums, in other words—not all of them, but those that are most innovative—have become precisely the kind of public spheres in which Hauser could find the discourses of civic life debated.

This book, then, resists the impulse to cover too much ground already ably trod by our current critical theorists in materiality, memory, space, and the body. Instead, I focus on identification, finding commonality with the Other, the pre-cursor to persuasion—and particularly on national identification. I turn to the work of a number of Burkean scholars to expand upon this Burkean concept, including Greg Clark's already mentioned *Rhetorical Landscapes in America* (which he subtitles *Variations on a Theme from Kenneth Burke*—that theme being identification). Rhetorician Krista Ratcliffe's *Rhetorical Listening: Identifi-cation, Gender, Whiteness* complicates the identification process by noting that "identifications, especially cross-cultural identifications . . . may be troubled by history, uneven power dynamics, and ignorance" (1)—a dynamic particularly apparent when discussing nationalism. Meanwhile, James Kastely and Bryan Crable bring to the fore Burke's understanding of division as a complement (and not merely a precursor) to identification, a notion that is particularly important, again, when considering the balance between individual anomie and communal hegemony in discussions of the effect of national identification on both indi-vidual and nation. The work of these scholars provides rhetoric with yet another point of entry into conversations of national identity fostered by such scholars as the sociologist Benedict Anderson and the narratologist Patrick Colm Hogan. Finally, in order to make my case for rhetorical identification in national museum spaces and its purpose outside museum doors, I draw from an international range of narratologists, political theorists, social scientists, historians, philoso-phers, and psychologists. The question of national identity cuts across many fields. Luckily, rhetoric is a versatile tool.

Plan of the Book

Chapter 1 provides an overview of the theoretical and historical picture of national museums. In chapter 2, I focus on museums as narrative spaces, exam-ining the dialogue between individual and collective narratives. Chapter 3 looks at the material side of museums, analyzing the selected objects that encompass, deflect from, and shape national identity as visitors move through particular crafted spaces. In chapter 4, I turn to how narratives and material culture combine to promote visitors' identification with the identity-story being presented in the museum. Chapter 5 applies that identification specifically to national museums, examining how identification builds nationalism in the museum. Chapter 6 disrupts that narrative by considering alternative museums, those that exist to counter the national narrative. I focus particularly on the possibilities of post-trauma museums for national truth and reconciliation. Finally, in the conclusion, I propose various reasons why this matters, why—and how—the practice of rhetoric inside the museum can have a real impact on the security and justice of the world outside its doors.

1

The Rhetorical Museum

You can't expect Iraqis to protect museums and ancient objects in the ground when they're desperate to protect themselves. . . . But this shouldn't exempt us from caring about our past. Politics have failed to create a national identity. Religion has failed. The sects have clearly failed. So who are we? That's the question. I think history is partly the answer, it's common ground.

—Jaffar Darwesh

Even in our digital age of big data and virtual reality, museum collections of foundational documents, old coins, iconic clothing, marble statues, and touchstones of popular culture still have a power to speak to a nation of its identity. National museums can provide a material demonstration of a national rhetoric that is voluntary, aesthetic, and polyphonic, and that can have a strong motivational effect on civic life. The visitor to a national museum is persuaded to create an individual self who is aligned with the communal self—in other words, to create a collective self—through an encounter with the architecture, the display spaces, the artifacts, and the signs that narrate the stories weaving through museum galleries.

How does the nation balance the ambiguity of identification within that collective self, between "I" and "we"? Some say it is impossible, that identification inevitably ignores the power differentials that make one group subsume its identity to another, and that the only correct move is to resist identification. I argue, however, that successful museums embrace ambiguity, composing out of the communal imaginary a collective narrative with which, to remain relevant, they must *invite* individuals to engage. In today's diverse nations, visitors are not merely told the story; they are encouraged by their experience of the space to re-create the story within themselves and thus to shape and distort it on the basis of their own internal narratives. That collective story is not limitless; it is bounded by the selection and display of artifacts and the narrative frame of events. Within such a scene, even resistance to collective identity takes place within a national framework. Put another way, the museum narrative of the imagined collective identity has boundaries, just as the nation itself has the boundaries of its geographical borders.

It is as if the visitor were handed a sheet of paper with the vague outline of the nation on it and a box of crayons, and were encouraged to draw a picture. The crayons are not limitless; they are constrained—there are ten of them, say, or twenty. The colors selected are multiple but compatible. Thus each picture drawn is unique to the visitor, fitting more or less into the given outline, but each will be in some kind of harmony with the drawing of every other visitor, and different from the drawings done in museums of other nations, with their own outlines and color schemes.

Kenneth Burke said this more theoretically in *A Grammar of Motives*, writing that the paradox of individual and collective motivations, "such as a concept of class, nation, the 'general will,'" seems to subsume individuals into a collective not of their making (1945/1969, 37). It may appear, then, that collective motivation negates individual will, but to Burke this is a paradox precisely because individual identity itself is already derived from the collective in which one lives: "Yet despite this position as dialectical antithesis of the individual motive, the collective motive may be treated as the source or principle from which the individual motive is familially or 'substantially' derived in a 'like begets like' manner" (37). To return to the outlined page at the museum, individual visitors who add to the drawing of any collective identity depicted in a national museum "choose" their scene, but they do so with its general boundaries already in view and its limited palette of colors already seeming largely (if not wholly) appropriate.

What Is a National Museum?

We might think we know the answer to this question—visitors surveyed by the Eunamus Project certainly did, with upward of 78 percent of visitors to Europe's national museums indicating that they knew they were in one at the time of the survey (Bounia et al. 2012, 120). The picture becomes more complicated, however, when we learn that two of the nine museums surveyed depict the history of places that at the time were not independent nations (Catalonia and Scotland). Another (the Rijksmuseum) is a world-class art gallery, while still another (the German Historical Museum) covers large swaths of history beyond the borders of today's Germany. Many visitors indicated that they knew their museum was national because it had "National" in its title (121–22). Standing in the Estonian National Museum, for instance, 82 percent of noncitizen visitors could identify it as a national museum, while only 73 percent of their fellow tourists in the neighboring Ethnographic Open-Air Museum of Latvia were sure of this (122–23). Visitors tend to define national museums *ideally*, most of them naming certain qualities that reflect the size and comprehensiveness of the historical collections and their ability to narrate a relatively "complete" story of important events from a "nation-focused perspective," as one Estonian visitor put it (126).

While individuals define their museums ideally, officials define them *operationally*—that is, certain museums are called "national" because they are funded by the national government or are officially designated as such. These operational definitions lead to great variety between nations. For instance, while Austria officially has no national museums, France officially has eighty. What France does not have, however—and what most clearly fits the visitor ideal— is a national *historical* museum, a fact that became a point of debate in 2011, in a changing France whose dubious attitude was captured well in the *New York Times*:

> But Mr. Sarkozy [the French president at the time] has now decided that he wants a cultural legacy after all. He has cooked up the Maison de l'Histoire de France, the country's first national museum of French history. . . . The idea is to distill centuries of Gallic gloire into a chronological display, supplemented by lectures, seminars and temporary shows borrowing materials from the country's already plentiful local and regional history museums.
>
> That's the plan, anyway. For months, protesters have taken to the barricades, appalled by the notion of the museum. . . .
>
> The problem? It boils down to a few issues: What does it mean to be French in the 21st century? And whose "history" should be celebrated? In an increasingly fractious and multicultural nation, the questions have no simple answers. (Kimmelman 2011)

Indeed, the whole idea became fractious enough that it was shelved before Sarkozy left office.

The United States officially has the National Museum of American History, but history is also officially displayed in the sister museums that make up the collection of Smithsonian museums in Washington, D.C., and New York City. There is also the National Civil War Museum in Harrisburg, the Museum of Westward Expansion in St. Louis, and dozens more run by the National Park Service—are they national museums? What about the National Civil Rights Museum in Memphis, Tennessee, founded and funded privately—or Cleveland's Rock and Roll Hall of Fame?

To overcome the conundrum of which museums should be considered truly national, Eunamus chose a practical approach. In "Comparing National Museums: Methodological Reflections," coordinator Peter Aronsson writes that "there are several ways to meet the question of defining the national museum. The *methodological* way . . . is to view the creation of the concept and the institutions as historical processes to be studied: concepts and institutions in the making in close interaction with knowledge regimes and politics" (2008, 7). Using a methodological process, Eunamus defined national museums as "those institutions, collections and displays claiming, articulating and representing dominant national values, myths and realities" (Aronsson and Knell 2012, 10). In a sense, national museums are national because they say they are and their citizens agree. "National museums are institutionalized negotiations of national values," as Aronsson and Knell put it (10). It is this *negotiated*, and therefore rhetorical, sense of "national museum" that I use in this book: national museums, are those places that both reflect and promote a national identity with which some significant portion of the nation agrees. Their collections might consist of sociopolitical history, natural history, art, or ethnography, as long as their claim to thus represent "dominant national values, myths and realities" is accepted as legitimate in the world of negotiated (and therefore continually revised) national values.

What was the first public national museum? A number of museums claim to be "first," but certainly there was a flowering of national public spaces in the mid- to late eighteenth century in Europe, and the great institutions of that era provided the model for national museums that was emulated around the world and changed little until the late twentieth century. Many of these great eighteenth-century museums sprang from the collections of Renaissance aristocrats, of which a few—such as the Galleria Doria Pamphilj, in the heart of Rome—still exist intact, providing a rare look at a pre-musealized collection. The Doria Pamphilj home is an eighteenth-century palazzo of an old Roman family some five hundred meters southeast of the Pantheon. Gilded rococo and intimate marble drawing rooms flank a long picture gallery in a quadrangle around a tree-filled courtyard hidden from the bustle of the modern city. In the

gallery are masterpieces by many of the chief painters of the fifteenth, six-
teenth, and seventeenth centuries, including Caravaggio, Guercino, Bruegel,
Velázquez, Titian, and Raphael. Paintings are hung in the traditional manner,
stacked floor to ceiling, with a more idiosyncratic order than the geographic
"schools" method commonly used in today's public galleries. Most charmingly,
visitors today, via an audio guide, are "personally" guided through the collection by the current Prince Doria Pamphilj, much as aristocratic visitors were
guided in the past.

The great museums of Europe, such as the Vatican (open by invitation as
early as 1506 but not really "public" until the opening of the Pio-Clementino in
1771, and springing from the collections of the Renaissance Borghese popes),
the British (a combination of three aristocratic collections left to the king at
their owners' deaths, opened to the public in 1753), and the Louvre (this former
royal palace was opened to the public in 1793, four years after the French Revolution), set the standard for most national museums for at least the next 150
years. These first "national" museums were the outcome of two phenomena
essential to their development: Enlightenment and empire. "It is almost too trite
to say that the British Museum was a product of its age, born into that period
of remarkable intellectual flowering, the European Enlightenment," writes Robert Anderson, the former director of the British Museum (Anderson 2003, 1).
The private collections of the Enlightenment, which comprised both discoveries
from the natural world and objects from the ancient, were displayed to selected
guests less to educate than to awe, and we can still get a sense of that initial
impulse in another surviving private collection, Sir John Soane's Museum in
London. Born the year the British Museum opened its doors, Soane amassed
a huge collection of arts and antiquities. Today, one enters the smallish rooms
of his seemingly typical Georgian townhouse, a few blocks from the British
Museum, to find them filled from floor to ceiling with hundreds of classical
sculptures, friezes, paintings, pieces of stained glass, one-of-a-kind timepieces,
and the largest collection of Chinese tiles outside China, along with thousands
of books, pieces of cutlery, picture frames, and furnishings, and a plethora of
fossils, shells, and other natural objects. The effect is astonishing: the sheer
quantity of the jumble of objects elicits wonder, but their display is not random;
it is personalized—the house, in fact, was designed around them by Soane, a
Royal Academy professor of architecture—and many of the objects are priceless today. Such would have been the awe-inspiring display of the original aristocratic collections that moved into the new British Museum, built to house

them. Anderson explains why imperial Britain would be the first nation to open the quintessential national museum:

> A major part of the answer to the question "Why did it happen in Britain?" is that collections owned by commoners of the size and significance of [Sir Hans] Sloane's simply did not exist elsewhere.... Conditions in Britain were especially conducive to the possibility of creating a large collection of international character. There was a high level of intellectual inquiry, fueled to a large extent by [Sir Isaac] Newton's revolutionary science and its aftermath. This was aided by the nation being relatively stable—at least compared with Continental Europe.... The Enlightenment in England and Scotland was distinctive from those varieties in other European nations and antipathy between the State and intellectuals did not exist as it did in, say, France.... The success of Britain's trade, for example through the East India Company (leading to "the British Discovery of Hinduism"), but also the activities of the American colonists, and by military action, was to bring all manner of exotic material to Britain. These acquisitions were frequently of significance: soon after the Museum's foundation, objects collected on voyages by Sir Joseph Banks [who accompanied Captain James Cook around the world] were to add a more rigorous scientific dimension to curating, while an Egyptian stele which found its way to the British Museum directly resulted in the understanding of hieroglyphic script. And lastly . . . the Protestant ethic . . . did offer a less constricting and controlling environment than Catholicism. (2003, 3–4)

In this brief summation, Anderson neatly ties together the idiosyncratic— Hans Sloane left his massive collection to the Crown—with what might be termed the "forces of history," including scientific ideals, the ability to take objects from other nations (I am particularly fond of the multi-ton Egyptian stele that "found its way" to the museum), and even the purported freedom of Anglicanism. He demonstrates, probably unconsciously, the enduring legacy of entitlement into which the first national museums were born.

As products of the scientific Enlightenment, then, these new museums took it upon themselves to rationalize the arrangement of their original private collections. Instead of the eccentric curiosity cabinets of Renaissance collectors, with their focus on the desire to awe and the individual connections between objects, these public Enlightenment museums aimed not for connection but for classification, not wonder but knowledge. Today, the Enlightenment Room in the British Museum preserves that rational arrangement. Located just past the café off the Great Court, the gallery duplicates the look of the original eighteenth-century institution. Wood-and-glass cases line the walls, floor to ceiling, of the long gallery, with glass-topped wooden cases in rows down its center. As in John Soane's house, the cabinets are chock-full of fossils and samples from the natural world, collections of human-made objects, artworks and antiquities, and ethnographic objects collected on the worldwide voyages of the empire's fleets. Unlike Soane's idiosyncratic jumble, however, items in the Enlightenment Room are meticulously classified and catalogued, and are normalized in those identical glass-and-wood cases. To cite but one example, Hans Sloane's substantial herbarium, which a botanist friend had already classified by "a string of Latin names," was carefully reclassified into the new Linnaean system when it entered the public museum (British Museum 2016).

In addition to Enlightenment and empire, these eighteenth-century museums are the products of one more phenomenon: the age of revolution. Rather than obedient subjects of the king, revolutionary peoples had to reidentify themselves as active citizens participating in a nation of thousands (or more) of strangers. Museums played an important role in this psychic transformation from local subject to national citizen, as museum scholar Sharon Macdonald notes in the first issue of the appropriately titled *Museum and Society*: "As individual identification with the nation-state and the numerous unknown 'brothers' could not rest on experienced social relations it had instead to be cultural—a matter of shared knowledge and practice, of representation, ritual and symbolism" (2003, 2). So in Europe under Napoleon Bonaparte, for instance, "in the name of the newly formed Republic, the spaces and things belonging to the king, the aristocracy, and the church were appropriated and transformed, at first in France and later across Europe" (Hooper-Greenhill 1992, 167), bringing the treasures of the aristocracy, now renamed possessions of the newly constituted republic, into the public realm in the reconstituted Palace of the Louvre.

That museums were established to promote the nation to people who were encouraged to see themselves as citizens for the first time was understood from the beginning; writers in the eighteenth and nineteenth centuries were quite explicit. Napoleon's officer in charge of bringing Italian works to Paris, for instance, wrote that public display of such trophies was a concrete example of the new power of the citizen in the republic: "Citizens of all classes of the population ought to be aware that the Government has given them consideration and that all will have their share of the great booty. People will be able to judge what a Republican Government means if compared with the rule of a monarch who makes conquests merely for the pleasure of his courtiers and the satisfaction of his personal vanity" (quoted in Wittlin 1949, 233). A few decades later, writing for *Illustrated London* in 1847, one W. I. Bicknell opined that the British Museum demonstrated the intellectual and cultural side of a British character more commonly known for its military and economic might:

> For these facilities every Englishman ought to rejoice, not merely for the personal gratification which he or even his countrymen, may derive from such an establishment; but also, for the advantages which foreigners visiting England, may possess of searching the hidden treasure of this inexhaustible *mine*. We repeat that there is a luxury in the recollection that we have *something*, amidst the everlasting *din* of trade and commerce, of which, as English we may boast, and to which we may direct a learned and enquiring brother, though he should have come from the very ends of the earth. (quoted in Siegel 2008, 214)

This sense that the national museum was founded for a state-building purpose was not confined to Europe. The Smithsonian's National Museum of American History, for instance, is not only the legacy of Enlightenment-era scientist James Smithson but also the "great engine of democracy" in a nation that at its founding had few schools and many immigrants, "teaching citizens civic virtue, cultural nationalism, and love of God," according to Joel Orosz (quoted in Roberts 1997, 4). Similarly, in the entryway to the Argentine National Historical Museum, a bronze plaque displays the original 1889 decree for a national museum, beginning, "Considering that the maintenance of the traditions of the May Revolution and War of Independence is of transcendental national interest and that concurring to this end, it being necessary that the monuments and other objects that pertain to that great time should be respected and conserved . . . those objects mentioned [should] be concentrated, collected, and guarded conveniently in a national museum" (my translation). And Flora E.

S. Kaplan, a specialist in African museums and editor of the first collection of essays on museums' role in nation-building across the developing world, wrote that "museums are purveyors of ideology and of a downward spread of knowledge to the public, thereby contributing to an historical process of democratization" (1994, 3). Such a socialization function is paradoxically both elitist, transferring the "proper" knowledge to the masses, and revolutionary, assuming that these masses will need and use that knowledge in their active public participation in the political life of the nation.

In sum, as institutions of the Enlightenment, national museums, as they arose in the eighteenth century, reflected an emphasis on rationality, education, and the ongoing classification of knowledge to understand the universe. As institutions growing in the age of empire, their collections reflected the power of certain nations to trade, or take, the artifacts of others as both symbols of power and objects of study. And as institutions blossoming in the nation-states of the age of revolution, they contributed to a new understanding of personal identity that included national citizenship, and they reflected the anxieties of the elites that these new citizens understand their shared history.

The world has been building national museums ever since. From India (1814), to Peru (1825), to the United States (1846), to Uzbekistan (1876), to Ethiopia (1976), to Australia (2001), to the United Arab Emirates (2016), these same issues of citizenship, education, and globalism continue to dominate national museum discourse. As Kaplan puts it, "Museums have long served to house a national heritage, thereby creating a national identity that often fulfilled national ambitions" (1994, 9). What has changed since the eighteenth century is the way in which that continuing discourse is presented. The display format of the early museums owed much to the concurrent rise of what Victorian essayist Thomas De Quincey (1848) called *the literature of knowledge*, or scientific language—that is, to the rise of clear, plain, supposedly neutral scientific settings as the descriptive force par excellence of the public realm. Large neoclassical buildings with glass display cases and explanatory placards: this version of national identity is still a feature of many museums. Yet two and a half centuries after the initial founding of the British Museum in 1753, national museums today serve a more contested national imagination, and they do so frequently with a nod toward the reemergence of De Quincey's other way of knowing, *the literature of power*, with its emphasis on the poetic, the narrative, and the affective sides of language—and therefore public space.

The Rhetorical Museum

So just how rhetorical can a nation-inducing museum be today? Pretty blatantly rhetorical. For instance, the State Museum of Temurids History (Tashkent, Uzbekistan) was opened in 1996, five years after Uzbek independence from the Soviet Union, to celebrate the medieval Temurid dynasty and particularly the life of Amir Temur, better known as Tamerlane in the West, nearly seven hundred years after his rise to power in the spice route city of Samarkand. Centrally located amid gardens in the center of the modern national capital, the round white marble structure, with its dome and porticoes, is adorned outside with blue tile, and inside its carved doors it boasts a vivid gilded domed ceiling, mural-covered walls, and graceful staircases that circle its atrium. It is a beautiful synthesis of modern and traditional Temurid architecture, in itself a rhetorical reassertion of historical Uzbek identity after decades of Soviet architecture. Is the museum rhetorical? Cultural historian Timur Dadabaev notes that the post-Soviet discourse in Uzbekistan invokes a glorious ethnic past as a counter to the Soviet discourse that had placed an emphasis on "civilizing" underdeveloped central Asia. Further, Soviet practice elevated particular historical figures and diminished others in order to promote particular social values (2010, 32). Thus it is not surprising to find that, as independent Uzbekistan reconstructs its national identity, Amir Temur—conqueror of much of central Asia, patron of the arts and sciences, ethnically non-Russian (he was Turkic-Mongol), and founder of the last "golden age" dynasty of the territory that many years later would become Uzbekistan—has taken on a mythic status. He was particularly promoted by the country's first and only president (recently deceased), Islam Karimov, and the state museum is a centerpiece of Karimov's efforts, as evidenced inside by the numerous marble plaques engraved with quotations from the president. Thus visitors climbing the staircase can read in Uzbek, Russian, and English Karimov's assertion that "if somebody wants to understand who the Uzbeks are, if somebody wants to comprehend all the power, might, justice, and unlimited abilities of the Uzbek people, their contribution to the global development, their belief in the future, he should recall the image of Amir Temur."[1] Since the Western image of Temur is largely shaped by Christopher Marlowe's sensationalistic play *Tamburlaine the Great*, with its oft-repeated depiction of Temur as the rampaging "scourge of God," it is helpful to add that carved into the outer wall of the museum are the words justice, enlightenment, honor, and friendliness, "reflecting the just policy of Amir Temur," as the Governmental Portal of the Republic of Uzbekistan puts it (2011). It is clear that the State Museum of Temurids History is making an argument for a particular view of the past in order to promote of vision of "who the Uzbeks are" today and the role that their "unlimited abilities" can play in the future. To be "rhetorical" here is to acknowledge a purpose that goes beyond history telling to persuade visitors of a particular view of themselves and their civic identity.

It is possible to argue that less nationalistic nations, whose museums are more purely aesthetic, are not as rhetorically focused as the Temurids museum, but I would argue that all museums attempt to use "language as a symbolic means of inducing cooperation in beings that by nature respond to symbols" (Burke 1950/1969, 43). For instance, the British Museum in London, that grande dame of the museum world, says in one of its visitor pamphlets that the museum "exists to tell the story of cultural achievement throughout the world, from the dawn of human history over two million years ago until the present day. The Museum is a unique resource for the world. The breadth and depth of its collection allows the world public to re-examine cultural identities and explore the complex network of interconnected world cultures" (Trustees of the British Museum 2012). Is this rhetoric, or is it merely a factual statement about the museum? The British does indeed have an unprecedented collection spanning the range of human history, and as a free museum open to all, it does indeed share its resources with the world. The travel writer Rick Steves famously tells his readers that a visit to the British Museum is like "taking a long hike through *Encyclopedia Britannica* National Park" (Steves 2014, 11). The two-acre classical gray building on Great Russell Street houses irreplaceable treasures in ninety-five rooms on three floors. But the museum trustees clearly mean their assertion of the museum's importance to be rhetorical as well as factual, persuading their audience as well as informing it. In this case, the museum is asserting its universality in a pamphlet arguing for its right—its duty to the world—to continue holding the Parthenon Marbles, more than half the surviving architectural adornments of the Athenian Parthenon, which were removed by Lord Elgin, the British ambassador to Greece, more than two hundred years ago. The Greeks have repeatedly demanded their return, and have in fact recently opened their own Acropolis Museum, with its Parthenon Gallery dedicated to the display of the missing marbles (another rhetorical move). It is within the context of a pamphlet on the British counterargument ("What has the Greek government asked for?" "What is the British Museum's position?") that the British trustees assert their museum's unique universality. This most iconic of all national museums, that is, asserts an identity that is stylistically performed as a disinterested service to the world, a service that *requires* it to continue holding—and aesthetically displaying—those objects gathered/removed from other nations over several centuries by the British Empire. The museum itself recognizes this as a rhetorical position, a stance that is its explicit response to an ongoing dialogue in which it seeks the world's agreement that Britain is the best place to hold such artifacts. That individuals can disagree over whether the British trustees are right marks this as a rhetorical position (rhetoric focuses on questions that have no clear right answer) and thus marks the museum itself as a rhetorical space.

The Epideictic Museum

When museums are rhetorical, we can consider the impact of the type of rhetoric they use. Traditional rhetorical discourse has been divided into three types: deliberative rhetoric, used in legislative bodies to exhort for future actions; forensic rhetoric, used in the courtroom to accuse or defend past actions; and epideictic rhetoric, traditionally used in ceremonies and festivals to unify the community around shared values and beliefs. Museum rhetoric is clearly epideictic, using past events to evoke a consensus around present-day values and identities, "both reminding [the audience] of the past and projecting the course of the future" (Aristotle 1991, 1358b). Aristotle's classic example was the state eulogy, that public performance at which the community gathers to reaffirm that it is indeed the kind of society that would honor the values and beliefs embodied by the dead. The task of the eulogist is to nudge the community closer to such values by naming them as qualities to be emulated. These emulated qualities, in turn, produce a communal identification, as literature scholar Jean Wyatt discusses (without the link to the epideictic). She notes that in Freud's psychology of groups, "'the ego is born' through mimesis—a formation of the self as a copy of the other . . . based on the desire to be the one 'whom one wishes to equal, to replace, to be'" (2012, 14). The emulated values of the Other, that is, form the basis for one's own sense of identity. To put it another way, there is no identity without identification with another, and epideictic rhetoric provides the attitudinal catalyst for that identification. It is *epideixis*, then, that works to persuade Uzbeks that if one really wants to understand who they are, "he should recall the image of Amir Temur" and his values of justice, enlighten-ment, honor, and friendliness.

Epideictic rhetoric is a part of the cultural glue that holds common beliefs together, but as rhetorician Cynthia Sheard argues, it can also help a commu-nity envision new possibilities (1996, 771), because upholding values reminds people to dream. "To praise a man is in one respect akin to urging a course of action," she writes, quoting Aristotle, adding that as such epideictic rhetoric "is an especially hortatory use of language because it is always ultimately about how we conduct our public and private affairs" (786). Historiographer Jeff Walker refers to epideictic rhetoric's ability to "challenge or transform conven-tional beliefs" (2000, 10) by focusing attention on the shared values that underlie (or do not) civic actions. In Sheard's words, "Epideictic discourse today operates in contexts civic, professional or occupational, pedagogical, and so on that invite individuals to evaluate the communities or institutions to which they belong, their own roles within them, and the roles and responsibilities of their fellow constituents, including their leaders" (771). When the old forms of promoting values (patriotic pageants, lengthy public addresses) no longer work in modern societies, epideictic discourse adapts. "We see examples of such discourse on the op-ed pages of our newspapers, on our televisions, in our classrooms, at confer-ences, in professional journals as well as in places of worship and other sites at which communal and institutional goals, practices, and values are reaffirmed, reevaluated, or revised and where specific kinds of behaviors are urged," Sheard notes (771)—and museums are among these other sites.

The world today is unbelievably diverse by ancient Athenian standards. Indi-viduals share national space with people who seem so different from themselves that the concept of unified civic space, much less shared stories, meanings, and values, is hard to grasp, and the anxiety this engenders fuels both hand-wringing and war. At the same time, tolerant people resist the call to tell others what to believe, how to act, what their identity "must" be as members of a nation. Muse-ums bridge the gap between these poles of hegemony and anomie as a modern form of epideictic rhetoric, a eulogy to the past nation whose values, revised, live on. When history museums present a narrative of past deeds that reaffirms present values and urges future actions in line with those values, then, they are using their assembled artifacts to construct an epideictic narrative. Through their stories, they aim to persuade visitors to embrace values that the nation collectively considers ideal.

good
term

Significantly, these values change with the times, and museums use the past to speak largely to present values. As epideictic *rhetorical* spaces, museums may encourage visitors to think about what they treasure and to reaffirm their commitment to those communal ideals, but as epideictic *aesthetic* places, museums may provide (though they do not all do so) what Amareswar Galla, director of the International Institute for the Inclusive Museum, is fond of calling "safe places for unsafe ideas"—places in which we can contemplate and debate opposing views. For example, the stately BELvue Museum in Brussels, a cream-colored luxury hotel from the eighteenth century, recently renovated the way it tells the national story of Belgium. It opened its twelve rooms in 2005 to tell the nation's history in a series of chronological galleries, yet only ten years later its permanent collection closed to "undergo a total transformation," according to its press release, which added, "The new exhibition will be organised around issues that are important for our society but which also represent the particularity of Belgium." Noting that 40 percent of its visiting audience is young, the museum staff convened a team of Flemish- and French-speaking eighteen- to twenty-five-year-olds to develop concepts for a new, less chronological, more thematic exhibit space. "'Our country has a young and tumultuous history and our society is witnessing rapid change. We feel it is important that a museum about Belgium also reflects the society in which we live,' says An Lavens, Manager of the BELvue Museum" (Oechsner 2015, 1). In a nation in danger of being ripped apart by language differences and immigrant concerns, and at a time when looking at the artifacts of constrained national history may be less a priority than it used to be, the BELvue is striving to renew its aesthetic form—to become more modern but also less monological—in order to remain a part of the existential conversation. Burke would approve. An overreliance on knowledge—on parceling out facts to an audience, or what he called the psychology of information—is unlikely to move visitors once they believe they have learned the facts. It is eloquence, the psychology of form, with its ability to transform one's own emotions into detailed examples arranged with power to evoke emotion in the audience, that keeps people returning even when they "know how it will turn out"—whether what they return to is a good book, a stirring symphony, or their national museum.

Museum Intersections

As rhetorical spaces, then, museums serve as points of intersection for various forces that are more commonly opposed in public space: the intersection between public and academic worlds, between pragmatism and idealism, and between the political and the aesthetic. Inside the museum, these dichotomies intersect dialectically.

By juxtaposing public and academic worlds, museum intersections redefine the role of "public intellectual," a role that is not always welcome around the world and that intellectuals by themselves cannot always successfully embody. At home in the intellectual communities of scientific inquiry, artistic expression, sociocultural and historical exploration, museums also understand the need to *communicate* both the knowledge and the passion of these fields to other audiences. In my travels exploring nationalism in museums, I frequently found myself enthralled by exhibits about things in which I thought I had no interest . . . until the museum persuaded me otherwise. Ancient amphorae, unknown artists, rabbits or glaciers or giant squid—the realms of intellect and popularity are intentionally bisected in museums because of their unique function: *museums exist to attract the public to knowledge*. As the ancient Roman rhetors would have recognized, museums practice eloquence in order to persuade an audience to consider their reasoning.

By juxtaposing pragmatism and idealism—the doable and the desirable— museums confront the helplessness engendered by competing expectations. Historian Stefan Berger notes that national museums in particular face four such "conflicting demands" from the nations that sponsor them. "There is a revival of national narratives," he writes, "and museums are increasingly asked to tell the uplifting story of the nation and provide citizens with cultural glue. At the same time, demands are being placed on museums to provide multiple forms of identity for different sections of the citizenry. They are also asked to relate the story of the nation to its neighbours and to wider spatial entities. Finally, museums are under pressure to educate citizens towards tolerance and cosmopolitan values" (2010, 1). Each of these demands—nationalism, identities, diplomacy, and ethics—is seen as a necessary component for modern citizenship, and therefore museums are tasked with promoting not only the desirability of all four visions but also their practical application. Their reliance on objects to anchor their exhibits helps them negotiate these conflicts, as objects come not from the ideal dream of a better tomorrow but from the pragmatic reality of a past or present-day reality.

By juxtaposing political and aesthetic worldviews, finally, museums help give the lie to the false idea that the latter are worth less in a data- and marketing- driven world. Rhetoric as it is manifested in museums provides the potential for a third way of reasoning that unites the logical and the emotional into thoughtful, action-oriented persuasion. To take action toward greater public commonality, people must first change their attitudes so that they desire that greater commonality. In parallel with the *political* constitution that unites a community, then, the humanities (channeled through museums) provide a *cultural* constitution promoting both stability (the manifested history of a nation) and flexibility (the freedom to negotiate ongoing issues of knowledge and policy). This was the message of Aronsson's final address to the Eunamus project as it gathered in Budapest in December 2012 to discuss possibilities for European cohesion at a time of increasing economic and political fragmentation. Museums offer the opportunity to reduce complexities to a more material plane, to place them within the context of the ongoing national story, and thus to address and to reconcile the divisions that in the external world may seem too amorphous, intractable, and unknown—and this gives museums, and the humanistic culture they persuade visitors to experience, a pragmatic role in worldly political debates over values and actions toward a better future.

As a Burke scholar, I emphasize this bridging aspect of museum rhetoric because Burke also strove to bridge the gap between politics and culture, pragmatics and vision, academia and the masses. He insisted on the real-world efficacy of aesthetic concerns: literature, as he famously noted, is equipment for living. Only by examining the attitude-driven language of aesthetic endeavors can social scientists begin to understand what he called the "trend of history": "It is precisely because the authority of words cannot be delegated ... that one must watch the 'poetry exchange' to learn what is really going on in the world. The usual 'parliamentary' method of gauging is ... [seen when one] draws up a simple questionnaire ... [and then] tabulates the results. . . . The future is really disclosed by finding out what people can sing about" (Burke 1937/1984, 334–35). The song, unlike the survey—even the "big data" survey of today's computer analytics—is not reaching for one answer but for several at once, not masquerading as logic but embodying the human complexity that manifests itself less in numbers than in the attitudes that lead one to action.

That, at any rate, is museums' potential. Some museums may seem to engage more overtly with the world outside their doors than others do—but, as a recent tragedy demonstrates, even the most aesthetic of museums may play an outsized role in the conception of national values and public identity. The Bardo National Museum in Tunis exists primarily to display the magnificent African Roman mosaics excavated from ruined villas throughout Tunisia. The rival of and then the breadbasket for imperial Rome, Tunisia two millennia ago was a

rich land studded with city and country estates, which its dry climate and limited population have combined to preserve, such that today it boasts the largest
collection of classical mosaics remaining in the world. According to Bardo officials, more non-Tunisians than Tunisians visit the museum. Its website is in
English and French, the colonial languages, rather than in the Arabic spoken by
the general populace. Yet the Bardo is unquestionably a national museum, even
a point of national pride in a nation whose infrastructure was threatening to
crumble when I first visited in 2012. Visitors are drawn in the entry hall to a
monumental, stunningly detailed mosaic of Neptune and his court, and from
there are guided through room after room of antiquities. The Bardo contains
little from the past ten centuries, and stepping into the airy, white, sunlight-
flooded space of its recently renovated entryway, just down the street from the
national Parliament, one might forget that a contemporary world of modernism
and revolution exists just outside its glass doors—that is, until March 18, 2015,
when its calm oasis of ancient permanence was the scene of a terrorist attack in
which twenty-two people were killed and more than forty injured. While initial
reports speculated that the attack was motivated by an economic or political
grievance, the statement of responsibility from the Islamic State (ISIS) described
the attack as a "blessed invasion of one of the dens of infidels and vice in Muslim
Tunisia" (BBC News 2015), thus making it clear that the attack was directed at
aesthetics, at the Bardo itself as a symbol of a Tunisia more tied to global cultural norms than to the radical isolationism of ISIS (see fig. 2). The seemingly
nonrhetorical celebration of ancient artifacts, in other words, was seen as rhetorically persuasive—as celebrating the values of a national identity that had, in
the eyes of radicals, to be stamped out.

"What is it about relics and ruins that keep on drawing fanatics?" asked
Middle East political expert Larbi Sadiki (2015) in an Al Jazeera editorial the
day after the attack, and I believe that the answer lies in part in their message of
permanence—what is unchanged and stable about public identity—which is
the opposite of the revolutionary change desired by radical groups everywhere.
Permanence and change (the title of Burke's first published work of cultural
criticism), as I hope to demonstrate throughout this book, are never neutral
states, rarely benign, and usually in tension. The one promises disruption of the
other, of the status quo, but the nature of that disruption—a *breath of fresh air*
or *cyclones of chaos*—and the nature of the status quo—*oppressively set in stone*
or *comfortably grounded*—is continually in debate. Museums, as culturally conservative institutions that yet hope to promote the best of what *could* be, are

2 | The lobby of the Bardo National Museum, Tunis, which was attacked by ISIS in 2015.

often in the middle of this debate. When they succeed—and they don't always succeed—they fall on the bias between our various intersections, combining aspects of both permanence and change to promote a glimpse of a stable while evolving sense of national identity with which visitors might, if they are persuaded, identify themselves.

In the next two chapters, I delve more deeply into the specifics of how first narrative and then material objects work through space and time on visitors to promote the kinds of identification and division that I analyze in the rest of the book.

2

The Story We Tell Ourselves

Understanding communication as collective memory . . . transforms what we would usually take to be a context for communication—a museum, a park, a preservation site, or other place—and implores us to see it as a mode of communication in its own right.
—Carole Blair

As we saw in chapter 1, the British Museum tells visitors that it "exists to tell the story of cultural achievement throughout the world." On the other side of the globe, posters for the National Museum of Australia proclaim that it is "where our stories live," while the Museum of Siam announces its intent to "tell the story of how Thai identity has developed over thousands of years." When people think of museums, they think of objects, but museums are filled with stories—they have fully embraced the "narrative turn" to tell their remembered story. As memory scholars Aoki, Dickinson, and Ott point out, "memory is mobilized symbolically and materially, spatially and temporally, and that is an embodied experience that often works affectively" (2013, 3). These are the themes I address in this chapter and the next as I set up the context for my discussion of national identification in the rest of the book.

History and Memory

History and memory are related, but more as cousins than as identical twins in the family story. Just as individuals' memories are framed by the scenes in which they live, the public persuades itself of its collective memories through the sharing of historical moments. The rhetorical claims made on a community are grounded in these shared memories, and they are both ideational and materialized. Sociologist Maurice Halbwachs's notion of "collective memory"—existing outside the individual, contributing to the shared remembrances of the groups to which one belongs—is a key assumption of public memory studies. Collective memory is both the "memory of a collective body, or a 'public'"—an idea—and the "visible manifestation of memory in the sense of making a memory public"—an object—as communication scholars Kendall Phillips and Mitchell Reyes note (2011, 1–2). Blair, Dickinson, and Ott describe six qualities of this public memory: it is activated by present concerns, issues, or anxieties; it narrates shared identities, constructed senses of communal belonging; it is animated by affect; it is partial, partisan, and thus often contested; it relies on material and/or symbolic supports; and it has a history (2010, 6). Blair, Phillips, and others would add a seventh quality, that public memory is emplaced, forged in the interaction between people and sites: "places of memory are *not* finished texts, but sites of re-collection in which individuals and groups selectively cull and organize re-collected versions of the past that are (not) shared by others" (Aden et al. 2009, 313). Public memory, we can say, is where place aligns with narrative to create a collective identity.

In his influential series on national identity *Les lieux de mémoire* (Realms of Memory), Pierre Nora makes a distinction between this ongoing process of memory and the notion of "history." For Nora, history is what memory becomes when it is reified and abstracted, moving from a living "milieu" to a past place, a "lieu," "the reconstruction, always problematic and incomplete, of what is no longer. . . . Memory takes root in the concrete, in spaces, gestures, images and objects; history binds itself strictly to temporal continuities" (1996, 8–9). Nora was most interested in how memories become history—how traditions are formed, how the use of history influences the present. Memory, he writes, "is always a phenomenon of the present, a bond tying us to the eternal present" (3), selectively re-creating the past for its own purposes. Museums, then, abstracting and renarrating collective national memories, become in Nora's work a category of "lieux," memory *places*. Indeed, to go a step further, as historian Dominique Poulot writes in an Eunamus study on historical narratives, "As has been shown by several generations of studies dedicated to the political manipulation of the past and to public uses of history, the collection of any museum is the product of reconstructions based on selection and choice, on selective omissions and voluntary commemoration" (2012, 7). Its displays are not just abstracted memory; they are *necessarily partial* abstracted memory (selected and deflected, as Burke put it), highlighting particular aspects of the narrated history and obscuring other aspects as the consensus of present-day individual viewpoints over what matters in the past changes with the times. As architectural theorist Eleni

Bastéa observes, "our memories would remain an amorphous mass were we not able to give them form, to shape them into a coherent narrative" (2004a, 10).

A clear example of changing present-day concerns breaking into depictions of the past is evident in the museums of many nations that address relations with their indigenous populations. Indigenous museums or exhibits in Sweden or Norway, in Australia, in the United States or Mexico all respond to present-day demands from native peoples to be written into the collective narrative. The Museum of the Nation in Lima, Peru, seemingly crafts one of the more muted displays of this native voice, but that voice has in fact been woven into Peruvian national history to such an extent that the collective memory of both past events and present identity has been altered. The museum itself is an imposing gray cube on a wide boulevard in modern Lima, but down a corridor from its cavernous interior, the galleries are more intimate, low-ceilinged affairs, housing a large permanent collection of artifacts titled "Unity in Diversity" and offering a journey through the history of Peru. Artifacts—case after glass case of objects sitting in rows on white-stepped platforms—are arranged thematically and then chronologically. Opening texts for each section tell visitors what they are looking at—"Textiles" or "Sacred Elements," with small tags further specifying "Domestic and Wild Animals," for instance—but there is not a great deal of cultural context. As the introduction to the exhibit notes, "The Peruvian territory is privileged because in it societies came together whose technological, artistic, and general cultural contributions continue to be of great importance for humanity" (my translation)—thus the significance and history behind these artifacts is presumed to be self-evident. The exhibit is instead creating a memory of the overarching *continuation* of various technological and artistic contributions within a pluralistic but unbroken forty-five-hundred-year history.

Now, many have read the history of Peru as a story not of continuation but of rupture, as the story of the sixteenth-century European conquest of the Inca Empire that resulted in near-genocidal population loss within decades. But that is not how the national museum remembers (or, as Nora terms this process, "rememorates") it. The "facts" of the museum history are arranged into a continuous tradition, materially demonstrated through a long, unbroken chain of pottery items, which change from epoch to epoch as the result of many conquests of one indigenous community by another, each conquest leading through melding to new pottery styles and techniques; in this story, the arrival of the Spanish, with their own pottery techniques, is just one more step in the changing but ongoing pottery-making tradition. As a nearby panel notes, "The arrival of the Spaniards to the Andean world brought as a consequence a wide and deep process of transculturation that covered all areas of society. . . . [This] produced a curious syncretism between ancient Peru and the European artistic vocabulary" (my translation). As the introductory panel asserts, "It is worth noting that we are the product of a long tradition, which denotes the survival of customs, technological management, beliefs, and forms of interrelation that come together in what today is Peru: a multiethnic, multicultural society." Modern Peru, a nation nearly half of whose citizens are Amerindians, has chosen to collectively rememorate and selectively narrate its past not as greatness lost but as greatness continued, not as separation but as unity. It is a story that transforms the old collective binary of conquest and disruption into the new national memory of survival and continuance.[1] As Sigmund Freud long ago pointed out, in the collective mind of a group, "testing the reality of things falls into the background in comparison with the strength of wishful impulses with their affective cathexis" (1955, 80). Emotion trumps fact when the collective examines its past.

How is this rememoration transmitted? Visitors are not blank slates for a new story to be written upon, and old and new memories often exist together: "As each generation modifies the beliefs presented by the previous generations, there remains an assemblage of old beliefs coexisting with the new, including old beliefs about the past itself," as sociologist Barry Schwartz notes (1991, 234). The old stories are less forgotten than reinterpreted to fill the present need. Between history and memory, memory is more malleable, more rhetorically attitude-driven. As Carole Blair asserts, "History claims for itself a legitimacy based on research norms. Collective memory, by contrast, is an overtly political and emotionally invested phenomenon" (2006, 53). Such memory is uniquely informed by—and seeks in turn to influence—the present. But the present is neither deus ex machina nor tabula rasa. To go back to our example of the changing depiction of indigenous histories, in sites from the Inca Museum in Cusco, Peru, to the Uluṟu-Kata Tjuṯa Cultural Centre near Uluru, Australia, present-day responses spark new attention to ancient presences, their historical signs narrated into (but not replacing) the collective memory that had previously ignored them. Thus collective memory adds a layer of indigenous survivance onto a story that may still, and *at the same time*, remember "civilizing heathens" or "taming empty land." As museologist Jennifer Harris points out, "The expectation of multiple and contradictory meanings in a postmodern institution poses huge challenges to museums in grappling with monumental topics" (2016, 17). However, these "huge challenges" shrink somewhat when placed in the context of the modern turn away from a belief in the purely rational. Sociologist Michael Schudson notes that "the notion that memory can be 'distorted' assumes that there is a standard by which we can judge or measure what a veridical memory must be. If this is difficult with individual memory, it is even more complex with collective memory" (1995, 346). Schudson gives the example of the U.S. Indian wars: "If you recall the wars between the United States government and Native Americans as part of the history of nation-building, it is one story; if you recall it as a part of a history of racism, it is another" (346). Schwartz would add that it is very possible to recall both, one layered on top of the other.

From the perspective of memory studies, then, what we call "history muse-ums" would be more accurately termed "places of public memory," as Dickinson, Blair, and Ott title their foundational text. Yet, as Harris notes, that is not what much of the public expects. Museumgoers surveyed by Eunamus overwhelm-ingly reported that the most important function of national museums is to "accurately" portray national history (Aronsson and Knell 2012, 28)—and most seem to think they do a good job. Aronsson writes, "museums are among the more trustworthy carriers of explanation of the world, much more so than schools or television" (2008, 14). Digging a bit deeper, however, we find that what visitors consider "accurate history" is not necessarily Blair's research-normed historical legitimacy but instead a negotiation with present-day mem-ory. A minority of those surveyed by Eunamus believed that museums should discuss *only* the past, while most visitors in the survey understood that muse-ums used the past to discuss the present (32.5 percent of those polled) or both the present and future (45.2 percent) (Bounia et al. 2012, 148). If museum dis-plays offer a window into the past, perhaps we value the window less for the assurance that we can climb through it into a forgotten past, and more because the shifting stories we glimpse through it illuminate the room in which we now live. Museologist Simon Knell asserts that within the museum, "no subject is more central to the construction of the nation than . . . the handling of the past" (2011, 8)—not the past itself, note, but its handling. This crafted past, enhanced by physical objects and enriched with data, is presented in a narrative. As the Uluṟu-Kata Tjuṯa Cultural Centre tells visitors to their website, "We carry our culture through stories which are handed down through generations from grandparents to grandchildren" (Parks Australia 2016)—and it is to narrative culture, the stories we tell our grandchildren, that we now turn.

The Narrative Turn

Part of the turn to overt narrative in museums comes from the shift from object analysis to human relations. Eilean Hooper-Greenhill explains that "'objects' in the modern age are no longer presented on the table of classification, where their morphology defined both their identity and their interrelationships. . . . Now material things present themselves in their relation to human beings. Material things are now constituted as objects through organic, historic links, through stories, and through people" (1992, 204). The museum educator, a twentieth-century addition alongside the curator and the administrator, is the personification of this move toward human relations. Indeed, storytelling and other interactive enterprises have become such major components of museums—with large panels, touchscreens, films, audio guides, docents, and performers competing for the audience's attention—that public historian Steven Conn was moved to title a book *Do Museums Still Need Objects?* While Conn was discussing science museums, history museums are most likely to use narrative as their representational strategy. As the Eunamus report on museum narratives put it, history "begins with the narrative, a coherent and developing discourse, and places objects and images to illustrate this narrative. While visitors may be asked to interpret the meaning of displayed items, these are subsidiary diversions from the controlling narrative" (Aronsson and Knell 2012, 37). In other words, curators see the museum object, that artifact upon which visitors focus their attention, as a tool of the narrative—those words that enter visitors' minds largely unnoticed. As we will see in the next chapter, rhetoric would counter that there is more to the story than this (indeed, I will refer to objects not as tools [agency] but as acts), but the narrative is still a powerful force.

The craftedness of the narrative *as* narrative relies on two qualities, according to narratologists: emplotment, or *temporality*, endowing the random events of life with a beginning, middle, and end; and reason, or *causality*, linking these events into a chain of meaning. In essence, according to rhetorical narrative theorist James Phelan, narrative is "a purposive act of communication . . . somebody telling somebody else on some occasion and for some purpose(s) that something happened" (2006, 297). Thus the narrative turn in museums can rightly be called as well the rhetorical turn, the addition of overt communicative purpose, with narrative's "power to capture certain truths and experiences in ways that other modes of explanation and analysis such as statistics, descriptions, summaries, and reasoning via conceptual abstractions cannot" (285). Moderns increasingly understand narrative in the same way that the ancients understood it—as the preeminent means of interpreting complex social occurrences.

Life Story Unity

Museum narratives are often presented through the perspective of a single narrator (the committee of museum staff), who narrates a communal life story through the selection of certain objects, their arrangement into a predetermined order, and the chronology of that order, which leads the visitor through the galleries. This process—a museum narrative linking the disparate events of national life, while slotting any new life events into the ongoing narrative— mimics the individual life story that each person constructs for him- or herself to make meaning of an otherwise random-seeming world. "It is through the construction of a life story that self and memory are intertwined," narrative psychologists Robyn Fivush and Catherine Haden write, and it is the life story of our past events, linked causally, that provides us a self-identity (2003, vii). This narrated life story is forged from real events, but in its telling it is crafted by the needs of individual and audience. As Fivush and Haden put it, "life stories are based on autobiographical episodes, but to a considerable extent reflect efforts to portray oneself in a way that makes sense within one's social and cultural context" (xiii). As narrative, that "making sense" of the story—both the personal story and the public one—relies on emplotment and causality and the ability to slot new data into an ongoing story. Planned a high-powered career and then got blindsided by a loved one's special needs? Considered your nation inviolate and then were conquered by invaders from across the sea? Your and your nation's ability to thrive, as we saw in the Peruvian museum, depends on fitting this new situation into the (revised yet ongoing) story you craft of your personal/communal identity. As narrative psychologist Dan McAdams puts it, "Stories are less about facts and more about meanings" (quoted in Bastéa 2004a, 11)—meanings that you, the narrator, supply. This meaning in a life story is created through both a *synchronic* integration, uniting the different roles each person plays in life in one "me" (*I am at the same time a scholar and a mother and a fan of the Beatles*), and a *diachronic* integration, uniting an individual's divergent life choices into one coherent timeline (*I pursued degrees in four different fields but they're all useful to my work now*) (McAdams 2003, 188–89). The life story is both "true"—composed of real events—and also necessarily selective, highlighting in any retelling only those events deemed most relevant to the individual's present-day values and future progress.

National museums undertake a similar process in constructing unified meaning from diverse national memories. In an earlier article, paraphrased here, I applied McAdams's life-story lens to the collective narrative in the Museum of London to demonstrate how a museum story works to unify a past that, as it was lived, no doubt seemed marked not by unity at all but instead by shattering disjunctions of invasion, disease, and disaster (Weiser 2012). The Museum of London, I noted, is a walk-through, multistoried space that sits astride Roman ruins in the heart of the city. It welcomes the visitor with a clear life-story narrative: "Start your visit to London here with over 450,000 years of history. Here you can discover prehistoric London, see how the city changed under Roman rule, wonder at the grandeur of medieval London and explore the effects of civil war, plague and fire on the capital. . . . Five new galleries show how the vibrant and unflagging energy of Londoners has shaped this global city" (Museum of London n.d.). The museum divides its galleries into seven periods that visitors walk through chronologically. Not surprisingly, the first 445,000 years ("London Before London") are highly selective, with necessarily brief glimpses of nomadic hunter-gatherers along the Thames. The next five hundred years, of "Roman London," get a comparatively larger amount of attention, complete with a re-created Roman street and walk-through villa, rivaled by the thousand years of "Medieval London," which includes a particularly moving caesura of a darkened circular room filled with voiced accounts of the Black Death. The bad times—"War, Plague, and Fire"—get their own room. As visitors approach the present, selections expand, such that while the empire of Lord Nelson gets a case, Victorian and Edwardian London gets both a re-created street and a stroll-through pleasure garden, and London during World War II gets its own section, complete with another darkened circular room featuring photos, voices, and film footage from the Battle of Britain to re-create a time still alive in visitors' collective memories. Thus visitors to the Museum of London are invited on a walk through the life story of the London-self. Those seven major periods, be they fifty years or five hundred thousand, and their episodes—flint tools, Roman street, voices from the Black Death or the blitzkrieg—unify the story *diachronically* across time, reconciling even the radically different paths occasioned by multiple invasions and disasters into the one identity "London." And those disparate groups—Britons, Romans, Saxons, Vikings, Normans, and immigrants from across the globe—are all unified *synchronically* into the one identity "Londoners."

McAdams's research with individuals demonstrates that the selected episodes of the unified-past narrative provide a purposeful argument for the future—your life story makes you into the kind of person who will act in x manner rather than y when faced with a new decision. A similar response to the collective life story could be seen in the Museum of London in 2010. Five new galleries depicted an optimistic London of the twenty-first century: a city with multiple waves of immigrants, embracing the diversity of the newest groups, a repeatedly rebuilt city that welcomed the structural changes of the upcoming Olympics, an enduring city facing even the potential challenges of climate change with a Wellesian futuristic confidence (see fig. 3). This last identity was materialized by the poster-sized picture of a dirigible-driven near future of elevated walkways, where "Londoners adjust to permanently flooded streets," and a distant future in which "space elevators take settlers to the moon."

The nature of the life story itself imposes constraints on the way the narrative can be resolved: making narrative meaning of the past impels one to diachronically unify those past events (as we saw in Peru), while a unified past prepares one to face the future with a sense of identity and self-confidence—whether the "self" is an individual or a nation. In an individual, this might make for a healthy psyche; in national museums, it means that it is more difficult to portray the national story as diffuse or purely tragic, so less optimistic options are not fully considered. That Wellesian poster in the Museum of London, for instance, came from a book (sitting below the giant poster on a table for the

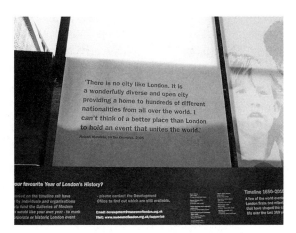

3 | A Museum of London sign paints a hopeful vision of future London.

visitor who cared to page through it) full of more grimly imagined future sce-
narios—but it was the optimistic scenario of unified identity that was displayed
on the wall in this museum.

Polyphonic Diversity

The *unifying* story, though, is not the only story in the museum. Just as individuals incorporate multiple epochs and multiple roles into an individual sense
of self, so too does the national story bring together diverse voices and multiple
perspectives. In fact, because the national identity story is *formally* compelled
to tell a unifying story, a museum can be particularly well suited as a space for
diverse voices: its parameters as "national" and its center as "unified" provide an
inherent stability that can allow it to balance what literary critic Mikhail
Bakhtin called the polyphony of multiple competing voices that exist both in a
novel and in life—including the interior life of each individual working to
unify a life story.

   In some museums, that polyphony is embedded in the narrative crafted by
the museum staff: "Ask any ten people what it means to be Australian and you
are likely to get ten different answers," reads a sign at the National Museum of
Australia in Canberra. Whether the polyphony is overt in the staff-crafted
narrative, though, it is still present in all museums, because those diverse
voices are carried in by visitors themselves. "Part of what makes cultural institutions like museums powerful forums for the creation of imagined communities is the fact that they are potentially ideal public spaces where personal,
private or autobiographical narratives come into contact with larger-scale,
collective or national narratives in mutually inter-animating ways," say social
scientists Shawn Rowe, James Wertsch, and Tatyana Kosyaeva (2002, 98).
This contact may not feel particularly "inter-animating" to museum staff, who
work diligently to ensure that visitors carry away some version of the narrative
that staff have crafted. Yet no matter how highly focalized the museum discourse, it is not the only story being told. As museum educator Lisa Roberts
points out, "in any given museum, visitors will probably encounter the same
raw material: an entryway, exhibits, and perhaps a restaurant or gift shop.
However, each will come away with an individually unique experience and
interpretation because every visitor is engaged in constructing a narrative
about what he or she sees" (1997, 137). Museologist Rhiannon Mason described

the experience of listening to residents of Newcastle visiting an exhibit of maritime artwork in which local amateur photographs were displayed in conversation with the paintings. The visitors to the exhibit did not discuss with one another painterly techniques or perspective angles—they talked about their own personal memories of watching ships being built and launched in Newcastle (later published as Mason, Whitehead, and Graham 2013). Personal memories might well tie an individual to a museum, but not necessarily in the way originally intended. Educator John Falk puts it succinctly: "Long-term meanings created by visitors from their time in the museum are largely shaped by short-term personal, identity-related needs and interests rather than by the goals and intentions of the museum's staff" (2009, 35). Indeed, Falk sees "building personal identity" as the primary purpose of visiting a museum (59), and he therefore argues in favor of those "inter-animating," idiosyncratic narratives that keep visitors from fully absorbing the official museum narrative. "Those who create tangible sites of memory, and those who make meaning from them, are participating in a cultural negotiation of considerable import," concludes communication scholar Janice Hume in her review of public memory scholarship (2010, 193)—to which I would add that those "creating" the memory site are both museum personnel and visitors.

John Bodnar (1992) describes the often contentious meetings of what he terms the "official culture" of the institution and the "vernacular culture" of the public in these sites of memory. Visitors' vernacular narratives might simply use the official story as scenic background for their own individualized tales, just as the official narrative might use the vernacular for "local color" without allowing itself to be influenced by these outside voices (Rowe, Wertsch, and Kosyaeva 2002, 108–9). But the relationship is usually more inter-animating, for while the collective dialogue is clearly shot through with multiple voices, those individual voices are also "filled with dialogic overtones" that "reflect the voice of others, including entire groups, who are not physically present in the immediate speech situation" (Wertsch 2009, 243).

The polyphonic encounter of the museum experience, moreover, does not happen in the abstract—it occurs as the individual walks through the museum space, not just *making sense of* but *sensing* the museum, seeing, hearing, touching (Aden et al. 2009, 320). Rhetorician Debra Hawhee has documented the importance, in both classical and contemporary rhetoric, of the physical body to the experience of mental persuasion. "It's only as a rational, cerebral, and yes, verbal endeavor that we have for the most part tuned out such features [as attention to rhetoric's sphere, interdisciplinarity, and its extradiscursive, nonrational features]," she argues (2006, 160), as she documents these ubiquitous, extrarational, but forgotten or overlooked roles. Hawhee returns to rhetorical notions of affective and sensorial persuasion along with the cerebral—the emotive audience response, in other words, to epideictic celebration. Historian Alison Landsberg calls this encounter between a person and a historical narrative a "prosthetic memory," the thing added onto a body to make it move, and she notes that these encounters occur particularly at places such as museums, where visitors *experience* the narrative (2004, 2). It is this sense of moving—both physically and emotionally—that Hawhee's work encompasses. A Burkean anecdote mentioned by rhetorician James Klumpp in his review of Hawhee's *Moving Bodies* illustrates the shift in perspective that this acknowledgment entails for rhetoric: Klumpp notes that he once confessed to Burke that he did not understand Burke's "new" insistence that *attitude* should be included in his persuasion schema, since Burke's other terms described an interpretive framework, whereas attitude was a mental process. Burke's response was to note that "attitude" did not only mean mental proclivity; it also meant the position of a body viz. its scene—that is, a stance (Klumpp 2010, 470). Bodies move through museums being moved by the stories they encounter (materialized stories, as we shall see in the next chapter) and being persuaded toward certain *stances* in response to those narratives.

Not everyone agrees with this interpretation of museum work. The Eunamus consortium put it bluntly: "National museums are about history: Most visitors surveyed said they came to national museums for social reasons, for entertainment and education. They did not visit with the intention of developing, understanding or crystallising their national identities. They believed these museums were about history, not identity" (Aronsson and Knell 2012, 28). Visitors, in other words, *resist* the idea that their own identity is being changed by their experience with the museum—perhaps because, unlike scholars, they do not view themselves as co-creating the reality they are experiencing. Visitors want to view the museum narratives as "truth"—but truth is always partially constructed by us. Our words and our stories, like our identities, are what they are because of our social scene. We may resist to some extent. But the polyphony of narratives—vernacular and official—might also inform one another, for either support or critique, so that both responses feature a meeting of engaged museum and engaged visitor at the point of the symbols that are both sensed and made sense of.

Spatial Narrative

The historical narrative that engages the visitor in a museum is also distinctly three-dimensional, asking the visitor to move not only through time, the chronology of an exhibit, but also through space, the architecture and arrangement of a display, in a way lacking in books, films, or any other form of narrative: "our histories are bound in space just as they are bound in time" as Bastéa writes (2004a, 7). The beginning-middle-end chronology of this boundaried spatial narrative is both present and diffused as visitors walk back and forth from case to case, through multiple galleries of their choosing, each trail through the museum intersecting with their own created narratives. The impact of this space on memory and emotion is one reason, I believe, why museums persist (even thrive) in a digitized virtual society. As Bastéa points out, *seeing* the object and *narrating* the object allow us to employ both the right and left sides of our brains, processing both holistically and analytically (9), which may explain our increased engagement with and memory of the experience presented.

Of course, as Bastéa goes on to point out, "mind memory" is enhanced by "body memory"—lived experiences, Hawhee's bodily rhetorics—and this is the other piece of the power of spatial narratives (10–11). In their walk-through, visitors to any museum gallery may move backward and sideways as well as forward, in and out of the designed narrative chronology, as they build an individualized path through the galleries. At the same time, the temporal disruption of this movement is constrained because the wandering visitor will stay within sight of the exhibit's overarching grand narrative as she moves about in it. The narrative mutually constructed by constrained visitor choices, then, is neither like reading a book from beginning to end nor like leaping, via links, from webpage to unrelated webpage. It is a bit more like reading a self-contained story or poem full of hypertext links, in which all the additional information remains within the overall frame of the main text—except that, in a museum, the original master narrative is always visible right there on the other wall, or back through the doorway that one may choose to walk through. In addition, as Michael Bernard-Donals (2012) notes, sensory affect in a museum is more bodily engaging than simply flicking one's eyes from main text to pop-up window online—for as museologist Sandra Dudley writes, affect is "fundamentally embodied and inseparable from the materiality of the body and the sensation of the material by sensate experience" (2012b, 98). The lived experience both outside and inside the museum, the sensation of walking through the exhibition, sparking the remembered identification with themes and objects, contributes to the affective persuasion of the material narrative. The winding path between towering monumental artifacts in the British Museum or the Mexican National Museum of Anthropology, the experience of hearing the birdsong of an extinct New Zealand forest or the voices of victims of the Black Death, the invitation to hold a three-million-year-old hand axe or taste pemmican—these sensory experiences punctuate the narrative and render it memorable.

These three-dimensional spatial narratives through which visitors move, then, vary by museum, but in their broad schema they can be divided into four categories, admittedly somewhat overlapping, that go beyond the causal chronology of a strictly linear historical narrative. I call these *multimodal chronology, interrupted chronology, polyphonic chronology,* and *lyric chronology,* and I will illustrate them with four national memorial museums.

Multimodal Chronology

The Kigali Genocide Memorial Centre, a memorial/historical museum on a hillside overlooking the capital city of Rwanda, follows a *multimodal chronology,* using various media and varying degrees of narrative openness. It chronicles the 1994 genocide of an estimated one million Rwandans by their countrymen over a hundred horrific days. Inside the museum building, the main exhibit flows in a circle around the exterior walls. Walking along a darkened enclosed corridor, visitors are told the story of the genocide step by step via well-lit placards. There is much text and few artifacts—mostly photos—and when I was there in 2011, visitors, both local and international, stood and read each panel, in order. The voiceless are given voice, and their story is given meaning, by the unity of a clear causal chronology: *this caused that caused genocide.* Yet, while the Memorial Centre makes sure that one history alone is presented, it does leave spaces for more than univocal learning. The circular corridor of the narrative surrounds an open center space filled with an eloquent sculptural grouping abstractly representing Rwandans before, during, and after the genocide. Multiple entrances to this circle allow visitors to wander at various points in the story from the chronology tunnel into the more aesthetic space. Two of these entrances also have niches placed in the outer wall of the curving tunnel, with several rows of carpeted steps rising to stained glass windows of hope brightly lit from outside. The effect is of small chapels, places to rest from the narrative. But the aesthetic counterpresentations go still further, as the "space" of the memorial itself is bigger than the building. It incorporates as well, in this year-round mild climate, a series of gardens that are just as much a part of the site as the history exhibit. These gardens are also designed to lead the visitor through the genocide, with separate gardens symbolically representing self-protection, unity, division, and reconciliation; there is also a forest of memory and a rose garden of victims—but the outside path is much more open-ended (visitors can wander, unlike in the tunnel, and the narrative of each space is only briefly defined). The gardens are what individual visitors make of them. As Harris notes, this type of display relies necessarily on visitor affect rather than rationality: "The turn to affect has occurred because expressing the inexpressible and representing the unrepresentable are the nearly impossible tasks of museums in the post colonial and post Holocaust eras" (2016, 16). In Kigali, finally, between the chronology of the museum building and the aesthetic experience of the gardens lies one more affective punch: eleven long, slablike barrows—mass graves where one hundred thousand Rwandans are now buried in long cement crypts (see fig. 4).

4 | Mass graves at the Kigali Genocide Memorial Centre.

In Kigali, then, as in all multimodal chronologies, the main story is largely monovocal, comprising the official chain of events that the nation has selected and renarrated (I discuss this further in chapter 6). The sidebars also tell the master narrative, but they offer more multidimensional affective spaces that allow individuals to weave a path in and out of that narrative and thus interact in multiple modes with this one historical memory.

Interrupted Chronology

Not all museums seek to tell such a uniform story. Some, in fact, purposely seek disruption via the second type of spatial narrative, the *interrupted chronology*. This narrative form uses its multidimensional space not to add or annex information to the main story but to counter its monovocal narrative. For instance, the Bundeswehr Military History Museum in Dresden, Germany, is a space purposely designed as a commentary on chronology. It began life as a nineteenth-century arsenal, a three-story solid block in neoclassical white, squatting on a hill overlooking the city. Architect Daniel Libeskind's 2011 addition, "a massive, five-story 14,500-ton wedge of glass, [dark] concrete, and steel," as his website puts it, "cuts into and through the former arsenal's classical order" (Studio Libeskind 2014) as it physically cuts through the center of building (see fig. 5). Inside, the museum leads visitors on a chronological history of the German military from Charlemagne to the present, while also exploring more abstractly the nature of violence. The chronological sections of the museum fill the two floors of the old arsenal, with vitrine-filled galleries representing the years 1300–1914, 1914–1945, and 1945–present. On each floor, that chronology is interrupted by the new wedge, housing themed exhibits designed to interpret critically the chronological narrative portrayed in the traditional spaces.

The thematic wedge of the Military History Museum attempts to dissociate itself at an architectural level from the chronology of pure narrative that is displayed in the traditional space. However, its intent is more than aesthetic—it aims to cause its *visitors* also to dissociate themselves from the narrative—and on that score I would argue that the museum ultimately falls short, because the experience of the *chronological* section is so much more visceral than the cerebral themed sections. In the chronological section, suits of armor stride forward in menacing formation, a frostbitten human foot graphically depicts the harshness of soldiering life, and a man and horse with identical gas masks gallop against a

5 | The exterior of the Bundeswehr Military History Museum, Dresden.

blood-red background. Against this compelling, even eloquent chronology, the
new thematic wedge is less powerful. First, it is less intrusive on the inside than
it appears to be from the outside. The elevator is housed within it, so visitors
enter each floor in the wedge, which makes it feel more like a large lobby than a
disruption—and once inside the chronological galleries, the wedged disruption
is left behind, so the wedge functions more like a chapter break. Further, the
narration of the wedge veers between overly abstract concept and overly minis-
cule detail. For example, the "War and Memory" display is introduced with a
text panel full of abstract concepts ("Wars are etched on the memories of peoples, families, and individuals. They are existential human experiences. Concepts of war range from glorification and mystification to the wish to abolish
war altogether to make way for 'perpetual peace.' Perceptions of war are determined by economic interests, religious beliefs or ideologies, traditions and rituals, art and mass media") and what appears to be a public archive of artifacts—row
upon row of travel books, film posters, and tin soldiers, placed in librarylike
movable storage shelving, nothing particularly emphasized. The themes, in other

words, have ignored the question of how to build a narrative bridge that makes the abstract concrete for the visitor and binds the (seemingly random) objects into an affecting story.[2] Architect Stephen Greenberg, critiquing a Libeskind building, says that "Libeskind's object-making vision has overwhelmed the experience and has taken precedence over the story and the characters in that story" (2005, 232). Ironically, Greenberg makes this critique not of the Military History Museum (which had not been built at the time of his essay) but of another Libeskind building that I find more successful: the Imperial War Museum North in Manchester, England.

In the IWM North, I would argue, Libeskind comes closer to achieving the kind of interrupted chronology he was aiming for in the Dresden museum, using multidimensional space to simultaneously manifest and interrupt a narrative. The museum is another modernist building, in the heart of old industrial Manchester. It tells the story of Great Britain's role in wars from World War I to the present. Like its cousin in Germany, the design symbolizes the fragmentation caused by war. "The design is based on the concept of a world shattered by conflict, a fragmented globe reassembled in three interlocking shards. These shards represent conflict on land, water and in the air," explains its website (2013). The architectural space celebrates the multifaceted nature of its narrative not only in the variety of individual stories, with multiple soldiers' letters and news clippings prominent among its collections, but also in the way it combines a chronological layout along the outer ring of the exhibit with a thematic layout of interior rooms and a large central space of rotating films and activity stations. The visitor entering the main gallery is encouraged, as in Rwanda, to follow "The Timeline," which narrates a selective account of British history in which World War I leads to World War II, the Cold War, Bosnia, and the present day. However, visitors may also opt to break away from the timeline at each display and enter a themed room that offers either a more aesthetic experience, such as the personal stories arranged as interactive file drawers in "Experience of War," or a call to critically reflect, as in the display on nationalist propaganda in "What Shapes Our Impressions of War?" In the center of the gallery, meanwhile, accessible (and visible) from the timeline every few yards, is a large open space where a series of "big picture" films on such crowd-pleasing topics as children in war and the home front in World War II play at regular intervals, alongside larger pieces of hardware (tanks and such) and various interactive stations. Still, whenever a visitor steps into the themed or central rooms, the timeline narrative always remains visible; the narrative is always right there—and unless the visitor chooses to leave the gallery, a return to the narrative must constitute "continuing" the experience.

The interruptions in this museum pay attention to affect and the ability to bounce in and out of the chronological narrative, meaning that these disruptions are placed within the larger story. A visitor does not need to try to hold both chronology and sidebars in mind at the same time—competing simultaneous narratives are held not only in the mind but in the eyes and ears as well. This is a juxtaposition handled relatively easily in aesthetic narratives, used as their audiences are to the interrupted narrative and range of emotional effects of, say, the postmodern film. It is the museum as *aesthetic* space, in other words, that allows this juxtaposed interrupted narrative to be effortlessly incorporated into our own developing stories. And with the multiple moods the visitor is asked to inhabit, ranging from celebration to hopeless despair, the space calls forth a synchronic diversity (multiple roles) within a flexible but bounded diachronic (timely) unity.

Polyphonic Chronology

In this way, the space of the IWM North can be said to demonstrate also the third type of narrative, a *polyphonic chronology*. In this kind of narrative, multiple voices are juxtaposed throughout, as in Bakhtin's polyphonic utterances, in which "the word never belongs solely to the speaker; instead, is it always 'half someone else's'" (quoted in Wertsch 2009, 243)—which evokes in the visitor a correspondingly more complex, more dialectical stance toward the narrative.

One of the finest examples of polyphony that I have experienced was housed for several years in Lima's Museum of the Nation and consisted of a photo exhibit titled *Yuyanapaq/Para Recordar* (To Remember) on Peru's twenty-year Dirty War against the Sendero Luminoso/Shining Path guerrillas. This exhibit spread through the bare rooms of the museum's upper story, gray cement walls alternating with whitewashed ones in a stark, boxy space. Sightlines were always considered. For instance, visitors entering the exhibit were greeted with a window looking straight through the center of the exhibit to its farthest point, framing the oversized bandaged face of a man. What this man represented was promised by everything between. Rows of enclosed rooms with gallerylike photo displays opened suddenly onto large open spaces with oversized photos like giant picture windows (see fig. 6).

6 | The artful use of space in the *Yuyanapaq* exhibit in the Museum of the Nation, Lima.

The interruptions to the rooms' chronology resided less in the space itself than was the case in the interrupted narrative, and more in the objects, voices, and retellings within the space. That is, the exhibit constantly disrupted its own narrative by presenting multiple "sides" of the conflict. For example, a series of placards arranged on pillars leading up to the life-sized photo of captured Sendero leader Abimael Guzmán told visitors on one pillar that the Truth and Reconciliation Commission considers Sendero "the immediate and fundamental cause" of the violence, while another pillar documented the socioeconomic causes of the uprising in chronically neglected indigenous regions, and a third pillar concluded that the war reinforced "preexisting authoritarian and repressive practices" in the police force, while torture and improper detentions "acquired a massive character." Through which of these lenses are visitors to look, finally, at the full-length photo of the jailed Guzmán? All of them? And while visitors thus gaze at a life-sized Guzmán, arm raised in a defiant salute, they have also within their sightlines photos of the shell of a Lima building blown up by Sendero *and* of the peasant leadership of the organization of rural family members of those who disappeared while in police custody. Which of these is the "real" story of the Dirty War? Can there be a "real" story? In a response room at the end of the exhibit, visitors were invited to ponder the "truth" of these conflicting episodes and to add their own reflective voices to the mix. Any too-easy diachronic conclusion was mitigated in polyphonic chronologies by the careful synchronic interplay of the "voices" of artifact, narrative, space, and the visitor him- or herself. The exhibit functioned in much the same way that Aden et al. describe in their concept of re-collection, whereby "we can examine how the confluence of the site as a re-collection of [re-membered] fragments and the individual interpreters as compilers of fragments produces different communities of memory" (2009, 324).

Lyric Chronology

Finally, the fourth category of spatial chronology, *lyric chronology*, we have already seen at work in the outdoor sections of the Kigali Genocide Memorial Centre, where visitors wander through gardens of beautiful plants with minimal direction, stopping to look at fountains or sit on benches, coming at last to the concrete slabs of the mass graves. The surprise here is that, compared to the rest of the site, the graves are largely unnarrated, almost understated. If voiceless victims are given voice inside the museum, and symbolically brought to life in the garden, here they are individually mute and dead, their rhetorical force lying solely in the foreknowledge of their silent numbers stacked on top of one another in rows beneath the cement. They are *atopos*, generically "out of place," and they therefore displace the visitor and challenge her to invest in interpretation, as rhetorician Joshua Reeves says of disruptive memorials (2013, 308). The power of the graves comes from their sudden, unexpected material *presence*, even as that presence can be understood and therefore engaged with only when it is combined with the stories woven into the total site. Through lyric chronology, visitors leave narration behind and are asked not so much to think about the events as to experience them in some bodily manifestation of (pre)emotional resonance. One final Libeskind structure works in a similar fashion, telling history as experienced lyric, and that is the Jewish Museum in Berlin, Germany, which sends arriving visitors down a long, dark stairway and into three intersecting "axes"—of exile, Holocaust, and continuity—designed to evoke in visitors something of the disorientation and entrapment felt by twentieth-century

German Jews. The axis of exile leads one through passageways where the floor and wall are slightly off-kilter, making walking more difficult and disorienting, with a heavy door at the end that—once opened, with effort—takes one out to a small garden. There are olive trees, refreshing after the bleakness of the passageway, but the trees are too close together to be seen clearly, the sky is far away, and any sense of a path forward is impossible to imagine. The axis of Holocaust leads past small glass cases of personal effects—a kind of mockery of the traditional museum display (Harris 2016, 36)—as the walls narrow and the light dims, until one reaches a dead end in the dark and claustrophobic room of a tall tower whose empty space looms overhead. The final axis, of continuity, leads visitors out of the darkness and up a long, multistory staircase—more affective hard work—to enter the more conventional remainder of the museum and follow a chronology of German Jewish history that, the spatial narrative persuades them, was interrupted for a time but has deep roots and spreading branches.

Deep Narrative

The wordless trajectory of the Jewish Museum, in fact, points toward one final type of spatial narrative that seems, paradoxically, to be nonnarrative. This implicit spatial narrative, guiding the visitor through underlying trajectories, I am calling *deep narrative*. It is embedded in the overall exhibit, which works to promote the unity and purpose characteristic of national life stories. This deep narrative implicitly tells visitors how they should interpret the artifacts, the placards, the supposedly neutral object-based epistemologies they are examining. By *deep narrative*, I mean to employ a kind of poetic dialectic between linguistic *deep structure*, the theoretical unity underlying seemingly different surface features, and postmodern *master narrative*, the overarching cultural story unifying smaller narratives. In the museum, then, a *deep narrative* operates both below and above the surface of an exhibit. Such a narrative might be seen in what is emphasized or deemphasized in the displays, what follows what in the galleries, or even what is or is not offered for sale in the gift shop or repeated in the marketing materials. Recall Aden et al.'s notion of memory places as "not finished texts, but sites of re-collection in which individuals and groups selectively cull and organize re-collected versions of the past that are (not) shared by others" (2009, 313). The deep narrative of museum space, intersected by visitors moving through it, makes for continuous created yet constrained stories operating at a level often outside our conscious awareness.

The deep narrative at work in the ancient history galleries of the recently remodeled National Museum of China in Beijing, for example, is arguably more persuasive than its more overtly narrated modern galleries. The museum itself is an enormous white structure along one side of Tiananmen Square, its two long wings stretching out from a central pillared courtyard that leads into its grand marble atrium of checkerboard ceiling and window squares. Its soaring central spaces divide history into a many-galleried first five thousand years and a smaller (but extensive) past 150. The recent history in its celebratory exhibit *The Road to Rejuvenation* in the latter has been criticized for "completely suppressing the shades of gray about [China's] past," as an article in the *New York Times* put it (Johnson 2011). In contrast, the museum's other major exhibit, *Ancient China*, seems more purely interpretive in its approach, with rooms full of astonishing treasures, in glass cases beautifully lit and spaced throughout the large rooms, accompanied by placards telling little more than their provenance. Compared to the extensive explanation and univocality of *The Road to Rejuvenation*, *Ancient China* seems content to let unnarrated observation guide the visitor. However, a narrative unfolds here too. First, the spatial architecture of each room moves the visitor chronologically from dynasty to dynasty over the course of five thousand years. Second, its chronology is very much a unifying narrative of both the diachronic events and the synchronic actors depicted by the beautiful artifacts. This unity is narrated repeatedly on the text panels that anchor the entrance to each room, many of which read like this one, on the rise of the Sui Dynasty: "A Unified Multi-ethnic Country: After 300 years of division and ethnic integration, China once again entered an age of unity and prosperity near the end of the 6th century CE. . . . This period marked another important stage in the development of a unified multi-ethnic country." Unity is the underlying message that incorporates even the Mongol invasion and conquest of China, which is portrayed not as the rupture it undoubtedly felt like to those who lived through it, but instead (as in the Museum of London with the Vikings, or in Peru with the Spaniards) as a unity narrative: "Multi-ethnic Regimes and Unification: . . . This period of polarized multi-ethnic regimes ended in the 13th century when the Mongols rose up and unified China." This unification narrative is spatially depicted as well, as for instance in the room on ethnic groups during the warring states period, in which the non-Han peoples, described as "on the peripheries," are also placed on the periphery of the room, which places artifacts from the central plains on display in its center. It is through the framing lens of continuous reunification that visitors move through the ages of sophisticated, stunning objects.

Thus, in the historical narration and formal display accompanying the beautiful objects that illustrate five thousand years of Chinese history, regional and ethnic separatism is repeatedly abolished by the centralized state, leading time and again to greater prosperity for the nation. The individual objects re-create history, their presence narrative evidence of national unity—a unity story that may be even more important to the continuation of the modern Chinese state than the more superficially propagandistic story of revolutionary triumph in the twentieth-century rooms. As archaeologist Gwen Bennett noted of Chinese archaeological interpretation, "One of the first requirements that [China's] new leaders faced [after the 1949 revolution] was to unify into one nation the territory inherited from the Manchu Qing Empire and comprised of multiple cultural regions where different languages were spoken, different lifeways were practiced, and different needs were paramount. One tactic taken among many to achieve national unity was the development of a national culture" (2012, 37–38). The deep narrative of the *Ancient China* exhibit naturalizes this unified national culture into five thousand years of unbroken history, and it projects the naturalized unification of periphery and center onto the present—as, for instance, in the display on Tibet, which is depicted on screens, with heroic accompanying music, in an imagined train journey that visitors would take from the Han center to its purported periphery. Would China's ethnic minorities and geographical outliers desire separation from the center? In the deep narrative of the museum, five thousand years of historic beauty would demonstrate that those voices were an aberration.[3] As Nora wrote, "history [is] less interested in 'what actually happened' than in its perpetual reuse and misuse, its influence on successive presents" (quoted in Bastéa 2004a, 9).

Deep narrative need not be instrumentalized for such a specific purpose, of course, to be present in a museum display. Narrative reinforces the sense of self—the way things just *are*, or what Burke called the pieties, what seems naturally to go with what (1935/1984, 74). Thus the genre of national narrative promotes individual identification with the collective—what goes with what— through the seemingly neutral facticity of objects. Even without the very real imposed narrative of such ubiquitous devices as guided tours or audio tours or multimedia tours, the deep narratives underlying crafted history that are present even in the more interpretive museums can be discerned through the interplay of the spaces within the museum. For instance, the National Museum of Ethiopia in Addis Ababa tells visitors on its orientation placard that the museum "has 4 different sections": paleoanthropology in the basement, the last two thousand years of archaeological and historical exhibits on the ground floor, "traditional and modern Ethiopian works of art" on the floor above, and an ethnographic collection on the top floor. The explicit narrative of these exhibits, or the narrative between them, or anything that unifies individual pieces or galleries, is very limited. It is, seemingly, an individualistically interpreted museum. But even here the museum's deep narrative clearly imposes linearity—diachronic unity—on the varied objects in its collection. Visitors are encouraged to begin their visit underground, where they are greeted by a life-sized screen of *Ardipithecus ramidus*, or Ardi, a friendly-looking hominid who lived some 4.5 million years ago in what is today Ethiopia. Lucy—*Australopithecus afarensis*, three million years old—rests further inside, along with other personalized prehistoric humans who embody a multimillion-year-old origin story. Climbing back upstairs, visitors circle through ancient (but historical) archaeological artifacts in vitrines that fill the main floor, while at their center are the (better lit) royal treasures of more recent centuries, followed by a suite of rooms of the last emperor, Haile Selassie, laid out as he would have used them. Once properly schooled in several million years of linear, diachronic unity—continuity from Ardi to Selassie—we are directed on the top two floors into synchronic unity, as (on the second floor) the varied art styles and then (on the third) the varied regional folkways of modern Ethiopia are displayed side by side around the outer walls of large open rooms. Visitors themselves create the missing narrative unity as they circle from one artwork or folkway to the next while keeping the national whole constantly in sight. The deep narrative of the building is clear: Ethiopian history, the history of a diverse but unified people, stretches back to the dawn of humanity and forward to today. In such a story, even the historical gaps between exhibits— and these are substantial, particularly on the ground floor—seem merely chapters temporarily shrouded in the mists of this immense timeline.

Aden et al. have also noted that as memory places "tell stories about the past, they re-collect the voices of those involved in the story in much the same way that Bakhtin outlines in his theorizing of the dialogic characteristics of the novel. That is, any single story/place holds multiple voices within it" (2009, 316). And Bakhtin's discussion of dialogic narratives includes his understanding that at times there is a "hidden dialogicality" that operates beneath the level of conscious purpose, in which people's utterances are formulated as responses to others, *because* others spoke—others who are not remembered as part of that larger conversation. "Individuals often state that they are simply reporting 'what really happened,'" writes social scientist James Wertsch. "The result is that we often fail to recognize the extent to which collective remembering is a fundamentally political process that is shaped by the dialogic textual resources employed" (2009, 245). Memory remembers the individual conversation; history provides the contextual discussion to which that conversation was a response.

What the spatial narratives of museums can show us, then, is that the scenic assumptions of the narrative, whether explicit or not, influence its utterances: every statement is at some level a response, a bit of hidden dialogicality. These dialogues unite the narratives across time, in recognized timelines, but they can also unite across space, building a story by proximity and juxtaposition of elements. As Aden et al. put it in their argument for a new, more holistic methodology for memory studies—an approach the parameters of which I touch upon throughout this book—"re-collection addresses all of the following: The place of re-collection as fragmented con/text, the discursive traces circulating within and around the place of re-collection, the discursive fragments that visitors bring to the place, visitors' sensory and embodied experiences within the place, and—importantly—visitors' individual and collective selection, and shaping, of all of these elements into a coherent orientation involving past, present, and future" (2009, 327).

While we can see in this book examples of museums performing each of these functions of re-collection, the process doesn't stop there, because the *formal* impact of narrative—the life story, polyphony, spatial and deep narrative—on the musealized history of a nation may play an even greater role in the telling of its story. Because all histories are in various ways narrated for an audience, as life stories (individual and national), they are inevitably stories of unification. The narrative genre imposes a preferential unity story on the raw materials in the national museum. The nation is *formed*, it is *created*, in a purposeful way that, seemingly inevitably, leads to the unified nation of the present, and unresolved disunities do not fit the pattern of the life story. Museums are cultural glue because, even with the hidden dialogicality of an individual encounter with collective memory, the hidden unification of the life-story narrative crafts these multiple storylines into one. The distillation of world events into narratives necessarily pushes a national story in certain directions and away from others. Museologist Jay Rounds could be speaking of Burke's selecting/reflecting/

deflecting vocabularies when he writes, "Museums are in that line of business. They take the stuff of the world, and they present it arranged by some principle of order. They provide vantage points from which the order that's invisible in quotidian life becomes intensified and visible in the space of an exhibition. Outside is the blooming, buzzing confusion of everyday life.... Inside the museum, the visitor finds a world laid out in order. The museum shows us a world that makes sense, and that is a world in which we can believe that our lives make sense" (2006, 140). Of course, the "blooming, buzzing confusion of everyday life" is in fact *not* left at the door but walks into the building in the mind of each visitor—but each "everyday life" is bounded, and answered, by the scene in which it is lived and the manner in which that scene is narrated.

The house of memory through which we walk, then, both in our minds and with our bodies in a three-dimensional museum gallery, determines the interplay between causal chronology and aesthetic experience that allows us to make meaning of life around us. The present breaks through into memory differently in a museum than in other kinds of narrative, using bordered three-dimensional space as a material commentary of past on present on past. Finally, visitors' movements in and out of the chronology simply *feel* more natural than they do in other, more cerebral media, because a museum audience consists of physical bodies doing what they naturally do, walking about in an exhibit space.

Narrative crafting, though, is just one aspect of the power of museums. I have been arguing that the museum is more than its objects, but even in this chapter those objects are present, playing a role in forging the aesthetic experience (as well as the verisimilitude) of the museum. Kendall Phillips, the public memory scholar, writes that by distinguishing between acts of memory, recollection, and remembrance we might better understand how "objects of remembrance invite us to understand our past in particular ways," and also to understand how "these understandings are reinforced by the mechanisms that discipline our recollection" (2010, 221). That is, the agency of objects in museums is determined to a large degree by their placement *in* the museum, their selection as a part of material culture. When visitors enter a museum, they are presented with the stability of great moments in their national history, Phillips's *remembrance*. They are asked to align their more fluid public *memories* with that remembrance. This is not unlike Bodnar's dichotomy between "official" and "vernacular" histories—but Phillips, like Ekaterina Haskins, adds a third option falling on the bias across the dichotomy: *recollection*, the existential space in which public memories are in the process of being shaped into—or resisting—

alignment with official remembrance. Phillips paints this as a struggle: "The space of 'public recollection' [is] a site in which public memories are disciplined in relation to the frameworks of public remembrance and against which recalcitrant public memories struggle in an effort to disrupt the dominant enthymematic logic and dispute taken-for-granted assumptions about the past" (219). I would counter that we all engage in the construction of unity, though we all seek to paint the picture as we ourselves see it. Whether struggle or creative endeavor, however, these remembrances are conveyed by more than a story—as Phillips notes, they are stories made material in objects that embody the events, "designed to both solidify the imprint left by the past and to maintain it in a certain form" (220). The rhetorical role of these material objects—existing in space, interacting with narratives, affecting visitors—is the focus of the next chapter.

3

The Object of the Story

By the very fact of selecting certain elements and presenting them to the audience, their importance and pertinency to the discussion are implied. Indeed, such a choice endows these elements with a presence, which is an essential factor in argumentation. . . . The thing on which the eye dwells, that which is best or most often seen, is by that very circumstance, overestimated.
—Chaim Perelman and Lucie Olbrechts-Tyteca

We never look just at one thing; we are always looking at the relation between things and ourselves.
—John Berger

Humans find significance within the material world, but we are largely alone in this. I might travel to the National Museum of Australia to see the heart, the National Museum of Victoria to see the hide, and the Museum of New Zealand Te Papa Tongarewa to see the skeleton of the great Depression-era racehorse Phar Lap—but no horse today feels the need to experience this exemplar of his species. Such objects, though, embedded as they are in story, are the bread and butter of museums and their millions of visitors each year. Objects may seem to convey forensic truths—*these events really did occur and here is the flag, or pottery shard, or painting to prove it*—but beyond forensic remembrance lies epideictic remembrance, the values of a society that are invoked by the material objects, thus encouraging visitors to identify with the remembered identity (to *recollect* that identity, in Kendall Phillips's terms). The national stories are not merely told but are crafted; the artifacts are not merely presented but are displayed.

Historian Eric Sandweiss describes early American city museums as relying on artifacts to trigger "revelation not cerebration, emotion not distance," much as a circus showman does (2004, 35). The epideictic revelation of objects, though, serves as more than showmanship. As historian Frances Yates notes in her treatise

The Art of Memory, for those trying to remember a line of argument in ancient times, objects were the subject matter of the speech, while words were what these subjects were clothed in (1966, 9). Yates quotes Aristotle's *On the Soul*: "It is impossible even to think without a mental picture" (33). Aronsson and Knell point out that while the modern narrative approach is historiographical, begins with the story, and "believes that the past is real and may in part be recovered and illustrated with the evidence of real things . . . reflect[ing] the historian's desire to marshal evidence into a convincing explanatory form," museums also commonly employ another, older method. The interpretive approach, used "frequently by art or natural history museums, begins with the object and builds upon the museological notion that knowledge can be retrieved from real things" (2012, 36–37)—that the painting or stuffed cougar on display can, without the context of historical narrative, say something on its own about a nation's shared past. As Steven Conn observes, nineteenth-century educational theory held that scientific curators could, through correct organization, arrangement, and display, allow visitors to understand the classification of the natural order "at a glance." This "naked eye science" was based on what Conn calls an "object-based epistemology," "predicated on the assumption that objects could tell stories 'to the untrained observer'" (2000, 4). Late in the nineteenth century, the Smithsonian curator George Brown Goode predicted that the museum of the future would have "a collection of instructive labels each illustrated by a well-selected specimen" (quoted in Sandweiss 2004, 36)—rather more "cerebration" than "revelation," but even then a sense that text and object worked together.[1]

The Material Museum

We might begin, then, with the scholarly debate over just what objects are—are they real (objective, agents)? Or are they intangible, woven out of narrative? Are they perhaps simply agencies, tools, of the narrative agents? I suggest in this chapter that one way to approach objects is to view them as Burke did poems, as *constitutive acts* that are created in their time, uniquely, and are also continuously created in the minds of subsequent observers. As constitutive acts, objects in a museum do not simply communicate wordlessly their innate significance, but they also do not serve as simple illustrations of the story being told. Instead, objects in a museum act in the world of people. Let me elaborate by discussing three ways in which objects, narratives, and visitors intertwine.

Objects as Proofs

First, there is certainly a degree of verisimilitude in what museum objects repre-sent. As visitors select from multiple (at times competing) memories to form the narratives that recollect national identity, selected memories are given their own artifact-filled rooms and allied with the "proof" of their material objects, whose presence reinforces the remembrance they are meant to represent. It is a cyclical relationship: A story is built from the material remnants of the past, reinforced by other remnants selected because they best fit into the growing narrative, serving then as proofs of the story they were selected to fit. The objects construct but also strengthen the narrative that they are selected to reinforce, thus doubly deflecting from any narratives that are not represented. Indeed, it is the act of selection itself that turns the object from "discrete lump" into material culture (Pearce 2012, 24).

In a national museum, this recursive process constructs what art historian Donald Preziosi describes as the *myth of nationality*. National narratives, he cau-tions, are not "ghosts" that preexist their staging in the museum (not forensic truths) but are "co-constructed and co-evolving. . . . Great national museums exist precisely in order to foster and perpetuate the belief in the truth of abstrac-tions such as national identity, character, mentality, or ethnicity: After all, right there in front of one's eyes, as the evidence right there in the vitrine you're stand-ing in front of, is the actual sacred relic of some person, people, place, or time" (2011, 61, 63).

Each object is therefore its own rhetorical process; or, in Preziosi's words, "Any exploration aimed at 'locating a nation in museums' is of course never an innocu-ous, apolitical, or purely instrumentalist enterprise, entailed as is the very notion of the nation with phantasmatic fabrications purportedly represented (that is, *re-presenced*) by collections of materials in fact precisely chosen for their per-ceived abilities to witness that which they purportedly are intended to prove" (65). The presented object is also the selected object, chosen because it best rep-resents the story it is proving. Preziosi's musealized version of Burke's selecting/reflecting/deflecting triad notes that any *collecting* that occurs is necessarily accompanied by *recollecting* the memory of who and what to remember (aligning with Phillips's *recollecting* of individual memories into the official narrative) but also by *de-collecting*, "the deliberate erasure of past meanings and functions" (59).

Artifact "proofs," then, are collected to aid in individual identification with the collective: "We imagine ourselves to be what our historical relics . . . can be

read as implying we have long been in the process of becoming" (58). The artifacts offer the material evidence that makes building the unifying life story that
much easier. Virtually any exhibit can serve as an example of this collecting/
recollecting/de-collecting act. For instance, on a wall of the National Museum
of American History in Washington, D.C., is a one-panel display titled "Getting
Out the Vote." The text explains that "Americans have a deep pride in the democratic process," and that in the nation's first century this pride turned presidential elections "from the concerns of a limited elite into a massive expression of
popular will." It goes on to tell visitors, however, that while "virtually every group
. . . has demanded the right to vote, many Americans who have this right do not
exercise it"; only half of those eligible, if that, vote regularly. "Increasingly," the
panel concludes, "national special-interest groups have sought to motivate their
constituents, who often seem indifferent to the pleas of the candidates." What is
re-collected here is the story, familiar to Americans, of a growing popular democratic movement now challenged by voter apathy and special interests. The
material evidence for this particular remembrance is a collection of historical
posters urging people to vote, from "Rock the Vote" to "Sigamos la Causa," to
"Protect Your Traditional Values," to "Don't Pass the Buck—Vote!" What are
de-collected by this narrative and these artifacts are the vociferous ongoing
struggles behind these posters, such as the struggle over the legal disenfran-
chisement of certain classes of voters (minorities and women, the previously
incarcerated, the very poor), the debate over the arcane indirect voting process
(primaries and the Electoral College), the battle over widespread gerrymander-
ing of congressional districts and the role of big money in political campaigns.
The virulent nature of these debates might well suggest something more than
"indifferent" voters and low turnout, more than populist voting campaign slogans about Americans' "deep pride in the democratic process"—but the artifacts
of these less straightforward features of the American political system remain
absent, deflected by the less ironic, more easily materialized evidence of decon-
textualized "get out the vote" posters.

Of course, the "proof" offered by objects is never fully hegemonic, because, as
we saw in the previous chapter, visitors bring their own stories and interpretations into the museum with them. As Sandra Dudley writes in her collection on
artifacts, "Museum objects constitute material 'facts' and evidence for stories to
be told, and at the same time are now understood, in our postmodern world,
within a frame of subjectivity—that is, we know that they mean different things
to different people" (2012c, xxvii). "Sigamos la Causa" buttons might remind me

of my first voting campaign, or of my virulent support for English-only or anti-immigrant policies, or they could mean nothing at all to me if I do not understand Spanish.

The potential polyphony of objects is sometimes a great concern in museums (*will visitors get the "right" message?*), and when it is, it is often the accompanying narratives that aim to convey an unambiguous historical truth that makes deviation seem impossible. In this setting, museum artifacts are merely the road markers that point from the unquestionable past to the inevitable future—and this is the role of propaganda rather than dialectic. When we acknowledge that artifacts can serve as proofs of narratives, therefore, we are acknowledging as well that these are not necessarily forensic proofs of *fact*, evidence of the whole historical truth, but are instead epideictic proofs of *values*, selected to evoke emotions and correspond to particular present-day concerns.

Objects as Illusions

Do artifacts, then, fool visitors into imagining that an epideictic celebration is a forensic truth—and if they do, should they be deemphasized? Simon Knell argues that eliminating objects would only exacerbate the unreality of museum stagings. In museums that divorce themselves from the evidence of artifacts, instrumentalized master narratives take over, or, as Knell puts it, the "interpenetrable object" is replaced by "mere assertion" (2011, 7). "Non-fictional narrative has its basis in historical writing, not in museum building" (7), he argues, and the museum loses its moral authority when it relinquishes the object. The artifacts provide a grounding, even if a compromised grounding, for the developing national narrative.

However, as Knell argues elsewhere, the significance and meaning of that grounding reside not in the objects themselves but in the minds of their viewers. "The material object cannot become an *art* object without additional interpretation," he writes in an argument for the "intangibility of things" (2012, 325), and the same may be said for an object of national culture. Knell, in fact, points out that the material reality of an object is illusory:

> The illusion, then, is this: that this one object is actually two, one tangible and real but not always present, the other intangible, the product of experience and negotiation, which seems to us to be the real object but is not.

The intangible object exists in our world but is made in our thoughts; it is ever present and inescapable. The material object also exists in our world but it never really exists in our thoughts.... Our thinking about an object, our surprise at first meeting it, even our involuntary bodily reactions to it, emanate from us and reflect our prior cultural experiences. (2012, 326–27)

Knell's point is that the significant object—the one that provides proof for some narrative we are asked to recollect—exists more in our minds than in the vitrine. "This intangible, conceptual, immaterial, evidential object *appeals* to the truth of the material object, but its connection to its material twin is detached and fluid—it lives in another world," he writes (328). It is, in fact, more *act* than object—and it acts upon its audience.

One way to allow for greater engagement with the *possibilities* latent in a museum object, or what Knell would call its intangible presence and what I am calling its constitutive act, would be to lessen the distance between viewer and viewed, removing layers of physical distance (like glass cases) or intellectual distance (through an overabundance of contextualizing text), as Dudley advocates (2012a, 6–7). We can see the effect of this more engaged, more dialectical depiction of material history in the Capital Museum in Beijing. It is a monumental building of polished black rock, immense open interiors, and five-story windows. On an upper floor, however, its monumentalism recedes into an exhibit called *Capital City Stories* depicting customs and street scenes from Beijing's iconic (and disappearing) *hutongs*, or neighborhoods of narrow lanes and alleys. The outer walls of the exhibit space display (or reconstruct) various idiosyncratic entrances to the classic one-story *hutong* courtyard structures, inviting visitors to pass physically through a typical entryway into the interior of the exhibit. There, the vast museum space becomes more intimate as well as polyphonic, with corridors winding between display cases and semi-enclosed room mock-ups, all rich with colorful artifacts depicting a variety of aspects of family life and beliefs of the people of "Old Beijing," from the Qing Dynasty through the republic. The exhibit space even includes an old theater with tables at which visitors can relax and watch a performance. Unlike the modern gallery in the national museum a short subway ride away, here in the city museum there is no inevitable march of history, no particularly unifying message—just daily life in its myriad forms, both in the courtyards and in the lanes themselves. A felicitous group of traditional statuettes just outside the "walls" of the "*hutong*" displays dozens of carefully carved and painted individuals in long lines of street

7 | Statuettes parade through Old Beijing in the Capital Museum.

markets and colorful parades (see fig. 7). Their intimate size, well under a meter tall, and vibrant, varied looks are juxtaposed with the empty black granite space of the building that houses them, and the views of smoggy modern Beijing skyscrapers visible through the floor-to-ceiling windows. Is this juxtaposition intentional? The bright, personalized spaces of "Old Beijing" do not include much signage about their provenance, and the visitors around me were not reading the signs as much as remembering to one another what life looked like in an earlier age—injecting their vernacular narratives into the official version. In other words, objects and visitors intertwined to re-create a version of Old Beijing—less a forensic truth than a value-driven version emphasizing communality.

Objects as Acts

Any preparation that primes visitors to "see" an object, then, begins well before its interpretive signage in the museum. Indeed, Debra Hawhee cites a hundred-year-old communication article that notes that sounds (and, by implication, language generally) "cannot carry any meaning not already present in the mind of the hearer" (2015, 7); thus the idea that signs speak to us ("carry thoughts" to our brains) is equally intangible. Illusory objects, intangible signs: Does the museum exist only in the minds of the visitors? If objects and narratives—or at least their significance—are both intangible, then visitors would seem to have a great deal more power than scholars generally afford them. Yet if both are tangible—if they are proof and justification—then this would seem to make them nearly hegemonic, impossible to resist. Knell hints at a resolution to this dichotomy by acknowledging the existence of both forms of the same object— the material and the intangible. More materialist scholars (Blair, Dudley) imply the same thing when they call for a renewed focus on the material object—in essence uniting the intangible thought with the tangible artifact. Another way to consider the object is to recognize its role in time as well as space, temporality as well as physicality, which is to say, to make the object an act.

Numerous scholars across multiple disciplines have discussed the ways in which objects comment on the present in their representation of the past. As Hawhee and Vivian report, "The flurry of studies in rhetoric and public memory over the past scholarly generation . . . has revived rhetoric's close association with memory in distinctively modern fashion: not as a performative technique but as a critical and historical mode of inquiry," and they cite anthropologist Marc Augé's concept of "the return" as the sometime need to forget the critical present "so that we may revisit an older one diluted of subsequent complexities and distortions" (Hawhee and Vivian 2009, 99). Whether Augé's return is ever possible, it is certainly not so in a museum, nor yet is his related concept, "suspense," which asks us to emphasize the present by "provisionally cutting it off from the past and the future" (99). In a museum, objects of the past always exist in the present as well. Material objects' proof of *facts* lies in their recounting of past events; their proof of *values* lies in their implications for the present and therefore the future. To fully experience the object in the museum is not to try to see it untainted by modern interpretation, as if one were in fact still that ancient person carving an icon or an arrowhead, but instead to see it musealized and narratized, providing a historical commentary on present-day values, showing what the nation today finds important about its origins.

We could say, then, that the object is a material thing created in and for a particular time that also exists in and for our own time. Historian James Loewen says that an object contains both a "manifest narrative" (in museums, this would be what the accompanying text says it is about) and an erection or preservation narrative (how it came to be displayed in the museum) (quoted in Balthrop, Blair, and Michel 2010, 171). Kenneth Burke more generally discusses the question of how to read a historical aesthetic object (for him, this object was poetry) by examining both its extrinsic qualities, as an object created by an author in a particular historical scene, and its intrinsic qualities, as a timeless statement. Critics in Burke's day debated between these two poles of interpretation, and Burke posited a third way. What if instead of considering it as an object, he said, we think of the poem (and here we can extrapolate to any object of material culture) as a "*constitutive act*," a kind of living record, "and after the act of its composition by a [creator] who had acted in a particular temporal scene, it survives as an objective structure, capable of being examined in itself, in temporal scenes quite different from the scene of its composition, and by agents quite different from the agent who originally enacted it" (1943a, 93). The object becomes both/and, not either/or. Considering the museum object as *act* rather than thing makes clearer that its role is *both* that of the uniquely material creation of a particular moment in history *and* the displayed commentary on present-day concerns. Indeed, exhibits that ignore their present role and consider objects only for their past proofs aim too hard to present one monological telling of past events, writes Knell, displaying a singular "manifestation of the nation rather than the nation found through democratic negotiation," and that in turn makes for "no division between propaganda and the supposedly objective narrative" (2011, 11).

Like Knell, Burke argues that "parliamentary babel" (Knell's more generous term is "democratic negotiation") is the preferred means of shaping visitors' attitudes. Only in hindsight might the historical path seem inevitable. To tell a more *truthful* story, the narratives and objects that are selected to explain the past need to tell a more *ambiguous* story. Artifacts as acts are doubly ambiguous, impelling interpretation that is at once invented long ago and happening right now. Furthermore, within the already ambiguous setting of a spatial narrative through which visitors weave their journeys, artifacts (as both things and acts) can be ironically juxtaposed alongside other similarly polyphonous artifacts. For instance, in the Mexica Hall—a high-ceilinged celebration of the Aztec civilization at the apex of the National Museum of Anthropology in Mexico City— visitors wander past the impressive large-scale floor replica of Tenochtitlán, the ancient monumental capital, and from one magnificent stone carving to the next of a deity or king or the iconic Sun Stone. Then, as they leave the hall, they see

8 | Ironically juxtaposed icons in the National Museum of Anthropology, Mexico City.

two objects placed side by side: a large Aztec god, utterly defaced, and an equally large, rough, worm-eaten wooden cross (see fig. 8). The signage—the manifest narrative—simply notes that Spanish missionaries often used defaced blocks to build new altars. In the spatial narrative of the gallery, however, in combination with the erection narrative that is the physical juxtaposition of these two objects, the message is the erasure of indigenous religion, perhaps even the erasure of indigenous personhood, and its replacement with a more rough-hewn, more primitive (even worm-eaten) religion, culture, civilization.

Beyond that "cerebration" response to conquest, already somewhat ambiguous, lies the emotional impact of the two objects and their placement at the end of a walk-through extolling the Aztec Empire at its height. This surprising juxtaposition calls for a new response from the nonindigenous visitor to the old narrative of European missionaries "saving" the primitive natives. After marveling at the Aztec material culture to this point, the surprise destruction of the Aztec deity evokes a response more visceral than cerebral—the evidence of what was lost is a felt pain. Further still, that emotional response at the end of the culminating gallery might jar some visitors into realizing that they have been *increasingly* identifying with the indigenous cultures of Mexico as they traversed the galleries from Olmec to Maya to Aztec civilizations. The arrival of the Spaniards who made modern Mexico the mestizo nation that it is may be suddenly felt—without need for didactic signage—as a destructive force. Or not. As Knell points out, the significance of the object is in the visitor's mind. As acts, however, the two religious objects—as extrinsic acts no doubt both carved with pious fervor by their creators and worshipped by generations, and as intrinsic acts both now brought together and displayed for quite a different purpose—continue to perform their multiple significances in this, their latest iteration. Such is the power of "what a museum experience can offer . . . not just as a step on the journey towards cognitive understanding of the story the object helps to tell, but as a potent and sometimes transformative phenomenon in its own right. . . . The physicality of the object . . . can trigger personal, emotional and sensory responses that may have a significance of their own" (Dudley 2012a, 3).[2] As rhetoricians Perelman and Olbrechts-Tyteca note in the epigraph at the start of this chapter, it is the *presence* of the object that gives it power—a presence heightened by the "experiential landscape" (Dickinson, Ott, and Aoki 2006) of an arranged museum space.

For that presence to be powerful, it needs its argument, its narrative, and its display, but these are most persuasive when they do not overwhelm values with too many facts. To be moved intellectually and emotionally, visitors need the existential space to contemplate multiplicities of meaning. It may be helpful, therefore, to advocate for objects as acts under the sign of what Burke called *poetic naming*, an aesthetic perspective on the world in which multiple ideas coexist in the same term (or object), a perspective he contrasted with *semantic naming*, in which a single term is made to correspond with a single idea. Instead of eliminating alternatives in the name of clarity, poetic naming plays up the ambiguities of multiple attitudes by "heaping up all of these emotional factors, playing them off against one another" (1941/1973, 148). For Burke, poetic naming was the contribution of aesthetics to social identity, an alternative to the scientistic desire of his day to find neutral language that would somehow describe everything with absolute clarity and without bias. Clarity was the intent of nineteenth-century curators like Goode, with his "collection of instructive labels each illustrated by a well-selected specimen." Such is not the intent of the modern museum and its more ambiguous, more affective object displays.

To illustrate how a more ambiguous object-act might affect not only materiality but also national identity, let me turn now to some of the most emotionally charged summations of narratives and objects to exist in museums.

Ultimate Terms, Mythic Images

As the vast repositories across the world demonstrate, nothing collects the items of national experience better than a museum—or, as Luís Raposo, president of ICOM Portugal, puts it, "When you want a nation, make a museum" (2012). Indeed, regardless of what those items are, the very fact that it is possible to accumulate roomfuls of objects that have national standing communicates to visitors that the nation has a real identity. It exists, real communities live simultaneously within its borders, and this is proved by the accumulation of objects—with both their intrinsic and their extrinsic values—that visiting individuals can see as representative of their consubstantiality, their shared substance. Historian Alan Greenblatt summarizes the historical trend: "As the age of small principalities and enormous empires gave way to nation-states and the global economic competition between them, a new type of nationalism emerged. The creation of symbols of national identity, including flags and anthems, became more important, while religious and linguistic cleavages were minimized" (2009, 325). Within these collected demonstrations of nationhood, though, even a cursory contemplation makes it clear that not all objects are equal and that certain objects hold a particular kind of power. Often, as we have seen, this power comes about by dint of their placement in the museum space and the narrative that surrounds them—but the visitor must in turn acknowledge this significance (*yes, that object is special*) in order for the act to be fully persuasive. We might consider this mutual acknowledgment an example of the object/narrative having adequate scope, being sufficiently reflective of the collective reality it represents (Burke 1945/1969, 60).

Words and phrases that have sufficient scope to sum up all aspects of an ongoing discussion Burke calls "ultimate terms" (1950/1969, 186). In a museum gallery as in a book, the ultimate terms of this summation may be signaled first by a title, as with the National Museum of China's twentieth-century *Road to Rejuvenation* exhibit, or the post-9/11 historical exhibition at the National Museum of American History, *The Price of Freedom: Americans at War*. Ultimate-term titles sum up both the topic and the attitudinal scope of their exhibits, and such summational titles abound throughout the world. For instance, at the Bangkok National Museum in 2012, the special exhibition *Dharmarājādhirāja: Righteous King of Kings* brought together disparate objects from King Bhumibol Adulyadej's personal collection in order to equate, as the exhibition catalogue notes, "the Enlightened Dharmarājādhirāja, the Buddha, and the secular Dharmarājādhirājas, the righteous kings, from the Thailand's [*sic*] past to the present"—including the then current king, "devoutly called by Thai people dharmarājādhirāja." "Righteous king," therefore, served as an ultimate term, encompassing a discussion ranging reassuringly unbroken from the Buddha through the royal lineage to the current king. Its scope thus worked to encompass, as well, the king's actions and those acts of mercy and enlightenment attributed to the Buddha, making an implicit argument for extending the people's response—devotion—from the Buddha to the king.

The ultimate terms chosen for an exhibit impose an order on the narrative and a hierarchy on its values; the terms signal a careful selection from among all possibilities and thus they deflect as well as reflect certain attitudes. The scope of this frame, though, is more than a simple semantic summation. To say that righteous king "means" devotion to the current king is like saying that *Moby-Dick* is about a whale hunt. Ultimate terms unite information and attitude in a more dialogical manner, acknowledging multiple layers of meaning. They are another form of poetic naming, promoting attitude in its more physical sense—moving audiences into a stance toward the thing displayed and the stories, and identities, behind it.

A particularly clear example of this poetic transcendence into multiple layers of meaning can be seen in the way "freedom" is used in the new South Africa museums. In the Apartheid Museum, for instance, a 2001 building on the outskirts of Johannesburg, "freedom" is the ultimate term for a postapartheid nation. Apartheid is narrated in the museum as "our imprisonment," or "the imprisonment of all South Africans." This theme is embodied in the overall design of the unique multilevel space, as visitors enter the museum through two corridors of metal cages that physically hold historical documents of apartheid identity. They are then led on a trail through more cages to witness the increasing number of laws promulgated by the National Party after its rise to power. Prison cells—including a re-creation of Nelson Mandela's cell on Robben Island—hold a prominent place in the center of the museum. The theme that apartheid imprisoned both black and white is reinforced in a sober photo display of conditions for black South Africans that channels visitors into yet another caged display of the world's growing condemnation of apartheid in the 1960s and '70s, and the statement that white South Africans became the world's pariahs, trapped in their country. The negotiations leading up to South Africa's first free elections in 1994 are chronicled in a bunkerlike room punctuated by the chaotic sounds of armed violence from various separatist groups, black and white, that threatened those elections, so that voting is renarrated as an action in the universal fight against chaos and for freedom. The themes of imprisonment and freedom are so thoroughly incorporated into the site design that the enclosed space of the museum opens, at the very end, onto a native veld overlooking the city, where a guiding sign reads: "Coming to terms with the harsh realities of apartheid and its lasting effects is a process of unburdening. It is painful to some and liberating to others. Take a moment to walk and contemplate the beauty of this, our country. Think of what has gone before and what is still to come. . . . And then walk away free."

The influential philosopher Maurice Merleau-Ponty argues that humans are "carnal beings who move around, smell, touch and hear, so that every visual contact with the world becomes a *lived-out*, not a *thought-out* experience of it" (quoted in Belova 2012, 121). Ultimate terms in themselves, however, are by definition abstractions, highlighting the illusory effect of what is, in the end, a material space. Objects and spaces may act together to make material the abstraction in the minds of visitors, as at the Apartheid Museum, where freedom isn't just a word but an empty jail cell or an open veld. Sometimes, though, a *single* object-act has sufficient scope that it can encompass the multiple competing abstractions of ultimate terms in one material form, summarizing in the material the abstract summary of ultimate terms.

In national museums, these material summations necessarily concretize the ultimate terms of the nation, making national ideals material. That is, certain national artifacts become so all-encompassing of national ultimate terms that they make Burke's concept of a "mythic image" material. As Burke described it in *A Rhetoric of Motives*, a mythic image is "a motive which, being *beyond* ideas, would not lend itself to statement in ideas. Only by going from *sensory* images to ideas, then through ideas to the end of ideas, is one free to come upon the *mythic* image" (Burke 1950/1969, 202). Rhetoricians since Roman times have been trained to realize the potential of an emotionally arresting image, for "ordinary things easily slip from the memory while the striking and novel stay longer in the mind," as the unknown author of the *Rhetorica ad Herennium* put it (Caplan 1954, 3.22). Burke's sense of the importance of certain images, then, resides in the classical tradition, but his mythic image does more. As myth, it constitutes a communal identity made into story. As act, it makes material the ultimate terms not as univocal semantic translation—one notion mirrored visually—but as ambiguous poetic transcendence, as multiple notions embodied in one image, with juxtaposed meanings that cannot be expressed as pure information alone. As James Kastely puts it, dialectical terms lead to transcendent, encompassing ultimate terms "that are then available to us as mythic images . . . that evade or exceed statement in empirical and even dialectical terms. Such images should produce not mystification but mystery, and this mystery should not be understood as merely beyond the reaches of reason but as a moment in which reason transcends itself" (2013, 189). Mythic images help us to experience affectively the unity we sense in seemingly opposed or disparate ideas.

Burke's discussion of mythic images in *A Rhetoric of Motives* (1950/1969, 197–201) received scant attention until rhetorician Bryan Crable's astute analysis incorporated both *A Rhetoric of Motives* and Burke's notes on myth. In Crable's reading, Burke's mythic narratives unify multiple voices in ambiguous dialogue: "According to Burke, then, myth does not connote falsity or fiction, but the dialectical shift to a non-empirical image. . . . 'Myth' [wrote Burke,] 'would use positive images, but poetically or figuratively, to symbolize motives not capable of being wholly and exactly encompassed by scientifically positive terms.' . . . Myth instead provides a *terministic* transcendence, reconciling parliamentary (dialectical) opposition with a 'summarizing,' but non-ideational, terministic order" (2009, 221–22). Crable specifies that Burke saw these summarizing images as mythic *origin stories*, "imagistic expressions of archetypes, 'firsts,' accounts of the 'mythic ancestry' of principles, or the 'ideal mythic type' at the root of principles. . . . Mythic transcendence is the imagistic depiction of the common origin of seemingly opposed principles or ideologies; it is the shift from the parliamentary jangle to 'another plane,' a unifying image of origins. Because it embodies the shared ancestry of these opposing voices, myth imagistically depicts these voices as 'successive positions or moments in a single process'" (222).

A mythic origin story such as Crable describes, uniting paradoxes, infuses the heart of the Kigali Genocide Memorial Centre, where the ultimate term "Our Rwanda" begins the exhibit with the assertion, "This has been our home for centuries. We are one people. We speak one language. We have one history." This imagining of a common origin for Rwanda's eighteen clans directly counters the division narrative that pitted Hutus against Tutsis and spurred on the genocide. It sums up in a mythic origin narrative the inchoate multilayered meaning of "Our Rwanda," the terministic transcendence that reconciles the parliamentary jangle of (genocidal) division. Such a use of the mythic image ideal is indeed generative, and Burke, thinking in literary terms, conceived of such images textually.

However, I believe that the space of museums displaying objects makes it possible to discuss a new, material kind of mythic image as well. In museums, Burke's "imagistic" myths can come out of the narrative realm and into the material. "Thus, the imagery could be said to convey an invisible, intangible idea in terms of visible, tangible things," as Burke wrote of such poetic objects (1950/1969, 86). In national museums, these "tangible things" provide their communities with a visual representation of national identity that speaks to the mythic origin of the nation, perhaps as a historical phenomenon but certainly as an epideictic one. As ultimate terms made material, mythic images would need to be poetic, to fall across the range of competing attitudes and ideas that make up a national ethos, carrying within themselves multiple narratives while imposing a hierarchy on the particular values held most strongly by *this* nation. It is this poetic materialization that makes it possible to talk about mythic images as objects.

Not every nation has a mythic image strong enough to stimulate national identification; but the United States does, and it provides a clear example of a mythic object carefully enshrined in its national museum while existing in the minds of its viewers, embodying multiple interpretations that provide the template for millions of similar images around the country. This is the star-spangled banner, the flag that inspired the national anthem. A closer look at the way in which this particular flag is presented in the National Museum of American History sheds light on the manner in which thinking of "mythic images" not only as origin narratives but as material image-acts may productively bring Burke's terministic realm into the material world.

The star-spangled banner has been on permanent display at the National Museum of American History in Washington, D.C., since 1912. The material fact of this particular flag and the anthem it inspired—an encomium the first verse of which ends "O say does that star-spangled banner yet wave / O'er the land of the free and the home of the brave?"—inspires the affective patriotic response so evident in a nation where flag imagery is ubiquitous. Richard Rathbun, then the assistant secretary of the Smithsonian, wrote to the flag's original donor in 1907, "Its presence in the Museum has caused a wave of patriotism, which it is very good to see" (Smithsonian National Museum of American His-

9 | The entry to the *Star-Spangled Banner* exhibit at the National Museum of American History, Washington, D.C., features a large metal representation of the flag.

tory 2008), while as late as 2014 the museum's e-mail fund-raising appeal used the line from its director, John Perrell, "I still remember the first time I saw the original Star-Spangled Banner at the Smithsonian. . . . It was an awe-filled moment." The star-spangled banner itself has been increasingly elevated in stature and distanced from common public interaction over the decades, such that a flag that at first was brought outside to display on special occasions, then hung for many years on a wall of the Arts and Industries Building and then in the foyer of the American History museum, now has its own multimillion-dollar gallery just off the central lobby of the renovated museum. Outside this gallery hangs a giant golden replica, which draws the eye (see fig. 9). Meanwhile, the flag itself rests behind thick glass at the apex of the new gallery. The horseshoe configuration of the gallery provides visitors with what Greg Clark terms the rhetorical preparation necessary for individuals to have a "public experience"—"a transformative personal encounter with shared symbols of a people's collectivity . . . an encounter, linguistic or extralinguistic, that has aesthetic form and the rhetorical function of transforming a self to cooperate with the other selves encountered" (2004, 106). In keeping with Clark's rhetorical preparation, visitors to the star-spangled banner gallery in the "entry" side of the horseshoe learn about the War of 1812 and hear the story of Francis Scott Key languishing on an enemy ship overnight, wondering if the fort (and by extension the nation) would withstand bombardment, and then, the next morning, seeing the flag still flying "by the dawn's early light." After this narrative preparation, visitors turn the corner and behold the same, surprisingly large, obviously old flag, laid out in a large sloping glass case that fills the back side of the horseshoe. The gallery space is intimate, the lighting is dim, period music plays softly, and no photos are permitted anywhere, all heightening the feeling of moving through "sacred space." The display presents the artifact as a mythic summation of the nation, and indeed, the flag's role as a mythic image is explained—if not in those terms—on the museum's online exhibition site: "When Key declared that 'our flag was still there,' he fused the physical symbol of the nation with universal feelings of patriotism, courage, and resilience. . . . The flag was no longer just an emblem of the nation; it became a representation of the country's values and the ideals for which it stands" (Smithsonian National Museum of American History 2013b). Knell's caveat about object intangibility, however, reminds us that it is not the flag object that is in itself a mythic embodiment; it is those who *endow* the flag with rhetorical qualities—significance, scope, ambiguity—that transform it into a mythic image in our collective consciousness.

Such is the function of national tourism, Clark writes; "it enables diverse individuals to imagine their national community in similar ways as they encounter the symbolic experiences that are available to them" (2004, 15). Museum-visiting tourists are encouraged by the material provided to endow the experience of a place with collective meaning and then to determine their own stance, or attitude, toward that meaning. Only in light of this active response can they be, as Clark writes, "prompted to recreate themselves in the image of a collective identity" (4)—one that both speaks to a sense of common values and is wide enough in scope to encourage inevitable variations. Indeed, it is the presence of a hierarchy of alternatives that provides the space for an individual to identify with the communal while recognizing that this is, in fact, a choice—that provides the space for separation and thus identification rather than unconscious unity. Merleau-Ponty scholars Fred Evans and Leonard Lawler note that, "like a dialogue, perception leads the subject to draw together the sense diffused throughout the object while, simultaneously, the object solicits and unifies the intentions of the subject" (2000, 4). It is the dialogue—enhanced in a museum because of the poetic nature of its display of material culture, I would argue—that allows for sufficient ambiguity in the mythic image to allow it to make a collective identity material.

This dialogical nature of the star-spangled banner is highlighted on the "exit" side of the horseshoe, which visitors encounter after viewing the flag itself. Visitors can explore the flag's contradictory history (an object of war sewn by a Baltimore homemaker and her African American slave), but, more significantly, at the very end of the exhibit they are reminded via video images of the great diversity of uses to which Americans put the flag—to praise and protest, fight battles and sell T-shirts. There are, admittedly, too few contradictory images in this laudatory exhibit, but even a small reminder of divergence awakens memories of difference because flag imagery is so ubiquitous in the United States: the flag planted at Ground Zero after 9/11 and on the moon by the crew of Apollo 11 is the same image set alight by antiwar protests and draped over veterans' coffins, displayed on the neighbor's xenophobic bumper sticker and the dog's bandana. Indeed, the laudatory nature of the museum exhibit itself raises questions about the flag's hegemonic role. As the Smithsonian website says, "As the debates over flag protection continue, memories of the turbulent 1960s continue to challenge and inspire Americans to contemplate the meaning of patriotism and the value of protest" (Smithsonian National Museum of American History 2013a).

Burke notes in *A Rhetoric of Motives* that in Kantian philosophy there is both a conceptual object (a physical structure) and a poetic object that "is built of *identifications*" (1950/1969, 85) (we can hear echoes here of Knell's material and intangible things)—and it is as poetic objects that mythic images such as the star-spangled banner build upon multiple identifications with national values and ideas. As a poetic object-act, the American flag piles up multiple layers of ambiguous meaning: this imagery "will not represent merely one idea, but will contain a whole bundle of principles, even ones that would be mutually contradictory if reduced to their purely ideational equivalents" (87). The thoughtful and deliberate consideration of the dialectical, competing values in iconic images that function as unifying forces may well be a hedge against oversimplifying the national values implied by those images. Experiencing the dialectical in the mythic image is not only a more accurate way to interpret its encompassing historical nature, then, but also a more radical maneuver in an age when the possibility of equally competing values is so often viewed negatively.

What other possible mythic images exist in the world's museums? I might include the Aztec Sun Stone in the Mexican National Museum of Anthropology, or the Declaration of Arbroath in the National Museum of Scotland. I might even include individual exemplars whose role in their nation moves beyond their original biography into the realm of mythic image. I have already discussed how the State Museum of Temurids History in Uzbekistan highlights Amir Temur's role as a model of indigenous strength, wisdom, and glory for the newly independent Uzbek nation. I would argue that Mustafa Kemal Atatürk, founder of the modern Turkish nation, has for many decades also played such a role in his homeland. One way to view Atatürk's continuing influence—and, indeed, the continuing debate over his legacy—eighty years after his death is to think of him as having become a mythic image for the nation, the material embodiment of its mythic origins and the means of imposing a hierarchy on the changing values under debate. All of this is on display in the Anıtkabir, Atatürk's mausoleum-museum, which takes up multiple acres on a hillside overlooking downtown Ankara (see fig. 10). The site still attracts millions of enthusiastic Turkish tourists annually, and it recently expanded its attached museum of the War of Independence (in which Atatürk played a leading role). From the entry gate, one walks perhaps half a mile up a wide stone walkway lined with pairs of lion statues invoking ancient Hittite sites, then up a broad staircase to an open square ringed by a series of neoclassical sandstone buildings that culminate in the large cube-shaped Hall of Honor containing Atatürk's tomb. A highly laudatory introductory film in a building near the square's entrance tells visitors (in Turkish and English) that Atatürk is "the symbol of independence," and it ends with the line "Atatürk lives on in the actions of the Turkish people." He is depicted in the accompanying museum displays in multiple roles: as military hero, rebel, nation founder, and government leader, as someone who worked for language reform, land reform, religious reform, women's rights, children's health, and education, and as a husband and father and a lover of fitness, finery, liquor, and high culture. The multiplicity of Atatürk's roles emphasized in the museum exhibits already allows multiple entry points into what it might mean for Atatürk to live on "in the actions of the Turkish people." It might thus spur visitors to contemplate multiple simultaneous attitudes (stances) as they stand before his tomb at the end of their tour of the vast complex.

In a country in which national values are in a state of flux, however, recent visitors are finding even more entry points into Atatürk's legacy. As political

10 | Atatürk's tomb in the Anıtkabir mausoleum, Ankara, continues to be a popular destination for visitors to the capital.

scientist Marc Herzog notes, the Anıtkabir "figures as a central space to many of the on-going debates and struggles about the identity and destiny of contemporary Turkey" (2012, 1). Increasing numbers of rallies have been held there over the past decade, as the current rural-based Islamist government instigates changes to the pro-Western, fiercely secular urban identity of Atatürk's Turkey. Notably, a rally in 2008 opposing the end of an Atatürk-era ban on head scarves in government buildings and universities drew some 125,000 protestors to the central square of the monument, as secular Turks identified their vision with Atatürk's. The ban was in fact lifted by the current government—and I was struck, visiting the Anıtkabir in 2012, after a twelve-year absence, by the number of women who came to the mausoleum wearing a head scarf.[3] These were not protestors but tourists. Despite the ongoing intense debates over Atatürk's legacy, these women, covering their heads while visiting the Anıtkabir, were identifying their individual Turkishness with different aspects of Atatürk's mythicized image than his role as a secular reformer. Meanwhile, Westernized Turks also continue to identify with Atatürk to symbolize the national identity they see as under threat. Part of the Gezi Park protests in Istanbul in 2013 against government policies was a series of silent vigils held before the ubiquitous public image of Atatürk (Fradkin and Libby 2013). Atatürk's persona, then, increasingly distanced from his biographical existence, is increasingly made into a mythic image—stretching, albeit uncomfortably, to encompass a greater diversity of Turkish identities while also taking on renewed significance as Turks debate among themselves just what their identification with the Turkish nation should look like, as the centennial of their nationhood approaches.[4]

The promotion of certain individuals, like Temur and Atatürk, as exemplars of their nation is in fact a fairly common form of musealized mythic image. The large special exhibit on Nelson Mandela at the Apartheid Museum in 2011, covering all aspects of his life from birth to retirement, made a point of highlighting not only Mandela's triumphs but also his defeats in a way that turned this revered figure into a more human, more complex, and thus more encompassing symbol for a nation engaged in its own continuing struggle to reach its potential. The Evita Museum in Buenos Aires, Argentina, promotes through its portrayal of Eva Perón both the populist policies of Peronism and the devotional attitude toward Peronism that many Argentines, including the former ruling party, continue to support—although its relatively small number of visitors might have suggested a changing identification, which did in fact sweep the Peronist party out of power in 2015. Similarly, the National Gandhi Museum in New Delhi, an older complex with peaceful spaces telling an understated story of dedicated rural communal life with simple personal artifacts (albeit accompanied by the sharp-minded writings of a master tactician), seems more suited to pilgrimage than to engagement with the contentious debates of modern urbanizing India— and it also was largely empty when I visited. Its walk-through ashram may be as anachronistic as Mahatma Gandhi's own chosen mythic image, the spinning wheel of village society. Perhaps this is why what continues to draw large crowds of visitors is not the museum but Gandhi's tomb across the street—just as the tomb of Mao Zedong draws thousands of pilgrims in Beijing. Both men hold a special place in their respective nations' self-identity, but now more as memorial than as participant in the current conversation about globalized national identity, and thus their one-time role as national mythic images, embodying the qualities of the present-day nation, has perhaps spent its force.

This raises the question of how much the mythic image, already partially intangible, is a preexisting reality and how much it is a reality selected (and promoted) by the museum itself. Global examples would seem to argue that the answer is complicated. Clearly, display craft plays a significant role—the object requires the affective delivery techniques of space and narrative to be seen as a national image. No matter the display, however, objects also need the collective assent of their visitors that they do indeed encompass a mythic embodiment of sufficient scope to represent the nation. The perception of the object needs to feel like a two-way, dialogical experience, in Merleau-Ponty's terms. A clear example of this dual responsibility for the creation of the mythic image can be found in New Zealand, where the effort to embody a new, more dialogical kind of lived "Kiwi" experience is embodied in a rediscovered mythic image housed in the Museum of New Zealand Te Papa Tongarewa in Wellington. Opened in 1998, Te Papa quickly became one the world's most notable national museums. It draws hundreds of thousands of foreign tourists annually, and it has a significant impact on New Zealand society. In 2016, more than one in five New Zealanders visited the museum at least once (Museum of New Zealand 2016, 13). Its curving, soaring, angular sand and gray stone blocks anchor the public space around Lambton Harbor. Inside the museum, an interior I discuss further in chapter 5, hangs an object that is explicitly promoted as an image for an emerging New Zealander identity—the Treaty of Waitangi. The treaty is an 1840 agreement between the British Crown and some 530 indigenous Maori chiefs that granted the Maori people land and civil rights as British subjects in exchange for British sovereignty over New Zealand. The treaty was then largely ignored by the British for more than a century, but more recently it has assumed the role of the "founding document" of the New Zealand nation. From the 1970s on, the Maori have used the treaty to redress breaches of their rights. The museum's signage informs visitors that the treaty deals with "ideas vital to modern New Zealand—government, citizens' rights, land and cultural heritage." Yet its purpose or promise in the modern nation is still a matter of debate, a dialectic in which the museum participates: since 2005, Te Papa has sponsored an ongoing series of talks called "Treaty Debate." The treaty itself, meanwhile, is displayed (in an exhibit given the ultimate-term name *Signs of the Nation*) in perhaps the most heavily trafficked and central part of the museum: next to the Wi-Fi-accessible, always filled café. As crowds of Wellington locals enter the free museum to sip their flat whites and check their e-mail, the artifact most prominently before them is the museum's large glass replica of the treaty, accompanied by oversized English and Maori translations. Perhaps visitors' attention is caught by one of the performances held in the open space between the hanging placards. If they wander over to the display area, they will be surrounded by half a dozen lighted speaker poles. These poles are not informational but attitudinal, playing diverse voices debating the treaty. Some voices praise it as transformational to New Zealand society while others are deeply critical and wonder if society has gone too far. Their diverse opinions are the voices of this modern nation trying to determine whether redress under the provisions of the treaty constitutes the "fair go" they envision as part of their changing identity.

The presence of these debating voices makes the treaty contentious, a current reality, an object-act of lively debate that engages individuals' identification with the changing nation. The juxtaposed divergent perspectives that unite (or attempt to unite) under the banner of a national identity contribute to the treaty's function as a mythic image of the new nation. Far from being a disturbance or distraction, divergent voices in the parliamentary babel bring the object to life, making it a *living* symbol of the nation.

As in the Museum of American History or the Anıtkabir, however, the dialectical stance of debating voices is not always appreciated, even among intellectuals. Historian Bain Attwood, for instance, in an article on the difficulties of mounting the treaty exhibit, takes issue with the conflicting messages it presents, noting that the "presentation of the Treaty . . . as an inspiring foundation for a unitary nation, was . . . undercut by the presentation of the interpretation of the Treaty as comprising two conflicting texts" (2013, 67)—but in this I would disagree. A display of pure unity would ignore the real ongoing debate, rendering the treaty less ambiguous and thus less in touch with the real world, less an act. The Treaty of Waitangi, then, can be said to demonstrate a museum's crafting, via its space, display, and narrative, the historic significance of an object with a tenuous hold at best on the collective memory. But this crafting would fail as much as Gandhi's spinning wheel to engage with the present day without the ongoing communal debate that forges a new collective memory. Its *role* as a proposed new mythic image is therefore historically crafted—but its *success* as this new image depends on the assent of a diverse audience in incorporating it into collective memory.

Material Space

I ended the previous chapter with a discussion of space as narrative, so it seems appropriate to end this one with a discussion of (displayed, designed) space as materiality as well. This will make clearer the interconnected nature of both object/display/narrative and collective memory/identity.

That architects and designers covet assignments to design museum space is hardly news. Daniel Libeskind, Frank Gehry, Renzo Piano, I. M. Pei, Zaha Hadid—many of the world's star architects made their names in part by designing museums. "There has never been a more challenging and a more exciting time in which to be devising creative spaces," notes architect Stephen Greenberg (2005, 226).Yet the context for Greenberg's point demonstrates spatial theorists' concern with this very movement toward the iconic museum—for Greenberg is talking about the need to incorporate "changing audience expectations and an explosion of new technologies" into design, to consider narrative (both spatial and deep, in my terms) and geographical context well before any attempt to come up with a blueprint. Indeed, the focus on the auto-rhetorical object that some rhetoricians find so compelling today seems to these museum practitioners more a legacy of the nineteenth century, when "museums were object buildings filled with objects in cases. . . . Exquisite installations and displays they may have been, but in the end the notion that the 'object must speak for itself, unmediated' became not only culturally and institutionally enshrined, but also a way of secreting knowledge. Access, engagement and connection were not on the menu" (226). The assumption that the object conveys meaning to the critical viewer becomes an elite sense that the "proper" viewer will have the critical tools to garner its meaning. Museologist Suzanne MacLeod's collection *Reshaping Museum Space* gathers architects, designers, museum directors, and museologists who argue repeatedly for a different viewpoint, one described by museum director David Fleming in reference to the now highly successful National Museums Liverpool: "Where we begin to generate uniqueness is in the narratives—the stories about Liverpool, with its exhilarating, roller-coaster history. The degree to which we are able to blend these narratives with the architectural space will define the success of the museum" (2005, 60).

Narratives, space—we appear to be back to the question of whether museums need objects, but MacLeod's collection makes it clear from multiple perspectives that they do, in the right context. Museologist Elaine Heumann Gurian, for instance, ends her essay with the observation that, "most importantly, [museums should] understand the importance visitors place on 'seeing the evidence' and so encourage interaction with three-dimensional experiences. Our special legitimacy remains visual access to physical things" (2005, 213). Sophia Psarra believes that the most important function of museum space is "to provide a place for the displays so that they can remain in our memory ... [giving] objects a context that is so well structured and so remarkable that we cannot help but remember them" (2005, 93). Greenberg suggests that we think of the material, the physical, at museums as a performance space, a "vital" museum space that seeks to transform visitors' experience with "imaginative interpretation and display with a resonant architectural setting" (2005, 229). His description of what that vital space looks like brings us back to polyphony—now not only with the stories told but with the physical means of telling such stories—as he comments on an exhibit at the Imperial War Museum in London:

> In a typical space you can find a seamless fusion of artefact display, home movie, testimony, newsreel, audio, cartography and biography and interior architecture. . . . As a consequence, it isn't just the story that is structured, but also the exhibition landscape that is conceived as a series of layers, which when plotted on paper are akin to an opera production; but in this case a production that integrates layers of text, personal testimony, archive and newsreel film and photography, alongside pacing and drama, alternating the principle [sic] mode of delivery in each space, the audio-visual plot and the lighting plan. (230)

A vital space is polyphonic in content and multimodal in display—and as with any dramatic performance, it exists in reference to both its internal content and the content of the external world around it.

We can see an example of the extent to which space—the space of the museum itself and the space it inhabits in its society—can determine response to an object by looking into the Museum of Egyptian Antiquities (the Egyptian Museum) on Tahrir Square in Cairo. The venerable 115-year-old red and white colonial-era building, sitting back from the square in a gated (and guarded) formal garden, houses one of the best-known collections of artifacts in the world. Its multiple cavernous rooms, interior courtyards, and long hallways hold a mind-numbingly vast collection of unspeakably priceless ancient objects, including one that would seem to carry the weight of a national mythic image as well as any—the golden death mask of Tutankhamun. Here, though, space and scene combine with narrative display to *deny* status as a national mythic image to one of the most renowned artifacts in the world. Eleven kilos of solid gold, molded into the likeness of the boy king and placed over his mummified remains nearly thirty-five hundred years ago, the mask, for outsiders, is as representative of the treasures of Egypt as the Great Pyramid of Giza. Indeed, when I visited in 2012, when the gift shop (which had been looted during the uprising of 2011) was still closed, the only guidebook sold in the museum (printed in Britain) featured the Tut mask on its cover.

The mask is displayed in one of the museum's only air-conditioned rooms, specially guarded, along with some of the other seventeen hundred objects on display from the excavations in the Valley of the Kings. It is clearly seen as very valuable, yet neither the mask nor the room in which it is housed is given any particular spatial prominence within the total museum complex. The room is not particularly prominent or even easy to find; it seems in fact an alcove cut into the wall of a much larger gallery. The mask is set in its own vitrine, but so are many objects. Indeed, the Egyptian Museum is stuffed full of both death masks and gold-covered artifacts, along with many giant stone statues, endless coffins, and shelf after shelf of grave finds—such that the affective message is that the Tut mask is *not* unique or iconic but merely one of many such treasures, in the same way that the *Mona Lisa*, hanging in a hallway of the Louvre, is just one of many priceless paintings.

Museological space alone, though, is not the only determinant of the mask's seeming lack of status as a national mythic image with which Egypt self-identifies. In a rapidly changing modern Egypt, it and its fellow artifacts in the Egyptian Museum seem left behind. The 2011 looting of the museum, limited in scope though it was, is still the most infamous example of the museum's lack of felt connection to the struggles of modern life. As the *Wall Street Journal* commented (rather hyperbolically) at the time, "A vast, impoverished underclass seems less taken with either the nationalist narrative of Egyptian greatness that stretches back to the pharaohs, or the intrinsic value of antiquities for all humanity, and more intrigued by the possibility of gold and other loot" (Joffe 2011). With Egypt now years into its crisis of identity, the museum is struggling so hard to remain *permanent* that asking it to confront change is particularly difficult, if not impossible. And yet it therefore remains outside the debates of the real world that would—as with the Treaty of Waitangi—give it national relevance.

In July 2012, I attended the opening screening of the Danish-Egyptian independent film *Sound from the Hallways*, shot in the museum in 2011 while the Arab Spring uprising was occurring just outside its gates. In the largely unnarrated film, sounds of the political protest of tens of thousands of people filter through the open windows of the museum as the camera plays over still, silent artifacts in unchanging cavernous halls. There is a performance going on, but it does not engage with an impassioned, changing audience. The film was scheduled to be shown at the museum itself, where it would be inserted obliquely into the ongoing debates. But while co-producer Mostafa Youssef insisted that the film celebrated the museum, museum officials disagreed and withdrew their support for this screening at the last minute, forcing a change of venue. According to the *Egypt Independent*, "The screening and its cancelation interrogate the level of openness of the Egyptian Museum as an incumbent house of memory for Egyptians and a bearer of one of the official narratives of the country's pharaonic legacy" (2012)—in other words, as a relevant participant in the national conversation.

As with any rhetorical narrative, the Tut death mask, like any other object in the national museum, cannot be a national mythic image without the consent of its audience, and Burke would argue that the museum's very reluctance to engage with the current conflicting parliamentary babel of national identity places the museum outside the possibility of that consent. Instead of polyvocal narratives that incorporate such voices as Youssef's in multimodal performances to engage the senses, the museum displays its objects one after the other at a distance, behind glass, in silence and under guard, spatially walled off from their contemporary surroundings. Reality is messier and more contested than any musealized narrative; material space of sufficient dialectical scope to encompass the real conversation must thus also be messier, more complicated, better able to use its space to engage with the babel of competing values.

Crable writes that rhetoricians interested in identification need to begin "by asking how symbols have always already interposed distance. How, in other words, have we taken the wordless, distinctionless realm of the nonsymbolic, and carved it, and ourselves, into the distinct substances that we take for granted?" (2009, 237). We strive—personally, as nations, as the world—to overcome division with unifying identification, but division is inevitable, built into the symbol systems that are our human means of communication. Striving to eliminate division leads only to the cessation of communication—the silent stasis of permanence while *life* goes on with the change outside the windows. Dialogue is not always possible. But when situations permit it, as we shall see in the next chapter, acknowledging the divisions of life can paradoxically allow for closer identification with the national audience. We can now start to move toward the social implications of these ambiguous narratives and objects—the world outside the museum doors—and that involves national identification.

4

Identifying with the Museum

Identification is affirmed with earnestness precisely because there is division. Identification is compensatory to division. If men were not apart from one another, there would be no need for the rhetorician to proclaim their unity.

—Kenneth Burke

We've seen in the last two chapters how national museums are performing history both narratively and materially. This performance promotes visitors' identification with a national story. More broadly, visitors identify with a national *experience*, a rhetorical ethos that aligns individuals with the particular sets of commonly conceived values and memories that make them American or Austrian, Australian or Argentine. Argentina, in fact, has a word for this common national ethos, *argentinidad*, and defining the multiple, varied qualities of the word (one Web commentator describes his fellow Argentines as "a compilation of contradictions . . . a collage of sensations") gives us a sense of how such national identification develops. *Argentinidad* is the focus of a popular 2004 alt-rock song ("La Argentinidad al Palo," by the band Bersuit Vergarabat) and also the subject of a 2007 book (*Idarg: Identidad Argentina*), available in Argentina's museums. The latter is a small encyclopedia of Argentine-isms with the rather serious "yearning" to "communicate a national identity to which we will aspire in an abstract universe of beauty and synthesis that betters the perception of our history as well as a future yet to be imagined" (Berdichevsky and Stecher 2007, 13). In both song and book, the items that signify *argentinidad*—everything from foods, to phrases, to places, to historical events—are all material demonstrations of diverse, contradictory collective memory. They celebrate the fact that a group of people across a long open swath of territory in the eighth-largest country in the world can hear the lyrics "The fingerprints, the cartoons / The disposable syringes, the pen / The blood transfusion, the 6–0 to Peru" (Bersuit Vergarabat 2004) and know together what they mean—and then *know* that they together know this. Indeed, the very fact that these qualities of the Argentine ethos can be grouped together into a list of traits that a broad cross-section of the nation can understand serves as reinforcement that all Argentines do indeed share a collective identity: their insider knowledge signals their communal possession of *argentinidad* and thus their communal identity as Argentines. At the same time, the wide variety of cultural references indicated in both song and book—this collage of sensations—might indicate *either* that to be Argentine is to embody diverse traits within oneself *or* that to be Argentine is to embody diverse traits within the collective and so acknowledge distinctly different individuals as also Argentine. In this chapter, I look at the tension inherent in collective identities such as *argentinidad*—the diverse individual or the diversity of individuals—that drives modern attention to the musealized display of national identity via accumulated narratives and artifacts.

I first explore the broad notion of identity—of both the museum itself and its visitors—before applying to the museum-visitor experience Kenneth Burke's notion of rhetorical identification. This analysis carries us into the next chapter, which examines individuals' identification with the diverse nation via its symbols and signs.

Museum Identity

As I hope the case studies so far have demonstrated, all museums are unique—but, like teenage nonconformists, they are unique in similar ways. They share generic features. Rhetorical studies of these features focus on the expectations that both speaker/writer and audience bring to a new situation—for example, that we will hear a eulogy at a funeral, or that when we tune into a presidential address we will not see an interpretive dance. Genres, wrote compositionist Carolyn Miller in a foundational 1984 article, are patterns that constrain both rhetor and audience by imposing a collectively agreed upon (but largely unconscious) set of content and form. We have only to recall the difficulty of navigating early webpages before conventions regarding spacing, color, hyperlinks, background, and so on became generic, to understand the ease of comprehension that such constraints allow. For similar reasons of visitor ease, museums follow genre prescriptions in both form and content.

First, museums have copied one another's architectural form, as Simon Knell has observed of European museums in the Eunamus publication *Crossing Bor-*

ders. The British Museum looks like the Parthenon, but the Greek National Archaeological Museum looks much like the British. So does the Hungarian. The Czech National Museum looks like the British Museum with a dome behind it, rather like Saint Peter's Basilica (the "other wing" of the Vatican Museum). The Louvre—like the Vatican, originally a palace—features similar long corridors lined with windows. Joshua Reeves argues that commonplace forms used repeatedly render themselves invisible (2013, 307)—but museums' copying of generic form, Eunamus is quick to point out, yields not a standardized "box" in each setting but a dynamically interpreted version of the generic type (Knell et al. 2012, 2). Museums are concerned with what classical rhetors called *decorum*—the necessary fit between genre and situation for the purpose of meeting audience expectations. "Research has shown," writes Suzanne MacLeod, "that architecture"—and we can include museum architecture, the space within which object and visitor encounter each other—"can be conceived as the outcome of a perceived social need, located in the specifics of time, space, and site" (2005b, 13). This decorous reproduction of other European museums fulfills the social need to provide Europe's museums with a sense of "Europeanness," even when such an identity is never explicitly discussed. "In national museums, Europe appears not as a subject but as a language through which the nation is performed," Knell et al. continue. "Nations seeking to express their identities to other nations have done so using borrowed symbolic forms . . . [that] have been regularised so as to function as a language European citizens can implicitly understand" (2012, 14). Because of decorous generic forms, Europe's museums create a sense of pan-national unity even as they promote individual national identities.

Further afield, national museums take a variety of forms, some clearly reproducing the European genre and others making conscious use of indigenous forms. For instance, the Indian Museum (Kolkata), is a rectangle with two floors of arched terraces around a central garden. Its form is echoed in the single-story arched colonnade/garden of the Peruvian National Museum of Archaeology, Anthropology, and History in Lima, which is in turn very similar to the Argentine National Historical Museum in Buenos Aires. The same form is echoed in the interior main hall of the Egyptian Museum in Cairo. All of these nineteenth-century colonnaded rectangles are reminiscent of the courtyard surrounded by arched corridors at the Vatican Museum (itself reminiscent of ancient Roman architecture). Museums built in the twentieth century, meanwhile, display different but equally globalized similarities, with midcentury national museums in Peru, the United States, Uzbekistan, China, and Tunisia (the renovated Bardo), among others, employing versions of the large stone cube of modernist architecture. The more recent, more postmodern National Museum of the American Indian (Washington, D.C.) and the Museum of New Zealand Te Papa Tongarewa (Wellington) share similar sand-colored curving walls, exterior gardens, and multistory open interior spaces, while the deconstructivist lightning-bolt architecture of the National Museum of Australia in Canberra is so notoriously similar to that of the Jewish Museum in Berlin that the Australian museum takes pains to explain the indigenous significance of its design. Still other museums take a more localized form—thus the brand-new State Museum of Temurids History in Tashkent gestures in white stone to the

11 | Counterclockwise from top left, museums in England, Peru, Australia, and Uzbekistan illustrate the different styles of national museums.

traditional central Asian yurt, the Museum of Anatolian Civilizations in Ankara looks like the former *han* (inn) that it is, and the Thai National Museum in Bangkok looks like a complex of traditional palace buildings—which in fact is also what it is (see fig. 11).

In fact, the Thai Museum in its idiosyncrasy illustrates a deeper generic identity, beyond formal architecture, that museums around the world share: museums all display their artifacts in a similar fashion, so that whatever the exterior of the building, visitors expect to walk into a lobby and be directed to separate exhibition halls that display artifacts and text panels. "Museums make sense to us because although they might introduce new material, they do so within narratives which are already well known, offering formulaic ways of making sense of the world" (Harris 2016, 27). Because of generic conventions, visitors look for an explanatory introductory panel when they walk into a gallery; they know that it's forbidden to touch the artifacts (which are often behind glass); and they have learned to piece together the artifacts into stories whose structure includes temporality, heroes, villains, defeats, and triumphs. These conventions that people "know" about quite different museums become apparent only when they're broken. The Thai Museum, for instance, is a complex of many buildings converted into museum galleries. Visitors walk back and forth along pathways and across green lawns to enter the different sections. In what order should they proceed? Are all the buildings open? Is the Buddha in that building that looks like a temple still a sacred object, or is it now an artifact? Can I eat my snack on that deck, or is it a site for prayer?

When museum architecture breaks generic rules of decorum, visitors are less clear about the rules—less "decorous" themselves. The purposeful disorientation of the Jewish Museum, as we saw earlier, thwarts the visitor's expectation that she will enter an informational lobby that will give her the necessary background to begin her visit fully in control. It disrupts the visitor's sense of Burke's "pieties" about "what properly goes with what" (1935/1984, 74). Burke believed that it was necessary first to make conscious our unexamined reverence for the order presented by commonplaces, if there was to be any hope of challenging our assumptions about the way the world "should" work. He envisioned a linguistic breaking apart and recombination of metaphors, the juxtaposition of terms that "should not" go together, in order to create new ways to describe the world—but here again, the materiality of museums makes possible a more extralinguistic, multidimensional, and material break from those generic expectations.

Second, museum objects themselves reinforce the generic expectations of museum visitors. Of course, uniqueness in display is part of the pride of national museums, and all museums highlight certain treasures. The Aztec Sun Stone, the Rosetta Stone, the death mask of Tutankhamun, the Anatolian mother goddess, the dancing Shiva, and the Neolithic jade dragon—these are all unique, at times mythic, treasures. They are also, however, *generic* unique treasures, in that they are works of art or culture made by distant ancestors who demonstrated a level of civilization that visitors are expected to admire today. It takes the unexpected "treasure" to remind visitors of the generic piety with which we expect to view a display of Neolithic, Bronze Age, or Iron Age artistry. The fossilized remains of *Ardipithecus ramidus* in Ethiopia, the display of Hills Hoist clotheslines in Australia, the ruby slippers from *The Wizard of Oz* in the United States—these treasures startle precisely because they do *not* speak the language of reverence for historic and prehistoric craftsmanship cultivated in identical ways in museums around the world. As Knell et al. point out, at the macro level, "a number of forces shape local conceptualisations and implementations of the museum. These include museum disciplines, such as art history, which shape thinking about particular categories of object," along with academic communities, politicians, and professionals. "The institution itself possesses a particular leadership and working culture that shapes a response or develops its own strategy" (2012, 8). Each of these forces represents a set of genre expectations that seek to impose an identity on the museum, which in turn asserts its own generic identity in dialogue with other national institutions both within and beyond the national borders.

As with the "indecorous" architecture, one's awareness of pious preconceptions about museum objects is strongest when the generic expectations are challenged or stretched. While we are all familiar with the musealized chair, with its "do not sit" sign, India's National Museum in New Delhi, built in 1949 in roughly the shape of the Indian *charkha* (spinning wheel), takes this musealization to another level. Inside one of its white-walled rooms, it houses "sacred corporal relics" from the body of the Buddha—some of the only ones in existence. In another setting, these revered relics would be objects of worship. Indeed, the Thai government gave the Indians a pavilion made of gold, teak, and diamond suitable to "enshrine" the relics, and the pavilion itself is now also musealized into an artifact to be gazed upon: a plaque informs visitors that the top section contains 109 grams of gold and the tip is made of diamond. Because the sacredness of such relics breaks through the genre expectations of museum convention, the National Museum has to place large signs on either side of the artifact, appealing to people not to leave "offerings and donations of any kind," which are "strictly prohibited." Similarly, the Museum of New Zealand Te Papa Tongarewa for several years displayed a carved *taunga atua*, or chosen dwelling place, of Uenuku, ancestral god of the island's first Tainui Maori inhabitants. The dwelling place, a nearly three-meter-high wooden post, was rediscovered in 1906 and is now permanently housed at the Te Awamutu Museum on the North Island. Signs at Te Papa warned visitors not to take photos of this important deity, who still apparently dwells within the carving, which had become an artifact to be gazed upon. Museologist Jan Geisbusch relates similar ambiguity whenever Roman Catholic relics (often the reliquary rather than the saint's bone, hair, or other body part inside the container) are musealized; modern visitors are rarely allowed to touch the venerated objects (2012, 206). The musealization of a holy object occurs as well at the Nordic Museum in Stockholm, where the object is used not only for display but also for cultural commentary. The sacred indigenous object is a carved wooden *seidi* that would have been placed at a special or sacrificial site by the Sami people of northern Scandinavia. The museum's rather more dialogical approach to its display included the *seidi* in its 2012 special exhibit on the Sami titled *Sápmi* (the indigenous name for Lapland). In the exhibit, the Nordic included in its signage comments from a Sami "exhibition reference group" that both explained and critiqued the objects displayed. Comments on the *seidi* read, "'Who assumed the right to desecrate the Sami's sacred places? I hold them in great respect and would never think of removing anything,' says Annelie Päiviö. 'A seidi unquestionably raises issues of morality, ethics and questions of repatriation and preservation,' says Victoria Harnesk." This criticism of the museum was juxtaposed with the *seidi* itself— which remains enclosed in its vitrine in the museum, not returned to Sápmi. The museum neither acknowledges nor denies the *seidi's* sacred status, perhaps leaving visitors to question their unstated expectations about, in Burkean terms, what should piously be worshipped and what should piously be musealized.[1] As Geisbusch notes, "While there can be no doubt that museums have saved many sacred objects, they have done so *in their fashion*, preserving their physical existence, yet bleaching them of energy and meaning. It is the museological gaze that Foucault saw as emblematic of Western modernity, imprisoning the object within discourse" (2012, 208). Museum identity, then, is both uniquely generic in its spaces across the world and generically pious when it comes to displaying the objects within those spaces. What of visitor identity?

Visitor Identity

In 2012, the European Commission, the governmental arm of the European Union, funded twenty-one separate projects in Europe alone that could be viewed as either directly or indirectly relevant to questions of European identity (Miller 2012). (One of these was the Eunamus project, on which I worked.) Yet as popular and important as it is in the scholarship of multiple disciplines, identity is a slippery concept to define.

As we saw in chapter 2, narrative psychologists view identity formation as the story people tell about themselves to others—and all identity theories have in common this dual internal-external focus on the self in society. Some theories, following psychologist Erik Erikson's work on identity formation, focus internally on the adolescent process of developing commitments to our values, beliefs, and actions toward and with others. Other theories focus more on the social forces that enable and constrain these choices, perhaps most famously articulated by sociologist Anthony Giddens's duality of structure—the idea that we make the structures that in turn constrain us in our potential choices. As Sharon Macdonald notes, Giddens recognized that in modern societies, identities are becoming dislodged from traditional collectivist structures like location and kinship, so that, while still constrained, modern identities are more individualized than premodern ones (Macdonald 2003, 6). In other words, moderns must form a sense of self with less of our script prewritten—and the script is our life story, the narrative of past choices and roles interacting with society, unified into a self-identity story that is then recounted to others. It is the self in society who both has the internal agency to determine selfhood and has that agency externally directed by interaction with the social scene.

Rhetoricians are among the critical theorists who have noted other constraints on personal agency—Raka Shome has argued that space, more than identity, determines the modern self; Debra Hawhee has argued for the central role of the body and its senses in determining one's perception of the world and thus one's sense of identity with respect to that perception. It is the position of this book that the self in society—as both corporeal *and* intangible entity, both individualized *and* collectively determined—is our "self" in continual, and necessary, flux. That ambiguous self is sufficiently defined as the one who moves through a museum, taking in (selectively) the selected stories presented and incorporating them (selectively if not always consciously) into a life story that, in the museum, moves toward identification with the collective. Social scientists

William Penuel and James Wertsch conclude that "identity may be conceived as formed when individuals choose on particular occasions to use one or more resources from a cultural 'tool kit' to accomplish some action" (1995, 90). The museum is the storehouse of this collective cultural tool kit.

Penuel and Wertsch argue that, rather than a static essence, identity is "a form of action that is first and foremost rhetorical, concerned with persuading others (and oneself) about who one is and what one values to meet different purposes" (91). Building identity requires building trust among one's audience. Yet rhetoric faces a dilemma when considering its audience as individuals who are themselves engaged in their own identity actions. Since Aristotle's *Rhetoric* first advised budding public orators to know their audience by knowing the *group* characteristics of that audience, rhetoric has struggled with the question of how to consider an audience of individuals. The communication goal encourages the illusion not of unique self-identity but of sameness, not division but unity. Thus teachers continue to encourage writers and speakers to *learn* the characteristics of their audience, or *imagine* the characteristics of their audience, or *create* the characteristics of their audience by their persuasive presentation, as if their audience were monochromatic. Similar issues are debated in museum studies. Should museologists engage in visitor studies to *learn* their audience? How much can they extrapolate from those data to *imagine* the whole self that is their visitor? To what degree should professionals *create* or *evoke* the desired characteristics in their visitors by certain displays, particular texts and artifacts, lighting, flow patterns, and so on? And what about interaction—how should the museum *engage* the visitor with touch screens, provocative questions, reflection zones, and all the rest that will encourage "the audience" to trust and therefore identify with "the identity" presented by the museum?

Faced with the audience's complicated collective identity, Burke's concept of the *personalizing of essence* provides a useful lens. Personalizing of essence links the essence of one's identity with the chronology of a narrated life story. Narrative, Burke notes in *A Rhetoric of Motives*, must by its nature historicize occurrences that do not actually happen sequentially, because narrative requires linearity—one thing must follow another. Thus one's essence, who one is, becomes the story of one's origins or destination (where one came from or ends up) when it is translated into narrative. "In either choice (the ancestral or the final) the narrative terminology provides for a *personalizing* of essence" (1950/1969, 15). Placing the essential in time, he explains, an individual translates the disparate events of her personal narrative into an abstract reflection, and then translates that reflection back into a narrative now larger than herself, a persuasive narra-tive. This is very like the process described by museologists for the identity work done by individuals in museums when confronted with a series of artifacts and a wall of stories. As a visitor moves through representations of the collective past, the abstraction that is the (essential) communal identity is narrated and object-ified into a causal timeline. That timeline is then personalized by interac-tion with the visitor's own life story, and—as she explores with her fellows the collective history presented—it is then collectively renarrated in a way that promotes her identification with the larger story by infusing her individual acts—and mine, and yours—with the more unifying presented ideal. Let me give a concrete example from the Library of Congress (Washington, D.C.) exhibit *Creating the United States* (2008–12), which focused on the ways in which key ideals from the U.S. Declaration of Independence, Constitution, and Bill of Rights have been instantiated through word and deed in particular cir-cumstances throughout the history of the nation. Thus, for instance, a citizen's individual acts of voting in local elections would be unified into a personal identity such as "I vote" or "I'm a voter." The Declaration and Constitution, in turn, by laying out the manner in which U.S. representatives govern "by consent of the governed," give each individual that common phrase to use in translating his individual (voter) identity into a communal identity: "We are the consenting governed." This abstraction is then retranslated back to the individual, infusing individual acts of voting with a communal identity that in turn described this new nation: "We are a nation in which individual votes determine who governs." This is the U.S. definition of democracy—made concrete in the museum through displays of artifacts from the leaders of the American Revolution.[2]

It is in this sense of forming an individual identity that intersects with collec-tive origins or ideals, and thus with collective identity, that, as Jay Rounds argues, "visiting a museum is both about construction of identity and signaling of identity. . . . Museums offer opportunities of affirming our identity, but they also offer a safe environment where we can explore other identities and gain materials to 'construct' ourselves" (2006, 138). Rounds's "other identities," I would argue, are the varied manifestations of the collective identity that each individual unifies for himself into a version of the collectivity with which he identifies. This museal "identity work," a term coined by Judith Howard in 2000, is unlikely to be the stated reason for visiting the museum; instead, it is a consequence of visitor engagement there. Identity as rhetorical *action*—the act of personalizing essence, the act of forging an identifiable collectivity—is malleable, "emergent rather than permanent," as John Falk puts it: "Our identity is a reflection [of] and a reaction to both the social and physical world we consciously perceive in the moment, but identity is also influenced by the vast unconscious set of family, cultural, and personal history influences each of us carries within us. Each is continuously constructing and maintaining, not one, but numerous identities which are expressed collectively or individually at different times, depending upon need and circumstance" (2009, 72–73).

Rhetoric itself becomes "the process of negotiating with others our notions of individual and collective identity," according to Greg Clark's examination of the aesthetic places where these negotiations occur (2004, 3). As Clark notes, individuals are prompted by the material provided (in a museum, the narrative) to endow what they are looking at (the object) with collective meaning and then to determine their stance on that meaning: they are "prompted to recreate themselves in the image of a collective identity" (4). We can see this kind of identity prompting in the entry halls of the National Museum of American History, where visitors are immediately confronted with the sheer physical abundance of artifacts stored there. Entering either of the large lobbies, they walk through corridors of "highlights" and gaze into shallow vitrines, much as they would study the collections of preserved nineteenth-century birds or insects in a natural history museum. Here, though, within a few feet of one another are the chemical balance Edward Morley used to determine the atomic weight of oxygen, a collection of political protest buttons from the past hundred years, a carnival mask from Puerto Rico, and the laptop computer used by the fictional Carrie Bradshaw in the television show *Sex and the City*. Visitors are confronted with three implicit messages about the nature of American identity: its material culture is vast, it is diverse, and it boasts a radical egalitarianism in which everything is a potential treasure (Weiser 2009, 29). The principal guide to the museum puts this plethora of artifacts into a nation-focused perspective, noting in its opening statement that "the [NMAH] . . . preserves treasures of the American past. From politics to popular culture, innovations to everyday life, the Museum's collections reflect the diverse experiences, beliefs, and dreams that have shaped the nation" (Kendrick and Liebhold 2006, vi).

The presence of these diverse artifacts in the national museum invites Americans to consider themselves within a populist collective identity. The America with which visitors are prompted to identify is not the nation of the Rosetta Stone or the head of Ramses the Great, of Winged Victory or the Mona Lisa, or of other symbols of imperial power and cultural triumph—it is the nation of the ruby slippers from *Oz* and President Lincoln's battered stovepipe hat. Such an identity is not likely to be wholly consistent with visitors' personal life stories, or even with their understanding of the life story of America, but the external generic constraints imposed by the space—its scene as the national museum, telling a story of the origins and ideals of the nation—encourage individualized identification along these lines more than along others. Eleni Bastéa quotes historian John Gillis to point out that "both identity and memory are political and social constructs, and should be treated as such. . . . Identities are not things we think *about*, but things we think *with*" (quoted in Bastéa 2004a, 8)—which is to say, the identity relationship individuals forge with a crafted collective identity becomes the lens through which they in turn view that collectivity.

Museum-Visitor Identification

In order to engage in the dialogical encounter with Burke's parliamentary babel of conflicting groups in negotiation with one another, such groups need to establish through some means "a shared sense of values, attitudes, and interests" (1950/1969, 138)—a baseline of consubstantiality from which to diverge (or, to use a different metaphor, an agreed-upon common boundary that embraces their differences). Burke called this a process of identification, talking one another's language via a shifting combination of "speech, gesture, tonality, order, image, attitude, idea" (55). This requires dialogue between parties, not monologue, and it is never entirely fulfilled because if "we" are to *identify* with "them," all must recognize both that we share commonalities and that we are diverse enough to not form one homogenous group of indistinguishable members. If they are to persuade, in other words, diverse people need to recognize their potential linkage *as* a linkage, a bridge across a divide, something needing to be worked on. G. Mitchell Reyes points out that within identification there is space for disagreement—identification with others is not the same as adopting their identity as one's own (2010, 245).

For Burke, what made this identification/division duality possible was the inherent ambiguity encoded in linguistic experience—the fact that words both unite and separate, and therefore provide enough scope to encompass the entire experience with the Other. This duality of encounter is carefully worked into the introductory text panel of the *Our Peoples* exhibit at the National Museum

of the American Indian. It asserts the individual identity of indigenous people
before contact with Europeans: "The people who live here are engineers and
artists, cooks and dreamers, hunters and students. They are scientists and kings,
farmers and revolutionaries. They aren't 'Indians.' They have never heard of
'America.'" They do not know the museum visitors. But by providing these
unknown indigenous individuals with familiar roles, the panel provides a way
for visitors to identify with them across time: modern visitors are also engineers
and artists, cooks and dreamers. Because of these common roles (i.e., this use of
terms to replace the term "Indians," which separates ancient peoples from non-
Indians), modern visitors are given the cultural tools that allow them to bridge
their differences while still recognizing that they are distant from one another—
that those ancient peoples have never heard of America. We may be strangers to
these long-gone ancestors, but (thanks to the museum) they are not complete
strangers to us.

Indeed, it is because of this need to acknowledge the division between peoples with whom we would imagine ourselves consubstantial that I suggest here,
instead of *consubstantiality*, Burke's earlier term from *A Grammar of Motives*,
dialectic substance, which takes as its starting point the nature of humans as
users of symbolic communication (words) and the fact that words necessarily
"define a thing in terms of something else" (1945/1969, 33)—a both-and paradox, whereby the idea of something *as* anything means also its idea as *not*
anything else. We are not ancient peoples. We are all inhabitants of this land
America. They do not know us. They share with us common attitudes and
actions. We are both consubstantial and divided (and thus we engage in identification).

As the very existence of the National Museum of the American Indian, along
with its new Smithsonian sister, the National Museum of African American
History and Culture, makes clear, the increasing effort to identify with diverse
museum audiences beginning in the late twentieth century means that museum
advocates went from interpreting the museum to these new audiences to interpreting the audiences back to the museum, incorporating a greater diversity of
experiences into the national narrative. Lisa Roberts emphasizes the back-and-
forth nature of museum-visitor dialogue in this identification effort: "It became
clear that the task of interpretation was first and foremost a task of connection:
getting visitors to connect to what they saw, on whatever terms that might be.
At issue was the legitimization of personal experience as a source of meaning
different from but no less valid than curatorial knowledge" (1997, 70). In the new

communal museums, personal knowledge becomes a part of the exhibit with which visitors are asked to engage, weaving their "visitor story" into the "museum story" in order to better identify with that collective narrative. For instance, "Welcome to the People's History Museum" reads the large yellow and red sign at the entrance to this blocky brown museum in the arts district of central Manchester, England. "Join a march through time following Britain's struggle for democracy over two centuries. Meet the revolutionaries, reformers, workers, voters, and citizens who fought our battle for the ballot." Here, immediately, is the use of familiar identity roles (workers, voters), the invitational "join a march," and the inclusive "our battle." The People's History Museum encourages audience identification with the working-class citizens whom museums like the British Museum ignore. Visitors are invited to "clock yourself in"—to punch a time card as they enter the exhibit hall. They are then immediately introduced to the world of exploited labor, as the time clock panel tells them, "In the past, the manager could put the mill clock back to make his workers work longer hours without knowing it." They face the photos and biographies of famous reformers and read their inspiring words. They are confronted with contextual place, learning that "five minutes' walk from where you stand a massacre occurred" in 1819. The People's History Museum employs a variety of interactional devices to promote engagement—and thus identification—with the themes of its exhibits. Visitors are invited to try on the costumes of previous eras' workers and handle the contents of individuals' "suitcases" as they read their personal stories, which are addressed directly to the visitor ("I don't own many things, but these are mine. . . . Take a look and you'll find out what I eat, what I drink, and how I earn my money. I work as a match girl for the evil Bryant and May"). They take on the workers' role as they walk through a cooperative store. And on video screens located throughout the exhibit halls, they follow the fortunes of multiple generations of one working-class family as their lives slowly improve thanks to the struggle for labor rights. For this experience to work on visitors, however, visitors must continue to be aware that they are *not* that family, and that they are in fact more empowered and enjoy greater rights today—rights that, the museum implies, they need to continue to defend. As the museum asks on its website, "Rather than being revolutionaries, reformers, workers or voters, have we become citizens?" (People's History Museum 2013). And, if citizens, do we choose to exercise citizens' rights, continuing "the march"? The museum's hortatory displays work to persuade its visitors to do so.

Engagement frequently aims to get visitors directly involved in the stories being told. Indeed, museum narratives can be constructed to *demand* a response from their audience, as museum educator Sue Glover Frykman observes, and this response frequently invokes a greater degree of visitor identification with the story: "Narratives can be said to be active in that they appear to communicate something to someone, interpret this, facilitate meaning making, stimulate the imagination and educate. They can also be said to be interactive in that they expect some kind of response from the reader or participant, encourage the expression of personal thoughts and feelings, facilitate interaction with others, lead to an exchange of views that can result in changed ideas and stimulate an understanding of events through participation" (2009, 315).

Promoting Identification

In order to promote identification, museums promote interaction, a kind of dialogue between visitor and exhibit identities. Around the globe, museums repeatedly use three approaches to encourage a high level of visitor engagement with exhibits, promoting identification with another's "speech, gesture, tonality, order, image, attitude, idea" in a way that bridges the divide between the individual and the collective.

Share Your Story

First, exhibits may ask visitors to *share with the museum their own personal narratives,* implying that the visitor's story is synecdochally connected to the official story presented to the visitor. Synecdoche, the rhetorical trope whereby a part stands in for the whole or the whole for a part, just as "longhorn" embodies an entire steer, or "hands" an entire ship's crew, places the seemingly idiosyncratic visitor story within the collective memory on display. Visitors are not so much asked to identify with one another as to identify others' stories with their own—each story is a piece of some collectively dialogical whole. This approach is used extensively in the National Museum of Australia in Canberra, the place "where our stories live." Perched on the shore of Lake Burley Griffin, in the center of the nation's capital, the museum's multicolored galleries tell many stories, many of them in the *Eternity* exhibit. Here, light boards display the life stories of fifty Australians—some famous or historically significant, others not—via text, still images, videos, and mementoes. Australians themselves are invited to do much more than learn about these individuals. The opening text panel encourages them to take these personal narratives as exemplars and add their own stories to the collection: "Share all the emotion as the selected stories unfold. And you're invited to add your own: in writing, through video, via sounds. Laugh. Feel fear. Fall in love. Take a chance." Each person's narrative is not a reduction of the greater whole, not less than the national story; it is an embodiment of the whole. As synecdoche, each individual's story is the whole nation's story told through yet another narrative.

As Dominique Poulot notes, such calls for personal memories "incarnate the utopia of a democratically shared past, where all participate in historical research and writing" (2012, 7). Poulot sees this strategy particularly in trauma museums (see chapter 6), but in fact it is becoming increasingly popular throughout the museum world with the advent of computerized archives and displays that allow visitors to add their own stories to those displayed. Visitors are in this way promised that as part of the collective, they, rather than curators, "determine" what constitutes the national identity (although, of course, curators retain control over the selection and presentation of the collective narrative).

Play a Role

Second, museums invite visitors to *take on the role of a participant in the official story*, thus asking them to identify their personhood with that of others and to unify this other identity into their own life story. The U.S. Holocaust Memorial Museum (Washington, D.C.) is famous for giving an identification card to each visitor who enters the permanent exhibit. Each identification card contains information and a photo of a real person, along with the narrative of his or her life just before, during, and (for approximately half of them) after World War II. This card encourages visitors to begin their chronological journey through the 1930s and '40s with a dual identity—their own and that of someone who suffered the effects of the history on display.

While the narratives in this museum are purposely constrained—no one is handed the dual identity of a Nazi collaborator—the identities imposed by the Apartheid Museum in Johannesburg include both the privileged and the oppressed. There, visitors are told, "Your ticket to the museum has randomly classified you as 'white' or 'non-white.' Please use the entrance . . . indicated." They pass through separate turnstiles into the introductory section of the museum,

12 | Entrance through cages in the Apartheid Museum, Johannesburg.

two narrow tunnels made of wire-mesh cages that contain enlarged identity cards of similarly white or nonwhite South Africans (see fig. 12). Both tunnels lead to the same life-sized black-and-white photo of one of the review panels that determined racial classification during the apartheid era. The narrative not only forces visitors' cross-racial identification in a nation in which racial categorizing was paramount, but it also makes an argument about the "randomness" of such classification, which ends with visitors standing together before the review board and reading statistics pointing out the arbitrary nature of apartheid-era racial categories.

Both museums, then, use "official" personal narratives to counter the vernacular narratives with which visitors may enter. "Today we face an alarming rise in Holocaust denial and antisemitism," notes the U.S. Holocaust Memorial Museum on its website (2013)—and so visitors' personal narratives become joined with that of a Holocaust victim or survivor. A statement by Nelson Mandela—"To be free is not merely to cast off one's chains but to live in a way that respects and enhances the freedom of others"—is featured both at the Apartheid Museum's entryway and as the epigraph on its home page (2013)—and so the deep narrative of the Apartheid Museum is less one of oppressor and oppressed than of everyone in chains, caged together by arbitrary racial separation and then, together, freed.

Become One of Us

The third way that museums encourage interactive identification is to ask visitors to *directly incorporate their own life story into that of the museum display*, not as a separate identity but as if they were in fact made over into someone else, in a radical reidentification of self as Other. Historical museums everywhere invite child visitors to dress up in the costumes of another age, look at themselves in mirrors, and perhaps take a photo of this "other" self, while stagecrafted walk-through displays invite visitors to feel what it was like to be in a slave-holding pen, or a World War I trench, or a primeval rainforest, or (in living history museums) in any number of old-time villages. But the Passion for Boca Juniors Museum in Buenos Aires takes its "you are there" approach to cinematographic levels. The museum is tucked into the wall of La Bombonera, the iconic stadium of the Boca Juniors, the working-class soccer team in the old immigrant neighborhood of the capital city. Boca's American equivalent would be the 1955 Brooklyn Dodgers, with equally passionate fans in a soccer-mad nation. There are the typical sports jerseys, trophies, and other memorabilia to look at, but visitors to the museum are first given a more visceral experience. Ushered into a room encircled by large screens above their heads, visitors are shown in 360 degrees a film that is shot from the perspective of the visitor. With the camera as his eyes and the narration employing the second person ("You run, trap, and kick"), "you," a kid in the poor neighborhood of La Boca, can trace your progress in soccer, from your first discovery by scouts for the club, through endless practices with fellow aspirants, to your first big chance to score a goal (and your heartbreaking miss), to your working harder than ever, practicing, practicing, practicing, finally running onto the field at La Bombonera, where the crowds surround you with deafening foot-stomping cheers as you and your teammates face off against your rivals, waiting for your chance, until suddenly a teammate passes you the ball—and there are your legs, running, dodging, shooting in a long arc . . . and scoring! GOOOOOOOAL!!! The crowd goes wild. Since it is safe to assume that this is the dream of nearly everyone who makes the pilgrimage to the museum, its personalized enactment on film immediately invites visitors to connect with the "passion" that is the purpose of the museum—which is, after all, not a place devoted to the Boca Juniors but to the "Pasión Boquense." The emotional hooks of "our" story heighten visitor adherence to the overall Boca story.

Overidentification

Jennifer Harris writes that for theorists of affect, the evocation of bodily responses to this third form of visitor interaction would be merely a private affair were it not for the concurrent "dissolution of boundaries" that such an emotional response provokes (2016, 30–31). We are *touched*, and therefore the boundaries between our body and the other body are minimized. For Matthew Brower and Sara Ahmed, the sensation that "I come to feel that which I cannot know" (Ahmed 2004, 31) opens up the visitor to a social response, to action with others to whom one is now closer. It is the bodily response, not the intellectual thought, that motivates action—action informed by the sense of consubstantiation with others.

Rhetorical studies, while acknowledging the action orientation of affect, has recently become more cautious about this emotional response, particularly when it involves identification with others who are suffering. Rhetorician Lauren Obermark cautions that emotional *overidentification* with another's life story can be problematic if one's goal is to persuade the visitor to identify with a perspective *different* from her own (and thus change her opinion): "While identification is generally viewed as the precursor to persuasion, over-identification can result in a simplified understanding of historical and contemporary civic issues," she argues, defining overidentification as that which is "often overly emotional, superficial, and [does] not allow for any exploration of difference, which I suggest inhibits cross-cultural communication and, ultimately, critical awareness" (2013, 39, 42). Indeed, influential feminist scholars, from Diana Fuss, Doris Sommer, and Sonia Kruks to Wendy Hesford and Krista Ratcliffe, argue that the conception of identification is so skewed toward the overcoming of division in the search for consubstantiality that it elides power differentials and erases important differences of race, gender, etc., in favor of the perspective of the powerful. They propose instead various forms of resistance to identification. I agree with their point that difference—division—is necessary, but I believe that their critiques of identification may miss two key points in Burke's conception of it: first, his lifelong focus on dialectic and his preference for a third way that falls on the bias between any two extremes (in this case, unity and division); and second, his equally strong attention to the place of ambiguity in all human affairs. I discuss each point below.

Dialectic

Without the dialectic, as feminist scholars point out, too great a reliance on sameness leads to overly comfortable erasure of critical differences. Hesford and Obermark note that the desire to overidentify is particularly evident when the Other is a victim of injustice, and particularly troublesome when the perpetrator is more like us. Obermark points to white visitors to the National Underground Railroad Freedom Center in Cincinnati, Ohio, for instance, who may appropriate the experience of African American slaves in a reconstructed holding pen not so much out of empathy for the slave as from a desire to escape from the guilt of white slaveholding. But this comforting belief that white visitors now "understand" slavery does not require them to use their differential power to counter present-day racism.[3] Jean Wyatt refers to this as imaginary identification—and her solution is, again, dialectic, "when two persons speak . . . because new and different aspects of the speaker are revealed over time" (2012, 17–18).

A similar kind of overidentification may be seen in the differing depictions of historical and present-day indigenous peoples in Mexico's National Museum of Anthropology, which opened in 1964 as one of the first truly modern museums in Latin America. As we saw earlier in its juxtaposed cross and deity, the museum is both a depiction of and an homage to the indigenous cultures of what is now Mexico—both before contact with Europeans (on its ground floor) and today (upstairs). The precontact floor, though, receives substantially more visitors than the upstairs, and its displays are more spacious, less confined to vitrines, and more coupled with the hallmark contemporary artwork that the museum envisions as part of a dialogue between modern Mexico and its ancient past (National Museum of Anthropology 2013a). The ground-floor rooms open directly onto the central courtyard, and thus, again unlike the upstairs, the rooms are fully integrated into the main museum design. The large distinctive "umbrella" of indigenous symbols in the central courtyard promotes a message, the museum website explains, that "highlights *mestizaje* [mixed heritage] as a factor in national identity" (my translation). The two long arms surrounding this courtyard lead visitors through multiple civilizations, "culminating," as the museum website puts it, at the far end of the rectangle in "the Mexica Room, showing some of the most emblematic works of world art" (National Museum of Anthropology 2013b). The layout of this room invites personal exploration, but most of all it encourages awe, emphasized by its culminating position at the far end of the museum, by the six-meter-high ceilings (double the height of much of the rest of the museum), and by the well-lit stone artifacts, which themselves culminate in the mythic image of the Aztec Sun Stone, set on a dais and mounted just above head height at the far end of the room.

We can hear echoes of Burke's temporizing of essence, defining one's identity by the story of one's origins, in the quotation now carved into the museum's entrance, taken from the museum's inaugural address by then president of the republic Adolfo López Mateos: "Faced with the testimonies of those cultures, Mexico today pays tribute to indigenous Mexico, in whose example it recognizes characteristics of its national originality" (my translation). The identification of Mexico with its indigenous heritage does not, however, mean that it similarly identifies with modern-day Amerindians. Indeed, in this narrative of the glorious past, the upstairs rooms of present-day indigenous life can seem like a forgotten chapter. In the midst of folkloric displays of costumes, festivals, and indigenous belief systems, the armed uprisings that engulfed the southern states in the 1990s–2000s, as indigenous people fought against their marginalization, are referred to only obliquely. The one panel referring to the Mayan uprisings in Chiapas and Quintana Roo is presented only in Spanish, as an "epilogue" to the story of today's Maya told from the third-person perspective of an outsider. It reads in part, "They want to continue being Mayas. Their leaders have said so in their distinct languages and in Spanish so that they are understood. They seek to maintain the principles of the community. . . . They also aspire to be considered part of the nation in equality of circumstances" (my translation). "They" want to be part of the collective—a collective that, downstairs, is invited to trace its essential history back to their ancestors but whose consubstantiality with this past people does not seem to include "them" today. Downstairs, as we saw, visitors are on the side of the ancient Aztecs facing the final indignation of the worm-eaten Spanish cross. Upstairs, their descendants are rendered as ethnographic folklore, and their current-day struggles to remain indigenous but be "considered part of the nation in equality" remain largely unexplored. Unlike the dialectical portrayal of indigenous uprising we saw earlier in the Peruvian *Yuyanapaq* exhibit, the Mexican indigenous dialogue with the modern nation remains, in its museum, stifled by that modern nation's over-identification with the victimhood of the past.

Ambiguity

As Obermark notes, overidentification with the trauma suffered by past victims may also, paradoxically, inhibit and impede the urge to action in the present. What began in the 1960s as a praiseworthy early attempt at the anthropology museum to incorporate into the Mexican story what had previously been a scorned indigenous past can become the overly comfortable unity that obscures the more critically minded, uncomfortable effects of ongoing difference. Mexico is far from alone in this tendency—indeed, Christa Olson's recent *Constitutive Visions* looks at similar appropriations of indigeneity by nineteenth-century mestizo Ecuadorans:

> For Burke, dwelling in that ambiguity [wherein by becoming consubstan-tial we become "substantially one" instead of "wholly one"] allows a public *"acting-together"* [of identification]. . . . The examples provided by the Ecuadoran context suggest, however, that such *"acting-together"* need not necessarily mean that "one" and "other" act together. It may, in fact, mean that one acts *on* or *in place of* that other. . . . The rites of identification can include a three-stage movement from identification to appropriation and then to dissociation that makes the other into self and, in the process, sets the other aside. (2014, 164)

Dissolving the critical distance from the Other through overidentification, then, leads paradoxically beyond unity to dissociation, denying the Other separate space in the world. It is precisely this kind of historical ventriloquism that has caused contemporary indigenous peoples (and other nondominant groups), from the United States, to Norway, to Australia, to curate their own museums and speak for themselves, and we'll look at their efforts more closely in chapter 6. For Burke, however, the "paradox of substance" (the paradox, that is, that "a given subject both is and is not the same as the character with which and by which it is identified" [1945/1969, 32]) is a real paradox, a real description of ambiguous human relations. Thus when two individuals identify with each other and are consubstantial, they are *at the same time* united as beings who find key parts of their identity mirrored in each other and divided as *two* beings, inherently separated from each other. To avoid the oversimplification that erases signs of difference, then, I prefer to call this *dialectic substance*, an identifying action that considers human motivation in terms of its antinomies, its paradoxical contradictions (33–35). *Dialectic substance* better describes the necessary ambiguity—substantially one, not wholly one—that marks Burkean identification.

As a partial solution to overidentification, Obermark, like Krista Ratcliffe, advocates a more critically focused, more ambiguous identification—one that builds on the affective bonds of community forged by emotionally and intellectually identifying with others but also reminds visitors of their historical/ontological distance. This, to me, is identification as dialectic substance: visitors are not those past people, in their glory or pain, but visitors can choose to act with others in the present on the felt bond evoked by a common ancestry or shared empathy. It is perhaps still debatable whether Burke gave sufficient attention to this ambiguous identification—the breaking apart of uncritical unity to include as well the awareness of distance. But there is general agreement that it is in fact a needed balance in a world increasingly aware that we are all one another's Others. Instead of simplified identification—particularly when representing traumatic events or power differentials—Obermark argues for the distance that historian Dominick LaCapra invokes with his term "empathetic unsettlement," which "involves the virtual experience through which one puts oneself in the other's position while *recognizing difference* and thus resisting full identification" with the traumatized Other (Obermark 2013, 42). Such a stance allows for identification with the common humanity of that Other while not appropriating her traumatic experience. Others call this idea *acting-together* (Olson), *nonidentification* (Ratcliffe) or *identifying to a degree* (Wyatt)—or, as I prefer, Burke's original *dialectic substance*, with his understanding that it necessarily, through language, contains the paradox of substance, both a part of and apart from the Other. Shudder as we may in the slave pen, we are never the slave, never the Holocaust victim, never the exterminated Amerindian. We may, however, use our empathy within the exhibit to take action where we have power, in the present-day world outside the museum's doors.

Because of its continual both-and ambiguity, this more critical identification moves between the erasure of distance common to overidentification and the erasure of criticism that other rhetoricians, perhaps best represented by Dickinson, Ott, and Aoki, warn against. In their critique of the Plains Indian Museum in Cody, Wyoming, in the United States, for instance, they argue that the encouragement of visitors' reverence—for the ancestral indigenous tribes and therefore for the value of difference in lifestyle, belief, etc.—distances nonnative visitors from any need to confront their guilt over the destruction of these precolonial lives. "As visitors move through the PIM, they avoid (even forget) the sins of colonization by participating in a discourse of reverence—a discourse that celebrates the Other without identifying with it," they write (2006, 28–29). Indeed, their critique that there is too little (real, critical, present-oriented) identification offers another way to analyze the Mexican Museum of Anthropology, thus demonstrating how overidentification and underidentification may well have a common core, which is the avoidance of the critical consequences of identification.

Categories of Identification

In order, therefore, to broaden our thinking about the multiple ways in which identification functions in the move from individual to collective identity, let me end this chapter by examining and combining two kinds of Burkean identification categories. In the two chapters that follow, I'll return to these combinations to analyze particular museum practices. First is the continuum of identification that Burke included in his introduction to A Rhetoric of Motives: "And identification ranges from the politician who, addressing an audience of farmers, says 'I was a farm boy myself,' through the mysteries of social status, to the mystic's devout identification with the source of all being" (1950/1969, xiv). In other words, identification for Burke ranges from the individualized sort that the individual uses to unite him- or herself to another individual or group of individuals for practical reasons ("I'm like you," "I know what you're going through"), to the collectivized sort whereby the individual becomes united with a collective class of others by the "mystery" of unifying choices of language ("Republicans," "Rwandans"), to the universalized sort whereby individual difference can become (temporarily) effaced in the mystical emotion of uniting with the imagined community in scenes both benign (an audience jointly enraptured at a concert) and injurious (suicide bombers jointly certain of the holiness of their actions). As one moves from individual to universal, the emotional appeal of the identification correspondingly increases and the sense of individuation from the collective decreases. Paradoxically, however, the potential for a more ambiguous identification, one more rooted in aesthetics than in logistics and therefore more open to the potential for *both* unity and division, also correspondingly increases.

At each of these steps in the continuum, we can see a different function of the desired identification predominating: *identification by antithesis, semiconscious identification*, and *identification as the means to an end*.[4] With *identification by antithesis*, opposing people or groups unite against a common enemy, such that to say "I was a farm boy myself" is most effective when the implied conclusion is "and my opponent was not"; to assert one's collective status as a Republican is to not be a Democrat; and to feel mystical antithetical oneness against an enemy can mean personal sacrifice on the football field or on the field of battle. *Semiconscious identification* weaves a narrative that advocates unity by highlighting the carefully selected affective sense that "we" are already one, such that we Americans mythically share the pioneer farm boy ancestry we celebrate at Thanksgiving, we share the social status of "Americans," and we share mystical values of "life, liberty, and the pursuit of happiness." Finally, with *identification as the means to an end* comes the notion of conscious manipulation of others for one's own (or a collective's) purposes. Thus a politician says, "I was a farm boy myself" to gain votes rather than simply to mark a shared past; the slogan "All Lives Matter" is used to evoke a shared collective identity that obscures the differential extent of oppression against African American "black lives" mattering; and "the people, united, will never be defeated" is used to create a mystical bond that impels groups to march together for justice even in the face of repression.

The most effective inducement of all, one that may or may not be invoked to exclude others and may or may not be consciously manipulated as a means to an end, is the story of "that tiny first-person plural pronoun, 'we'" (Burke 1967, 50). Thus, around the world, "we" are now not Hutus or Tutsis but Rwandans, the Islamic State appeals to "our brothers" to come join "us," and "we the people" celebrate the American creation story every Independence Day. As we can see in the examples, each of these combinations of function and collectivity can have both positive and negative outcomes. While academics tend to see the dangers of unification and policymakers the dangers of division, I want to explore further the potential benefits of both. Thus, in chapter 5, I consider the consequences of national unity, crafted in the museum, with the world outside—and particularly with that most ambiguous of constructed unities, the nation. And in chapter 6, I examine the potentialities of national divisions, culled and critiqued in alternative museums.

5

Identifying with the Nation

When we consider museums as providing material settings for the performance of the nation we need to understand that this performance, and the material settings which permit it, have a direct relationship to the world outside; indeed . . . we need to understand that the processes of musealisation involved in the performances of both settings are essentially the same—but also connected. And we do not need to walk through the ruins of an ancient city to feel this connection; it is everywhere.
—Simon Knell

As we saw in the last chapter, individual and collective identities interweave in complex and unpredictable patterns in the rhetorical space of the national museum, but their identity narratives also follow various conventions of genre and form, mandated by the rich interplay of space-time in the museum. In this chapter, I move from examining communal identification inside the museum to exploring the implications of such identification beyond the museum doors, as a nation constructs itself from the material memories that it then houses in its national museum.

What we call national identity, writes narrative theorist Patrick Colm Hogan in his study *Understanding Nationalism*, is really two kinds of traits. Practical identity is what people do or can do; categorial identity is how they view themselves vis-à-vis other groups. Hogan describes practical identity as "the set of habits, skills, concepts, [and] ideas" that guide an individual through daily life. Just as with the formation of self-identity, this practice is not an individual act but functions "most importantly insofar as these enable his or her interaction with others. Thus two people share practical identity to the degree that their . . . memories enable them to achieve common purposes" (2009, 27). This is the kind of identity open to Burkean identification, in which two people identify with each other as they share values, attitudes, and interests. Kenneth Burke would agree as well with Hogan's later point that people are not really aware when practical identity is shared with others, only when it is different (28). In contrast, categorial identity is "any group members that I take to be definitive of who I am" (29)—that is, those with whom I identify via a terministic label such as Catholic, Thai, or male—labels that, as Burke argues, cause me to view the world through their particular terministic lens. Categorial identity, then, calls forth class identification.

According to neurobiologists, says Hogan, individuals respond quickly to people whom they perceive to be members of their terminological category, and warily to people whom they perceive as Other (30–32), as outside the social classes with which they identify. The goal of nationalism, then, is to encourage individuals to identify themselves with a particular national term (Indian or Argentine, for example)—a semiconscious identification made manifest by the shared practical terms of the kind we saw in the previous chapter with *argentinidad*. While the terministic boundary markers are categorial, then, practical identity is critical to making the categorial identity persuasive, since "every functional identity category must comprise not only a label, but an inclusion criterion," a set of expected actions (38). It is through labels and their (assumed and enacted) shared memories, ideologies, and habits that individuals forge the national identity Australian or Azerbaijani, just as their geographical boundaries determine whether they are physically in territory we term Australia or Azerbaijan. What rhetoric adds to this formulation is the acknowledgment that such shared traits are often crafted—we *persuade* ourselves that we share substance. Greg Clark adds that such identification with the nation occurs through "our encounters with each other's symbols that enable us to make and to change the identities that act and interact with common purpose" (2004, 22).

The national museum, then, operates within a larger context of national symbol systems, all working to persuade individuals that they share an identity with thousands or millions of others. The more people, the more difficult the persuasive act of nation building. Communities that seek to promote "the establishment of national identity above all potentially competing categorial identities" (Hogan 2009, 57), therefore, must attend to five parameters, according to Hogan: salience, opposability, functionality, durability, and affectivity. Each of these is addressed in varying degrees by the national museum, as we shall see.

What Is National Identity?

Hogan's first quality, *salience*, keeps national identity in the public eye. Hogan points out that "nationality generally lacks intrinsic salience, [so] nationalists must work particularly hard at making national identity relationally salient" (59)—thus the continued emphasis on the term "Belgian" in the national BEL-vue Museum, for instance. Indeed, the very existence of a *national* museum contributes to the salience of national identity. Earlier, I described national museums as children of the age of revolution (the changing role of the state), Enlightenment (the interest in categorizing), and empire (economic pressures and colonial power). These same three forces, during the same era, played their role in nation formation as well, moving communal identities beyond the known local level. Philosopher Ernst Renan's famous 1882 lecture "What Is a Nation?" was delivered after a century that saw the demise of dynasties and the rise of new nation-states. "What are these new entities so many have fought and died so passionately to create?" he might have been asking, and responses have been as varied and passionate as nations themselves in the intervening decades. These new nations, made up of (national) citizens rather than (localized) subjects, needed physical proofs that they were now one people—and these proofs were housed in new national museums that displayed material objects from through-out the national territory.

An example of the tension between local region and imagined nation in these Enlightenment museums can still be seen today in the anachronistic Indian Museum in Kolkata. One of the earliest national museums outside Europe, the Indian was established in 1814 in what was then the capital of British colonial India. The neoclassical structure, crumbling around the edges but still a lovely white marble around a manicured courtyard centered by a nonworking fountain, invites us to step back in time.

Many of its exhibits are still in their original Enlightenment-era wood-and-glass display cases. Dimly lit rooms are open to the heat and humidity of an Indian summer and packed with the collections of various scientific societies straight out of Jules Verne. Giant mollusk fossils, eight-legged goats in formaldehyde, stuffed polar bears black with age—the museum has it all. Some vitrines even sport their original hand-lettered placards from a long-dead curator, all of this adding to the feeling of having entered a Victorian museum frozen in time (see fig. 13). Within this context, the museum's collections of art, natural history, and ethnology are categorized largely by region. Persian, Mughal, Deccani, Raj-

13 | The nineteenth-century cases and handwritten placards in the Indian Museum in Kolkata demonstrate what many museums would have originally looked like.

asthani, Pahari, read the directional signs at the end of one row of the Painting Gallery, delimiting the paintings by locale. The geographical provenance of the collections of rocks and animals is also clearly identified, while the Cultural Anthropology Gallery depicts local village life (of prior decades) in case after case of life-sized dioramas from across the subcontinent. A highlight of the museum, the Archaeology Gallery's extensive collections of unmatched stone sculptures from Indian history are grouped around geographical "schools" situated only vaguely in time but very localized in space: the Gupta Sculptural Art at Sarnath, the Mathura School of Sculpture, Bharhut near Satna in Madhya Pradesh, Gandhara Art, etc. This collection of regionalisms on display throughout the museum is the essence of the regionalized nationhood of India itself— indeed, the very existence of both the Indian Museum in Kolkata *and* the National Museum in New Delhi speaks to the competing regionalisms implied here. Each separate collection forms the nation in much the same way that an anthology collects diverse authors in one book, with separate locales merged together to forge a national identity that does not (and cannot) supersede regional differences but instead highlights them.

We might well ask how India, or any multiplicity of locally active identities, ever moves beyond the local to forge nationhood. Sociologist Benedict Anderson sees this identification with the collective of unknown Others as the fundamental concern of national identity. This identification, to be successful, would happen along all points of the continuum discussed in chapter 4—between individuals, collectives, and universals—but Anderson's (and museums') greatest concern is with the semiconscious unification of an individual with others as a class, a unity that is achieved through symbols. To return to Renan's question, what is a nation but a collection of strangers believing themselves to be somehow united? Within the realm of museums, we might first identify three conventional responses to Renan's question and say that, as museums portray them, nations are made up of the persuaded unification of ethnicities, of memories, and of the imagination.

A National Identity Is Ethnicities

Scholars in Renan's day saw a world in which nations were defined by shared ethnic background, shared language, or shared culture. More recently, sociologist Anthony Smith founded a field on the argument that the ethnic past is the root of "the nation's explosive energy and the awful power it exerts over its members" (1995, 19). There is substantial debate over this view. For instance, Raka Shome argues that at the turn of the twenty-first century, political and economic hegemonic ties are stronger than any sense of national commonality. "Today there is a 'third world' in the 'first world' and a 'first world' in the 'third world'; America is in Asia and Asia finds itself in America. In such a context, theorizing relations of self and difference that are located only along lines of identity, say national identity, is not completely adequate," she writes (2003, 40). Contemporary historians agree with her—but in spite of critics' dismissal of ethnicity as a factor in nation formation, it continues to motivate popular debates over national museums. Museologist Sheila Watson finds from her research throughout Europe that narratives of the ethnic origins of nations are pervasive. One hundred thirty years after Renan declared that "the most noble countries, England, France and Italy, are the ones where the blood is most mixed" (1882/1992), and that religion and language are optional identifiers, Watson found that "national museums, whether deliberately or unwittingly, promote such ideas [of historical blood ties] in their galleries even when, as for example, in Scotland and Sweden governments adopt an official civic nationalism that attempts to ignore history and ethnic ties to the nation, replacing it with something akin to an allegiance to common values" (2012, 558). A sign at the recent exhibit on the Sami at the Nordic Museum in Stockholm asks, "Who was here first? (Does it matter?)" But frequently, still, it does.

Hogan's national identity quality of *opposability*, making boundaries clear between "our nation" and "other nations," is often a product of blood ties and perhaps the quality that antinationalists most fear, in museums as in life. Its danger is real, as it can so easily lead to scapegoating and war. To enhance opposability, strongly nationalist museums narrate a history that separates one national group from its neighbors (neighbors who, as Shome points out, may only recently have been identified as co-members of the national space but are now regarded as outsiders). After the bloody breakup of the former Yugoslavia, the Baltics represent a strong sense of such opposability. "Do national museums keep conflicts alive? Bosnia Hercegovina's History Museum retains the scars of the siege of Sarajevo," reads a caption in Eunamus's final report (Aronsson and Knell 2012, 6), under a photo of a giant placard on the side of the bullet-pockmarked wall of the Historical Museum of Bosnia and Herzegovina, a placard that invites visitors in Bosnian to "visit our permanent exhibition 'Besieged Sarajevo'" (my translation).

Opposability, in its function, is an extreme of Burke's *identification as antithesis*. We are *not* them. Cast in this light, opposability may seem a negative trait, but Burke and Hogan remind us that antithesis is necessary for identity—establishing borders is a necessary function of building both a personal and a collective identity. The problem lies in an excess of opposability, the kind that breeds exclusivity. Rather than accept that our cut of Burke's universal cheese (which "can be sliced in an infinite number of ways," even as one finds one's own cuts best [1935/1984, 103]) is one among many, it becomes the only real slice. A nationalism built too much on opposability forgets the necessarily dialectical nature of our collective identities, the identification that acknowledges the importance of both (seemingly intrinsic) unity and (seemingly extrinsic) division. Shome points out that the "here" of nationalistic spaces is "a product of relations that are themselves active and constantly changing material practices through which [the nation] comes into being" (2003, 41). Such relations are driven by power, and those in power determine whose presence in the national space is counted as legitimate—and that "legitimacy" is frequently conceived as temporal, a birthright.

Once seeming Others enter that legitimate space, then, it is the job of museums to narrate the unifying history that overcomes perceived threats to that space by "aliens." The specter of social disintegration pushes museums toward identifying any and all commonalities, some of which are based on (narratively crafted) historical blood ties and their supposed link to present-day values. This sentiment was demonstrated in the Dutch debate in 2006 over whether to build a national museum, framed by the unease about Muslim immigrants in Dutch society. A national museum, supporters hoped, would provide the common background lacking in DNA and culture: "A National Historical Museum that coherently exhibits our history does not even exist.... It seems we do not share a common identity any longer," complained two parliamentarians (quoted in Van Hasselt 2011, 317–18). Such attitudes are what I call the "push-factor" of nationalism, the "push" being a fear of social atomization that is often sparked by the arrival of groups who do not share the same blood, and therefore the same histories, as the group residing in the national space. It is resolved in the museum by narratives emphasizing a nation's commonalities (including, often though not necessarily, common origins). The expectation is that museums will temporize essence—historicize identity into a diachronic story of common ancestors, in much the same way that in the nation of (relatively recent) immigrants that is the United States, the historical narrative still calls the framers of the foundational documents 240 years earlier "our Founding Fathers."

Because of that assumption of temporal blood ties, however, museums may also ask visitors to *reconsider* their assumptions about these origin myths. For instance, the message of the Museum of Siam in Bangkok is strongly multiethnic. "Suvarnabhumi, a Multi-ethnic People," reads one text panel on the inhabitants of prehistoric Thailand, in the center of a collage of modern Thais from a clear variety of ethnic backgrounds. "Ayutthaya: A Melting Pot," reads another on the medieval capital. "Who Created Bangkok?" asks yet another, the introduction to a room of small cabinets filled with the possessions of daily life of the Cambodians, Vietnamese, Chinese, Moors, Mons, and others who flocked to the new city in the 1800s. Only toward the end of the museum trail is it made clear what this emphasis on multiethnicity is responding to. "Racialist Propaganda," reads a panel set in a wall of racist cartoons, photos, and text depicting the early twentieth century. As the Kingdom of Siam began to "reinterpret the concept of Nation," replacing its absolute monarch with a constitutional model, a radical nationalism took hold of the country, culminating in the National Socialist regime that in 1939, as a text panel explains, proclaimed "that the country is henceforth to be called 'Thailand' in accordance with its racial[ly] pure 'Thai' inhabitants who were genetically superior to other 'lesser breeds.'" Those who resisted the dictatorship were no longer racially pure Thais—a clear example of Shome's argument that "issues of exclusion and inclusion are better understood and captured through a spatial logic . . . through which inequities are produced and maintained" (2003, 45). Therefore, the choice of name (Museum of *Siam*), for a museum whose purpose is to "tell the story of how Thai identity has developed over thousands of years" (Story, Inc. and Pico Thailand 2013), suddenly takes on present-day significance, even as the museum avoids direct confrontation with existing structures, instead presenting "Thailand Today" as a multiplicity of video-screened voices, and "Thailand Tomorrow" as statistics and visitors' own hopes for the future. "What is 'Thai' anyway?" asks a screen over the reception desk—and the Museum of Siam makes it implicitly clear that whatever it is, it is not (or not only) an ethnic designation.

A National Identity Is Imaginary

This createdness—the semiconscious construction of a collective identity—is what Benedict Anderson terms the "imagined" community. In his famous formulation, he emphasizes the simultaneity of free and equal cohabitation—synchronic unity—in a bounded geography that is divided from other bounded geographies as the essence of nationhood:

> I propose the following definition of the nation: it is an imagined political community—and imagined as both inherently limited and sovereign. It is imagined because the members of even the smallest nation will never know most of their fellow-members, meet them, or even hear of them, yet in the minds of each lives the image of their communion. . . . The nation is imagined as limited because even the largest of them . . . has finite, if elastic, boundaries beyond which lie other nations. No nation imagines itself coterminous with mankind. . . . It is imagined as sovereign because the concept was born in an age in which Enlightenment and Revolution were destroying the legitimacy of the divinely-ordained, hierarchical dynastic realm. . . . Finally, it is imagined as a community, because, regardless of the actual inequality and exploitation that may prevail in each, the nation is always conceived as a deep, horizontal comradeship. (1983, 6–7)

The attempt to unite the nation synchronically, then, forges identification with one another's values, beliefs, and interests through shared practices, and this persuaded consubstantiality is the cultural glue that creates the terms that name a nation. As any collective grows, it faces a moment when it moves beyond the local group to "different" people with whom it needs to imagine itself in community. This might lead in three directions: into forced assimilation of these Others (Turkey's historical position toward ethnic Kurds); into the imposition of supposed "authentic" norms (citizenship tests, or debates over what constitutes a "real American" or a "true Frenchman"); or into an affirmation that what makes the society homogeneous is its culture of syncretism, tolerance, and freedom (such is the ideal, if not the reality, of Western liberal democracies, or of Singapore). All three motives, though their effects are different, are equally aimed at creating a shared cultural heritage, a common practical identity of habits and ideas that lead over time to expanding the collective identity of "us" beyond the known group.[1]

Burke's version of the created quality of communal identity is his theory of dramatism, the understanding that language does not simply convey meaning in the world but makes meaning—and meaning makes action. And it is *dialectic substance*, he said, the paradox of unity and division inherent in language, that is the "overall category of dramatism" (1945/1969, 33). Dramatism assumes that words generate attitudes (one's stance in the world), that attitudes shape our perception of reality, and that differing perceptions cause us to experience differing motivations for the courses of action we choose to follow. Because they affect our actions, Burke insisted, these imaginary perspectives created by words are in fact quite real, made of "real words, involving real tactics, having real demonstrable relationships, and demonstrably affecting relationships" (57–58).

In dramatistic terms, then, a nation talks (and writes, and displays) itself into being because of the ways in which a particular group of people name their egalitarian communion with the "speech, gesture, tonality, order, image, attitude, idea" of some classes of strangers (Burke 1950/1969, 55) and not others. For instance, the debates over Scottish independence that played out in the UK for several years included such questions as who was "Scottish" enough to have the right to vote in the independence referendum of 2014—and these identity issues are also on display in Scotland's recently renovated national museum (here I am indebted to Sheila Watson's work). The National Museum of Scotland in Edinburgh gives pride of place in its medieval section, "Scotland Defined," to the fourteenth-century Declaration of Arbroath, written by "the Barons of Scotland" to convince Pope John XXII of the justice of their fight for Scottish independence—or, as the museum's text panel puts it, "These still-resounding words appeal for freedom in the face of conquest by England." Indeed, to emphasize their emotional power, stirring parts of the declaration are inscribed in large black script on the two walls framing the artifact: "For we fight not for glory, nor riches, nor honour, but for freedom alone, which no good man gives up except with his life," reads one, and the other: "As long as one hundred of us remain alive, we will never under any condition be brought under English rule." Other pieces of the declaration (its class origins, its declaration of war, its concern with the pope's opinion, its own depiction of the mythic origin of the Scots as Scythian immigrants) are deflected in the museum display of the textual imagining of Scottish identity, leaving a selected narrative of honorable independent-mindedness and not-Englishness—whether political or in spirit—with which a present-day Scot can identify.

Watson's ongoing research focuses on the ethnic origins of nations within national museums, but, as she notes, these origins are as imaginary—and as motivational—as the Scythian myth was to those Scottish barons who are now themselves the originators of the historical Scottish identity myth: "Within all museums the origins of the nation reflect not so much what they once were nor, necessarily, what they are now, but how they aspire to be seen today and in the future" (2012, 563). In fact, the ambiguity and universality of the text highlighted by the museum—"we fight . . . for freedom alone"—allow the contentious deliberative issue of Scottish *independence* to be removed to a rhetorical level whereby all self-identified Scots can identify with the more abstract epideictic value of Scottish *nationality* as a freedom-loving people, for the descendants of those barons who would "never under any condition be brought under English rule" have in fact maintained an ethnic identity as Scots even as their political identity has been tied to English "rule" for three hundred years.

The focus on freedom as an epideictic value, then—freedom-*loving*—reframes what otherwise becomes a practical issue dividing Scots and turns it into the synchronic unity of the imagined nation.[2] Indeed, the very nature of the epideictic focus on building communal adherence to present-day values means that there is less need to uncover past truths of memory or ethnicity. Do the Scots and the English share a common ancestry or not? Do they physically inhabit one United Kingdom or two geographical spaces, Scotland and England?[3] The factual answers to these questions are less important than what people *believe* to be their level of identification with common values, in accordance with their understanding of "freedom-loving." To feel the value of nationhood, one must only accept the story, independent of any factual commonality. *Epideixis* operates in the realm not of fact but of feeling.

The need for present-day communal adherence may not guarantee what historians would consider accurate representations in museums—people will believe whatever best corresponds to their current situation as they see it. But communal adherence does leverage certain built-in parameters of the narrative. When personal experience and communal representation do not correspond in a museum display, as museologist Susan Crane argues, a "distortion" occurs (2000, 44), and individuals no longer find the museum relevant to their sense of communal identity. Stray too far from the national mythos and people stop feeling compelled to make the pilgrimage to the museum. Thus the successful museum navigates public memory, that space between official and vernacular narratives that seeks to perform an imagined, but accepted, communal identity (Bodnar 1992, 14–15). It is the performance, the active engagement, that is its key to continued relevance. As Clark notes, "When individuals encounter things that have been rendered collectively significant they are, essentially, enacting privately a public ritual. . . . And like all rituals, the transformative power of this one resides finally not in its words, but in the personal experience of enacting it—at least imaginatively if not actually. . . . Such experiences have the rhetorical function of constituting among the individuals who share them a common sense of public identity" (2004, 97, 102–3).

By their display of the artifacts of national identity—and in such a way that the mind is stirred to active identification with their ideals—national museums contribute to the imaginative creation of a unified national identity. This creation is not yet the full mystical encounter whereby the individual loses her sense of self, but it is on the continuum from more to less conscious choice, less to more emotional affect. This constructed national identity, though it is constructed from the past, is really "about" the present, and to be sustainably effective in this present it must walk a thin line between a supposedly stable past and a supposedly changing future, as I discuss in the remainder of this chapter.

A National Identity Is Memories

In contrast to some of his contemporaries, Renan in 1882 insisted that what makes a nation is not shared blood but shared memories, along with the determination to continue valuing them. This view of memory-identity is now widely held by historians, according to Alan Greenblatt, who notes that "many historians have become convinced that what truly binds a people together is a shared sense of the past" (2009, 316). This shared past is created, as we have seen, from shared public memories that are renarrated with particular iconic touchpoints (like *argentinidad*'s cartoons, blood transfusion, and the 6–0 to Peru), and that serve as demonstrations of the collective quality of communal identity. According to historian Rosamond McKitterick, as nations construct their histories, they are simultaneously constructing a national identity by coming to agreement about what in their past is fundamental. In Burke's terms, they reflect their chosen reality by selecting certain topics that necessarily deflect from others, thus building a particular unified identity from among the possibilities offered. McKitterick emphasizes that if this selected history is to be perceived as collective—as the construct of a national identity rather than a purely individual one—"it has to have some resonance with memories of people whose identities it's shaping" (quoted in Greenblatt 2009, 322). That is, the 6–0 to Peru must not only be *remembered* but be *important* to the collective if its memory is to promote the shared national ethos. Nationality as a series of remembered traits tends to be highly *functional*—Hogan's next identity parameter—citizens are "rewarded" with collectively recognized rights and privileges not granted to noncitizens. While less important in national museums, citizenship does usually convey the ability to read the signs and recognize the stories (when this is not the case, it is increasingly viewed as a problem to the inclusive museum, as we have seen); it may mean that citizen visitors are invited to contribute their memories to the exhibits, and it sometimes means they pay less to get in, privileging their right to enter this public space.

That their historical national memories are in fact constructed is made particularly manifest in Anderson's argument that nationhood is less than 250 years old, about as old as the earliest national museum (1983, 4)—yet within museums the historical memory of nationhood often stretches back to the dim mists of time. Such is Hogan's parameter of *durability*, in which national museums reach back into the remote past for their origin stories. This is nowhere more evident than in the sense of historical time on display in the National Museum of Ethiopia. "Hi, I'm Lucy," reads the text of a light panel display of the hominid skeleton that greets entering visitors. "I'm almost 3.2 million years old but am walking fully upright. Please meet my world-famous ancestors and descendants, all from Ethiopia." It is safe to say that none of the hominids living 3.2 million years ago in the Great Rift Valley considered themselves Ethiopian. But it is equally clear that a part of modern Ethiopian identity is the knowledge that the Ethiopian nation is—as a postcard I bought in the museum puts it—"where it all began."

Even in nations that are self-consciously aware of their break from a remembered past, moreover, that past can be appropriated and forged into national memory if it reinforces national identity. This is evident today in Turkey, which is undergoing a revival of attachment to its past as the center of the far-flung Ottoman Empire. While the Western-looking Turkish Republic was conceived in 1923 as a deliberate break with the discredited empire, the nation is retelling its Ottoman history today in design, on television, in movies, in museums— even in a planned theme park, according to the *New York Times*. In 2012, *Conquest 1453* became the highest-grossing film in Turkey's history, while the recently opened Panorama 1453 Historical Museum in Istanbul draws huge crowds. A 360-degree multistory, multimedia sound-and-light display of the 1453 conquest of Constantinople by Ottoman Sultan Mehmed II (the Conqueror), the museum opened in 2009 next to the old city ramparts. The conflation of Ottoman and Turkish history, and thus the extension of Turkish national identity to a more distant past from which it had historically broken, is unwittingly demonstrated by a local guided tour for foreigners captured on YouTube: "Here is a painting of Fatih Sultan Mehmet," says the tour guide, pointing at the panorama, "and these are the famous cannons of the Ottoman army. . . . And you can see up there on one of the towers, there is a Turkish soldier . . . he's waving the Turkish flag on one of the towers" (airepal 2011). The Turkish flag, adopted in 1936, is indeed a version of a similar Ottoman flag, but even that flag was not adopted nationally until 1844, four hundred years after the conquest. Whatever that *Ottoman* soldier would have been waving, it would not have been the Turkish flag that modern visitors assume. The appropriation of Ottoman history as Turkish, in other words, is a crafted memory, a narrative designed to bring the past into diachronic unity with a present-day national identity that is more closely tied to the Ottomans than had been the identity of the past several generations of Westernized Turkish nationalists. As the *New York Times* reporter observes, cultural critics have mixed feelings about this popularized reappropriation of the historical past: "'The Ottoman revival is good for the national ego and has captured the psyche of the country at this moment, when Turkey wants to be a great power,' said Melis Behlil, a film studies professor at Kadir Has University here. But, she warned: 'It terrifies me because too much national ego is not a good thing'" (Bilefsky 2012). Bringing the Ottomans back into the collective identity, then, layers new "memories" on top of older memories of the Turkish revolution (themselves a layer over yet older Ottoman identities), with or without (as in the case of the Panorama 1453 Museum) the more ambiguous critical discipline of multiple historical perspectives.

The shared memories that bring a nation together are constructed from the raw materials of events—but as narrated identities they are not the events themselves, no more factual (or not factual) than any of an individual's own personal memories that form the basis of an identity. The unity that individuals may experience—the ties from event to event—is of their own creation, a story imposed onto the past to better unite them individually into a collective class in the present.

A National Identity Exists in the Present

In sum, national identities as displayed in museums tend to demonstrate ethnic blood ties to the past, a celebration of common memories, or a terministic encapsulation of imagined synchronic unity. What they all share, however, is a (usually unacknowledged) dependence on present-day concerns. *Affectivity*, Hogan's most critical parameter, measures emotional engagement with the national category, and that engagement can only occur in the now. "None of this matters if we are not moved to act on this categorization," writes Hogan. "Labels become associated with particular emotional experiences. . . . We have emotional responses to the routines of homogenized practical identities, to in-group and out-group prototypes, to the land, and to other components of national identification" (2009, 63). Museum interactions exist in large part to trigger that emotional, affective response. The epideictic function we have traced throughout comes into its own as exhibits seek not only to inform visitors about the past but to move them to want to identify themselves with the current national territory, its people and their values. Debra Hawhee locates this emotional/intellectual response in the "sensorium," and she quotes anthropologist Joseph Dumit's definition of the "sensing package that constitutes our participation in the world" (2015, 5). Rhetoric as a field—epistemic rhetoric—tried for some decades to ignore bodily, sensorial motivations, but rhetoricians such as Hawhee (and museologists such as Elaine Heumann Gurian, who has written about the need to consider such things as comfortable seating when theorizing space) have welcomed their return. National museums, which focus much more on moving audiences than on simply informing them about objects, can be a particularly clear setting in which to study the sensorium's effects. As Gurian notes elsewhere, "The citizen visitor's motivation for seeing these [national] museums leans more to patriotic pilgrimage than ordinary museum-going. People visit who otherwise would never go to a museum in their hometown. The iconic nature of the national museum becomes its most important aspect" (2006, 54). The sensorial role of affective *epideixis* is not only to lure visitors but to change them, to encourage their participation in crafting the present-day national imaginary through a semiconscious identification that relies on both affect and intellect.

Historians Stefan Berger and Chris Lorenz, in their introduction to *The Contested Nation*, agree that only the concerns of the present create interest in the past. "The astonishing growth of interest in 'the nation' among European historians since 1989," they write, "is undoubtedly connected to time. It is related to the discourse on a united Europe and to the unexpected comeback of the nation in East-Central Europe" (2008, 11–12). Historian François Hartog calls this the "presentist regime of historicity," or the view that the past, no longer a grand narrative that provides origins and precedent for modern lives, exists now as a series of discrete narratives that allow moderns to explore alternatives that interest them because of present-day concerns. The classical regime "captured by Cicero's formula *historia magistra vitae* [*est*] [history is the teacher of life] has given way to the 'modern' regime," Berger and Lorenz write. "Instead of the past being authoritative for the present in the form of practical *exempla*, after the French Revolution the future became the point of practical orientation in the form of a *telos* [end or goal] in the making, especially [the goals of] the nation and its 'special mission'" (13). In the modern world, the past is no longer the teacher but a fellow student, to be chatted with or not as one chooses, in a class that is focused on the future.

Berger and Lorenz note that Hartog and the presentist historians have a "spatial" conception of history—of a past that does not temporally affect the present (as it did, for example, for Freud) but instead exists simultaneously *next to* the present, as an alternative, not a direct causality (16). Anderson, we recall, claims that *spatial* simultaneity is necessary for individuals to imagine common cause with unknown others in their nation, so perhaps *historical* simultaneity, as Hartog conceives of it, provides greater possibilities for identification with the masses of anonymous ancestors whose lives can be scrutinized in museums.

Rather than causal precursors, they may become alternatives with whom present-day peoples can communicate in dialogue. A simple attempt to jump-start that dialogue can be seen in Stockholm's Nordic Museum's permanent exhibit *Traditions*, where past and present are intermingled. In its display cases of Swedish cultural practices, time is downplayed: Is that a Christmas scene from today or a hundred years ago? Is that burial practice ongoing? To keep this mixture from becoming overly essentialized, furthermore, pink stickers attached to the vitrines provide updated facts from modern life. Thus at the "Teenage Traditions" vitrine, visitors look at the white shirt and chalice of confirmation, learn on the text panel that confirmation was once "the big step into the adult world," are asked to consider whether today's bridge to adulthood is "perhaps leaving school and celebrating with special parties—at least in Sweden," and then read on the pink sticker that "around half of Year 9 pupils claim to have been drunk at least once." The teenage rituals of the past have no more stated causal impact on the present than vice versa—instead, both exist side by side, ready for consideration.

We might well consider, then, whether the surge in historical interest that followed the 1989 postcommunist revolutions, like the surge of nationalism in newly reemerging nations like those of eastern Europe or central Asia or South Africa, is sometimes something more than many cultural critics in the West fear it is: the rise of dangerous exclusivism of a people reasserting blood ties or historical "lessons." Perhaps, instead, it is (*or it could be shaped toward*) an imagined simultaneity situated in both Anderson's social sense (strangers leading parallel lives) and Hartog's historical sense (past lives as parallel alternatives to present ones). Such a postmodern view of national identity allows for identification *across* the boundaries of space and time, rather than marking those boundaries as the outer limits of those with whom the modern nation will identify. Such a simultaneous view of Others in space-time, then, would call upon a nationalism that is less aggressive than we often imagine. It would be a more dialectical nationalism, allowing for multiple alternatives.

Is it possible for museums, as they create new identity narratives for newly emerging or reemerging nations, to present the past as simultaneous alternative rather than nationalistic exemplar? This more dialectical view might help visitors view the Others in their past, and the Others in their present, as more akin to neighbors than outsiders. "We" may do things the way I like best, but "your" way is also legitimate. I am reminded of my deep, heartfelt affinity for forests of birches and pines—the look of my northern childhood—while my husband loves the rolling scrubland of his Texas plains. Neither of us believes that our version of sublimity is the only one possible, even as we both opt for our own. Recall the previous chapter's discussion of dialectic substance—that we "necessarily define a thing in terms of something else" (Burke 1945/1969, 33). That is, Minnesotans are not Texans in some ways, but they are not Canadians in others. Canada is not the United States in some ways but not the Old World in others. In similar fashion, we can consider a collective history as both *is* and *is not*: Turkey today is not Atatürk's Turkey but also not that of Mehmed the Conqueror; Scotland is neither the independent land of those barons at Arbroath, nor is it simply England. In all cases, these Others across time and space are likely to embody identifiable qualities that allow those contemplating them in *this* time and space to better consider their own identities. As Samuel Taylor Coleridge noted, "us" and "them" are opposite banks of the same stream.

Seeing the past as a dialectical neighbor—a neighbor whose significance we interpret through our own present-day cultural lens—encourages the visitor to "expose the anthropological strangeness of [his or her own present-day] society," as Simon Knell writes. Discussing the same exhibit at the Nordic Museum, he notes that "the curators privileged a commonality of human experience across time in order to evoke this sense of strangeness. In doing so they had swept aside that historical distancing which also tended to distance the subject from the viewer as something academic, arcane, and rather irrelevant, approachable only through empathy, sympathy and reminiscence" (2012, 334). Instead of the past as inevitable forebear to the invisible present, past and present dialectically interrogate each other, blurring the lines between "self" and "other."

The Problem of Dissociation

Renan thought he had a means, of sorts, of facilitating a greater identification with a less aggressive nationalism. In his famous formulation, "the essence of a nation is that the people have many things in common, but have also forgotten much together. No French citizen knows if he is Burgundian, Alain, Taifale, Visigoth; every French citizen must have forgotten the St. Bartholomew's Day massacre and the massacres in the Midi in the 13th century" (1882/1992)—to which Anderson adds a layer making clearer the ambiguity of such "forgetting," as he points out that in order for a Frenchman to understand Renan, he must of course *remember* the Saint Bartholomew's Day massacre (of Huguenots by

Catholics in 1572), in the sense of knowing what it is. What he must forget is the emotion that such a memory might have generated in the past. Such a "forgetting," Anderson says, occurs through narrative: "Out of this estrangement [from one's past] comes a conception of personhood, *identity* . . . which, because it cannot be 'remembered,' must be narrated" (1983, 204).

And so, we might reasonably ask, following Anderson's interpretation of Renan, whether presenting past events without their attached attitude leads to greater community with others. One museum that seems to take this approach is the German Historical Museum in Berlin, which uses "WIR SIND EIN VOLK" (we are one people), a sign from the demonstrations that led to German reunification in 1990, on one of its identifying posters. In a seventeenth-century armory on the main street of the former East Berlin, the museum houses several thousand years' worth of historical artifacts—from the eras of Charlemagne, Martin Luther, the Thirty Years' War, the Napoleonic Wars, the Industrial Revolution, and Karl Marx—in its enthralling, highly narrative space. But what is inevitably most fascinating to outsiders is how Germany narrates its own twentieth century, and "scholarly neutrality" is perhaps the best way to describe its approach. On the causes of World War I, for instance, a sign explains the various self-interested motivations of each participating nation, deflecting attention from questions of instigation, invasion, or blame: "With the war the German Empire sought to gain economic supremacy as well as territories in Western and Eastern Europe. Great Britain was primarily out to preserve their colonial hegemony. The French objective was to win back Alsace-Lorraine and secure their own position as a great power." World War II is explained in carefully neutral language. On the rise of the National Socialists: "The Nazi Party saw its most important task in the struggle against the Jews and the Versailles Treaty. They were deeply contemptuous of parliamentarianism and the Weimar Republic. [The Nazis] saw these as the cause of the social differences, and the *unnatural division of the people*" (emphasis in the original). On the start of the war: "The German invasion of Poland on 1 September 1939 marked the beginning of the war for *Lebensraum in the East* which Adolf Hitler had long planned." On the Eastern Front: "The war in the East, unlike that in the West, was carried out as a war of annihilation. . . . Hence, the death of many millions of Soviet citizens was an integral part of the plan." On the Holocaust: "After the Nazi leadership decided upon the genocide of the Jews in 1941, millions from all over Europe were deported to specially-made extermination camps and murdered there." The museum counters its dispassionate text, in part, with its unflinching display of racist propaganda posters, rockets, photos, and canisters of Zyklon B, but it offers very little in the way of personalized stories or attitude-inducing language.

In rhetorical terms, it is a presentation driven by logos (reason) and *pragma* (things) rather than ethos or pathos, character or emotion. How to present an account of unprecedented fanaticism and untold suffering, and to enable this past to become a part of present-day identity? In the German Historical Museum, it is done by collecting (remembering, selecting) history and weaving it into a narrative that de-collects (forgets, deflects) personalized emotion, much as Renan recommended.

It is notable, then, that the level of emotional identification written into the text increases substantially with the end of the war: While "between 500,000 and 600,000 Germans lost their lives in Allied air raids" during the war, afterward, "[in] 1945, millions of refugees, war orphans and those bombed out of their homes *began the difficult search for a new home in a Germany transfigured through loss and destruction*" (emphasis added). They faced "Hunger, Poverty, and Misery," suffering deeply, being divided by wall, fence, and border checkpoints (as is the physical space of the museum gallery, which is literally bisected into east and west by artifacts and fragments of the Berlin Wall), and then were jubilantly reunified, an event portrayed with very little text but with those iconic signs and banners from unity marches and with video screens of the fireworks and celebrations at the Brandenburg Gate—narrated logos giving way to pure pathos. The past might call on us to remember the events while forgetting (or letting go of) the pain, but the present and future are clearly about the visceral joy of unity.

Does the German museum's dry approach to the past war—its dissociation from emotional identification with the passions of those years—allow the war's lessons for the present to be heard? Historian Mark Bevir argues that it does, that using rationality (and deflecting emotion) imparts responsibility "because actions and practices depend on the reasoned choices of people, they are the products of decisions, rather than the determined outcomes of laws or processes. . . . Hence, history instantiates a concept of rationality" (2007, 301). The linguists of Burke's time, such as Chicago's Alfred Korzybski, also would have approved of the rationality of such neutral language: By presenting facts rather than calling forth emotion, Korzybski and others believed, the intellectual side of the human mind was better able to come to rational decisions and take unbiased action.

Burke, however, would have disagreed with the idea that language could ever be neutral. The erasure of ambiguity in the name of banishing irrationality was precisely the danger Burke foresaw for such language. How, he would have wondered, did a conflicted people make the choices they made? He began his 1939 review "The Rhetoric of Hitler's 'Battle,'" "Here is the testament of a man who swung a great people into his wake. Let us watch it carefully"; his aim was to understand how Hitler's "irrational" arguments could convince others—and perhaps, someday, us, unless we become aware of their ongoing emotional appeal (1941/1973, 191). In the terms of the previous chapter, does discounting the unconscious emotional persuasion of the mystical union make it more or less likely to hold sway with audiences today? Clearly, the German museum considered the joy of reunification a tale to be told mostly in terms of the mystery of emotional identification. If an ancestor from 1930s Germany were to sit next to me in the museum, how, beyond the terms of rationality and irrationality, would we talk about the appeal of the Nazi message and its results? I might wish for an expanded version of the pink stickers of the Nordic Museum, which remind visitors of present-day situations (Germany's current leadership in admitting and resettling millions of Syrian war refugees springs to mind, as does the rising anti-immigrant nationalism in much of Europe and the United States), which could, if visitors ponder them, sit alongside these dark atrocities of the past and encourage critical engagement with the present.

Forgetting the emotion of the past, after all, may rob it of the very humanity that engages the critical faculties necessary to act in the present. I am reminded of the exhibit "*Bockscar*": *The Aircraft That Ended WWII*, displayed at the National Museum of the United States Air Force in Dayton, Ohio. This B-29 Superfortress, visitors are told via signage, "dropped the Fat Man atomic bomb on Nagasaki on August 9, 1945, three days after the atomic attack against Hiroshima." Visitors are then regaled with data about the technical specifications of the aircraft. An adjacent placard responds only obliquely to any questions about the human costs of this aircraft's mission: "Whether Japan would have surrendered prior to an invasion without the use of the atomic bombs is a question that can never be answered." Indeed, it cannot, but the debate that led to the decision, and the emotional enormity of the lives on both sides affected by it, and the continuing effects of the decision to construct the bomb, make history's "lessons" less about inevitability than about the need to weigh real-life options carefully.[4] Memory scholar Bradford Vivian calls this kind of erasure "public forgetting" (2010), and Ott, Aoki, and Dickinson give a powerful description of its impact at the Cody Firearms Museum in Wyoming, where six thousand firearms are framed as "tools, commodities, technologies, and objects of curiosity and beauty," while their role as weapons that kill and maim is "forgotten" (2011, 215). There are times, in other words, when objects and events that changed the world need to be described—poetically, attitudinally—as objects and events that changed the world. Our affective, *means-to-an-end* identification with them in the museum might well function as the beginning of critical engagement.

This kind of self-aware, means-to-an-end identification with the past is on view in Norrköping, Sweden, in the Museum of Forgetting, a collective "nomadic museum" project of cultural critics Erik Berggren and Kosta Economou, designed to tackle head-on the line between reason and affect, politics and aesthetics, in its series of traveling art installations. "Our projects . . . come together in the ambition to look critically at current political issues, memory and forgetting," they assert on their website. In a 2012 exhibit on political art called *The Political Is Collective—Factions*, their introductory text notes, "Any political articulation must, ideally, be anchored in the real, but hold the potential to liberate the mind from the immediate present 'reality' that embeds us and maybe even sometimes blinds us. . . . Western politics seems today pervaded in a complex way by 'homesickness,' expressed through a plethora of fictitious renderings of that which is 'home' and that which is abroad, outside and foreign, as well as equally fanciful longings to glorified pasts, fictitious futures nourished by a persistent forgetfulness about the present" (Berggren and Economou 2012). Forgetting the emotion of the past and narrating the story dispassionately may be intended to keep a people from endless recriminatory bloodletting, but such a view of the simultaneous ancestors may also remove visitors so far from the past that they cannot critically confront the emotion-laden realities of their own present—for humans do not live dispassionately. As Berggren and Economou point out, without this awareness of the present, past and future are mere fictions that we use to entertain wishes and dreams. And as various communication scholars have noted (see Marita Sturken's review of the Vietnam Veterans Memorial, for instance, in Sturken 1997), the voices selectively "forgotten" in these fictions are those of the less powerful and less successful, the ones most likely to make easy identification more problematic.

A National Identity Builds the Future

To sustain an imagined identity, then, national museum displays walk a fine line between showing and telling, between the poetic and the semantic, and across multiple expectations. One of the strongest expectations they navigate concerns their place between a stable past and a changing future. On the one hand, museums are seen by their nation as fortresses of the national past: "National museums were formed to build walls around communities, to act as cultural armaments that defined the self and the other and to establish world views through the lens of the nation" (Aronsson and Knell 2012, 11). This fortress mentality can be seen not only in the historical development of museums but also in present-day proposals motivated by fears of new outsiders in the national space. On the other hand, this very expectation of the museum as heritage armory gives it the authority to promote new perspectives: "As trusted purveyors of national orthodoxies, more than any other institution [national museums] have the power to re-imagine, to construct histories that build bridges between communities and nations" (11)—to be agents of change in the national scene. It seems a paradox—that "as trusted purveyors" of the past, museums are best able to help a community reidentify its present and future, with the implication that such reidentification aims toward less reified orthodoxies. Yet there are many museums that play this role, existing in tension between their functions as cultural goad and cultural glue, though there are fewer such national museums. Further, it is often as easy for visitors to imagine the cultural glue side of museums—as storehouses of the nation's treasures—as it is for museum educators to envision the cultural goad role, pushing society forward. What a nation needs, though, is both.

We can see a clear nod to the tension between the difficulty of change and the comfort of stability in the two Thai museums, the Museum of Siam and its counterpart, the National Museum, both located in rapidly modernizing Bangkok, a buzzing international city of eight million people. Change has been a part of the Thai story for more than a century, as both museums make clear. In response to late nineteenth-century Western attempts to colonize "uncivilized" Siam, visitors learn in the National Museum, King Chulalongkorn "visited other civilized countries to bring back modern technologies in order to bring Siam up to the level of other countries." It was "the first time in Thai history that a king had traveled abroad," and it led to Westernizing adaptations in everything from fashion to firearms—and also to repelling Western imperialists. The Museum of Siam concurs: with a proudly independent heritage, Siam in the late nineteenth century "was ready for change and capable of meeting the West on equal terms." Globalization, however, promised difficulties. "Though the West and its technology provided new answers to old problems, at the same time the West created new problems. The old world had ceased to exist. . . . From now on, the easy way of life at the water's edge was to become land-oriented as roads became more important than water-ways; horse-drawn and motorized vehicles replaced man-powered boats, and steam took over from sail." Visitors learn these facts in quiet, softly lit, air-conditioned rooms in a former mansion from that "easier" time. The extensive grounds of the National Museum are even more removed from the bustling city, with multiple beautifully adorned former palace buildings and temples set amid well-tended flowers and lawns, along the river and across from a park (see fig. 14).

Outside the doors of both museums, traffic-choked Bangkok traverses the uneasy path between tradition and modernity that they describe. Inside the museums, however, models of an earlier era—in Ayutthaya, amid the ancient

14 | The peaceful grounds of the Thai National Museum, Bangkok.

carvings, with the generations of the royal family—keep that "easy way of life" alive in material memory. Such an approach in turn eases the way for the Museum of Siam to help visitors tackle some of the challenges of modern life with its "Thailand Tomorrow" electronic whiteboard, mixing statistics ("Thai people consume fish sauce 4 times more than recommended for good health") with publicly displayed visitor reflections and comments, written on touch-screens in front of the floor-to-ceiling wall.

The shifting between the comfort of cultural glue and the challenge of cultural goad is yet another way to describe a national identity that requires both unity and division, or, to put it temporally rather than spatially, both *permanence* and *change*. Burke gave his first book of cultural criticism that title—*Permanence and Change*—because, in the midst of the Depression and the threat of war, he wondered why people were so recalcitrant in the face of proposals for a better life. It was not that the change message was insufficiently broadcast, or that people were stupid; instead, he argued, if people were strongly attached to the old story, the permanence, they could not be expected to change their responses automatically as situations change, even if a new situation were "named" didactically for them. Instead of being instructed, people had to be *induced* to pull apart their old allegiances and seek new alliances, new stances (1935/1984, 100–125). The historian Peter Catterall identifies their necessary recalcitrance as the modern importance of the past: "Memory is, in a globalizing world, if anything more important to people. It's something to hold onto, it becomes a more crucial part of identity" (quoted in Greenblatt 2009, 331).

The starting point for any inducement is not change, then, but permanence—the values currently held—and it is these values that museums make material in their role as cultural glue, even as their message may goad viewers to adopt a new cultural vision. Thus the fine line museums must walk: if they focus too much on permanence, stability, the past, their audience sees them as irrelevant to the present; but if they overlook the values of permanence in the quest for future change, the audience resists.

To illustrate, let me give an extended—and contrasting—example of induced change from two antipodean national museums, the National Museum of Australia and the Museum of New Zealand Te Papa Tongarewa.

The National Museum of Australia in Canberra opened in 2001 as an aggressively deconstructed building awash in primary colors and sculptural forms outside and large open display spaces inside. As one of its founders put it, "No rows of dull exhibits. No glass-cases of curiosities. No skulls and skeletons. No labelled snippets of this fact and that. . . . It would be . . . a place of animate display where the public mind and heart could both be stimulated" (National Museum of Australia 2004, 2–3). When I visited in 2009, the guidebooks, the oversized *Land, Nation, People* and the slim *Yesterday Tomorrow*, made it clear that the museum exists to "bring Australia's stories together," as the latter puts it. More than collection or preservation, its function is an education that it links specifically to narrative: "Exploring the past, illuminating the present and imagining the future—that is the Museum's vision, and it shapes the way we see the Museum's role as educator, collector, researcher, and, primarily, storyteller" (National Museum of Australia 2004, ix). The stories it tells are explicitly linked to national identity: "One of the biggest tasks for the Museum, as for all ambitious storytellers, is to deal with the big questions. What is the national story? Who has the right to tell it? How can it best be told within a finite space? What should be included and what can be excluded? Opinions differ on these issues, and the Museum should be a place that acknowledges that they do—where people feel encouraged to consider and develop their own views" (x).

The museum repeatedly disavows metanarrative, opting instead for the kind of polyphonic narrative most evident in its *Eternity* exhibit, discussed in chapter 4, which *Yesterday Tomorrow* describes as telling "the personal stories of 50 ordinary and extraordinary Australians [each relating] to one of ten emotions . . . [whose] lives and experiences act as windows onto moments, events, figures and movements in Australian history" (2001, 15–16). This museal narration generated some controversy, including the charge that the museum had ignored the stories Australians had grown up thinking of as their nation's imagined collective history—it had ignored permanence, in other words, in its attempt at change. Museum educator David Arnold documents some of the newspaper reports on the museum's opening in 2001, which included "Museum offers tangled vision of Australia," and "the underlying message of the National Museum of Australia . . . is one of sneering ridicule at white history" (2007, 46). The director at the time, Dawn Casey, initially attacked the museum's critics as "'outraged traditionalists' wanting a 'master narrative'—a strong, authoritative voice with a simple chronology of civilisation and progress" (quoted in ibid., 44), but the museum's attempt to shift the locus of interpretation from one authority (the museum) to multiple authorities (the visitors) was not well understood. Criticism was severe enough that a year after the National Museum's opening, the Museum Council convened a review commission to rethink the presentation. This commission did not recommend a master narrative, but it did argue for a greater nod toward permanence, toward the museum's role as the cultural glue of the nation's identity:

> The Museum's principal weakness is its story-telling—the NMA is short on compelling narratives, engagingly presented dramatic realisations of important events and themes in the Australian story. And there are too few focal objects, radiant and numinous enough to generate memorable vignettes, or to be drawn out into fundamental moments. This is, in part, a problem of translation of narrative into museum practice. It has led to some incoherence. . . . Bewilderment makes it nearly impossible for curiosity to be aroused and satisfied. Without engagement, there is little likelihood of inspiration, reflection or education. (Commonwealth of Australia 2003, 68)

The review commission required that the museum "tell the Australian story—and by means of compelling narratives, where possible focused on enthralling, significant objects. Its aim is to inspire, to arouse and satisfy curiosity, to educate and to entertain" (66). The museum responded to this charge by shifting from narratives of change to narratives of permanence, as can be seen in the approach taken in two museum publications. In the preview coffee-table guide *Tangled Destinies*, director Casey celebrates the debates that went into "the selection, treatment and presentation of issues," because, she writes, "museums are a battleground of ideas and histories" (2002, 21). Later in the book, architectural critic Charles Jencks contends that "national identity is a composite of puzzling oppositions" (2002, 64). For identity to cohere, however, as the narrative psychologists would remind us, these oppositions must be unified—a position that the postreview book *Land, Nation, People* (2004) attempts to adopt. The battleground of tangled *interpersonal* destinies of the preview publication becomes the tangled destinies between *people* and *land* in the postreview book, and this land-based approach is reflected also in the museum galleries, which describe the diversity of Australian experiences as a product of regional differences. Cowboys in the bush herd cattle with rough and ready trucks, while suburban dwellers dry laundry on their Hills Hoist clotheslines—two iconic objects now showcased in the museum.

Indeed, the new Landmarks Gallery specifically ties its narrative of social differences to regional differences: "We often talk of Australia as if it is a singular entity, as if all Australians are the same and 'the nation' an undifferentiated concept. In contrast, Landmarks explores how all Australians live in particular locations and how the tenor and trajectories of our lives are both similar to and shared with Australians in other places, and different from others' experiences" (National Museum of Australia 2013). The multiple voices are still there, but they do not become "entangled" in debate (much less in opposition) with one another; instead, they make up a mosaic of identities resting geographically side by side. This is, in fact, the very phrase used in *Yesterday Tomorrow* to describe the "Garden of Australian Dreams," a giant outdoor walk-on map of the continent that unintentionally reinforces both the regionalism and the separateness of Australian identity. All locations on the map include both Aboriginal and settler names, a possibly entangled image that the guidebook smoothly separates by explaining that it allows these place-names to "rest side by side . . . reflecting the mixture of people and cultures that is Australia today" (2001, 34). This comfortable spatial distinction is further embodied in the museum's architecture by the placement of the First Australians Gallery (indigenous history/ethnography) in its own wing off the main entry hall. This placement highlights the gallery but also separates it from the more centralized galleries of European (and other) settlers' histories. Instead of Casey's envisioned battlefield, the museum becomes, as *Land, Nation, People* puts it, "a place . . . where people feel encouraged to consider and develop their own views" (National Museum of Australia 2004, x), without needing to confront others'.

The history of Australian colonialism is thus presented spatially in a fashion similar to that of the multiple Smithsonian museums—of American History, of the American Indian, and of African American History and Culture: indigenous and black perspectives are present as an alternative, resting beside those of European Americans rather than directly engaging with them. Such neighborly alternatives are, as we have seen, an improvement over the earlier view of one civilization succeeding another in time—but what is missing is Burke's parliamentary babel, the two alternatives in (potentially emotional) dialogue. Yet merely to promote entangled debates, pushing change without accommodation for the permanence of the old perspectives, invites backlash, as the Australian museum discovered. That museum is now "seeking to avoid contested and circular discussions about what constitutes an Australian identity or a national character . . . about which it is difficult to achieve a consensus," writes Arnold (2007, 50)—and the very ambiguity of his statement (is this a good or a bad thing?) forms the crux of the permanence-versus-change dilemma.

A rather more transcendent approach, uniting a nation across acknowledged divisions, is visible two thousand kilometers to the east. In the Museum of New Zealand Te Papa Tongarewa, "identity" is such a focus that its logo is a giant fingerprint. What does it mean to be a New Zealander? Te Papa, opened in 1998, addresses the shifting nature of that question head-on with its bilingual English/Maori name and signage. Much as modern multicultural education efforts deemphasize "ethnic week" or "women's month" in favor of a curriculum infused with diversity, Te Papa, from the moment you step inside, naturalizes a bicultural New Zealand (Attwood 2013, 51). At the same time, it embraces its role as the nation's cultural glue: "te papa tongarewa," for instance, translates as "the place where treasured things are held" (Keith 2010, 8). "Te Papa is the guardian of New Zealand's national collections," its guide tells visitors, and "as your host, we welcome you here" (3). This construction is different from the celebrated debates over collections at the Australia museum—at Te Papa, the implication is that New Zealanders already have an underlying common collection of "treasures," now held for them by the museum.

Like its Australian counterpart, the museum uses narrative to discuss identity: "As the national museum, it must answer a big question: 'What is unique, distinctive, and typical about this country?' The collections tell the stories that respond to this question" (17). These "stories," such as those explaining the geographical and geological forces that shaped the New Zealand islands, include both scientific research and Maori legends. These intertwine so that earthquakes, for instance, are explained by displays of plate tectonics intermingled with stories of Rūaumoko, the Maori earthquake god, while the popular simulated "earthquake house," where visitors are treated to shaking floors and rattling objects, is a material engagement with the commonality—the earthquakes—underlying both explanations.

The spatial layout of the museum also emphasizes commonalities before delving into differences. While the overall architecture of the museum divides the building into Tangata Whenua (Maori) and Tangata Tiriti (European or Pākehā) wings, this division is not very apparent on the initial floors. The first floor of exhibition space is devoted to the formation of the islands and their unique flora and fauna, all of which, in semiconscious identification, become "ours" on the signboards (our plants, our landscape). The first anthropological exhibit is called Ourspace and features a full-room interactive floor map on which visitors' footsteps trigger the museum's preset images of New Zealand's people and places (see fig. 15), along with a wall where visitors can upload and

15 | The interactive map of the *Ourspace* exhibit at Te Papa Tongarewa, Wellington, embodies a diverse mixture of official/museum and vernacular/visitor images.

add their own images to the preexisting mix to "create your vision of New Zealand . . . mix it, own it, share it," according to the in-house guide *Te Papa Explorer* (Museum of New Zealand n.d., 6). Such images, unlike the stories uploaded in Australia's *Eternity* exhibit, do not "rest side by side" but are necessarily "mixed" and "shared" by the software.

Shared appreciation of the "awesome forces" shaping the land leads, on the next floor, to shared responsibility for the dramatic changes that human settlement—both Maori and European—has occasioned. "Welcome to *Blood, Earth, Fire*, the dramatic story of how people have made their home in Aotearoa New Zealand," reads the introductory sign, using both Maori and English names for the land. "It's about the disappearance of many original inhabitants. It is also the story of how people have come to love and care for this land." Videos in the Blood, Earth, Fire Gallery showcase sheep ranchers alongside environmentalists, outdoor adventurers, and city dwellers, among them Maori, Europeans, and Pacific islanders, all of them "show[ing] you the place in Aotearoa New

Zealand that is most important to them, their place," a sign tells us. Finally, the shared heritage of all New Zealanders' ocean voyages and settlement is highlighted—a difference from Australian history that the New Zealand national story capitalizes on repeatedly. Maori settlers arrived in Aotearoa only several hundred years before Europeans. The fifty-thousand-year disjunction between Aboriginal and European settlement of Australia is thus replaced with repeated references to the journey of Kupe and his wife, Kuramarotini, from Polynesia to these islands in approximately 1200 C.E., with an emphasis on the parallel ocean voyages of later explorers like James Cook and the nineteenth-century settlers. Museologist Richard Sandell would identify this as a "pluralistic spatial device" operating within Te Papa, accommodating "multiple forms of difference" within a "unifying interpretive framework" (2005, 191). Such displays, which he notes are the most radical efforts undertaken by museums that want to promote social equality, support differences that allow diverse groups to maintain their identity, but they also emphasize sameness—"shared experiences, values and beliefs between different groups" (192).

It is only after several floors of these commonalities of experience—the emphasis on what is permanent and uniting in the New Zealand identity—that the museum delves more deeply into divergences, including separate galleries of (highlighted) Maori cultural treasures and (rather deemphasized) European artifacts, and—in its most "entangled" exhibit—a look at the many social changes of twentieth-century New Zealand called *Slice of Heaven*, whose final placard sums up the Te Papa message of continuity alongside continual change: "Us and Them: Entering the 1950s, New Zealand society seems prosperous, peaceful, and integrated. The 'us' behind this image of unity are heterosexual Pākehā blokes (male European New Zealanders)—the country's dominant players. Other groups, however, find themselves marginalised. In the 1970s and 80s different voices start to speak out. Women, gay-rights advocates, and anti-apartheid activists are among those protesting. . . . By the century's end, many diverse groups have a say in New Zealand society and politics. 'They' have become part of 'us.'" The *Essential Guide* to Te Papa defines this new "us" as someone with "Kiwi identity," which it then explains in clearly hortatory, future-oriented terms:

> Kiwis live in a broadly egalitarian society and believe that everyone deserves a "fair go." . . . Widespread [antiwar, antinuclear, antiracism] protests . . . have reflected Kiwis' willingness to oppose injustice or back a

principle. . . . Today's Kiwi is just as likely to be innovative with a modem
cable as with number 8 wire [for ranching]. . . . Kiwis have grown wings—
many have travelled extensively or lived in other countries. . . . [But] Kiwis
retain a strong identity. . . . Home or abroad they feel a strong affinity with
the land. (Keith 2010, 46–47, 50)

In chapter 3, I discussed the museum's exhibit on the Treaty of Waitangi—
its assertion of Maori rights in the old-new New Zealand, and its acknowledgment that this assertion is still being worked out in practice, still contentious.
For Maori and Pākehā, united as Kiwis who "believe that everyone deserves a
'fair go,'" the museum provides space for the parliamentary babel between
groups that might (it attempts to persuade us) have surface divisions but the
deeper selves of which are unified by more permanent identities. Burke's dictum
on hortatory language is clearly at work in building this melded Kiwi identity:
"Men induce themselves and others to act by devices that deduce 'let us' from 'we
must' or 'we should.' And 'we must' and 'we should' they deduce in turn from 'it
is'—for only by assertions as to how things *are* can we finally substantiate a
judgment," he wrote (1945/1969, 336–37). In Te Papa, the vision of a Kiwi nation
of globally innovative people settling a unique, beloved land and motivated
by the principle of a fair go for all becomes both an announcement of identity
to the outside world (*it is*) and an inducement to local Kiwis (*let us*) to identify
themselves as that version of "us" that the museum's rhetoric implies *they should*
be. That is, it becomes a call for semiconscious identification with the Kiwi
social class. Of course, this "us" is never fully stabilized (for instance, as various
writers have pointed out, the increasing interest of Pākehā New Zealanders in
Maori cultural artifacts may be shifting control of the artifacts—and thus of the
culture—away from the Maori),[5] and the new permanence is no less susceptible
to change than the old—it is a dialectic. Thus the inducement to determine who
"we" *should be* is a never completed project, always contentious, but therefore
always engaged.

This is the key to building a nation in a museum: selecting and narrating
particular objects to demonstrate to the nation that its desired way of being
already exists, is already a part of the past—*Look! It's right here in the museum!*—
and needs only to continue, even if its "continuation" is a movement toward a
changing future. We are already *ein Volk*, we already possess Kiwi identity, we
already are a unified multiethnic country, we already prize freedom together,
national museums assert, so let us live into that reality. This terminological

identification with the collective class—not only an identification of words here but of symbols—may well be semiconsciously aware of its antithesis to some other group (often "traditionalists," sometimes "change agents"). It is certainly promoting the collective *Volk* or Kiwi nation as a means to the end of national unity. But a museum traversing the dialectical spaces between permanence and change walks most clearly the space of semiconscious identification that invites the visitor toward unity as an emotional and intellectual choice.

Of course, a national museum filled with affective symbols of unity can also be precisely the kind of scene that engenders nationalistic boosterism of the most exclusive kind. Where are the differing, even opposing voices that make up the full extent of national history and the national experience? Where is the call for change in the midst of that potential for so much permanence? They may be in the national museum, as we have seen. But if they are not, then the psychic need for those voices to be heard often engenders an alternative space, another kind of museum to fill the perceived gaps in the national story created by the selection and deflection process of the national museum.

In the next chapter, I shift gears and take a look at these alternative museums. They still often promote national unity, but their affective strength comes from the ways in which they emphasize differences and uphold the antithetical voices of those who would otherwise be too easily overlooked or ignored in a world clinging stoically, fearfully to unity.

6

Alternative Identifications

Far from being nostalgic for national histories, perhaps it is time we started to tell the histories of networks of peoples. Perhaps we should craft histories of all sorts of overlapping groups only some of whom attempted, more or less successfully, to construct national imaginaries and to impose those imaginaries on others.
—Mark Bevir

The resonant, relevant national museum, preaching a nonoppositional identity among diverse people in dialogue with one another: This is not the world of the twenty-first century. In this chapter, I look at several reasons why open-ended narrative, affective mythic images, and communal *epideixis* fail to achieve the vision of egalitarian dialectical unity, but also at how societies have worked to fill the gaps through their alternative museums. Openly embracing diversity, these alternative museums may teach us to how to build a more poetically ambiguous (thus more relevant, more realistic) collective identity.

Museum Illusions: Neutrality and Inclusivity

We have looked at the use of narratives and artifacts to promote collective identity and have examined the ways in which individual visitors identify with symbolic actions. And we have seen that narratives and artifacts work together to provide emotional appeal, contextual unity, and an impression of veracity in a way that neither does as fully on its own. However, two issues arise as museums grow increasingly sophisticated in their display methods: (1) the mistaken assumption of many museum visitors that the stories narrated there are neutral and nonpartisan, backed up by the "evidence" of artifacts, and (2) the related assumption of many museum professionals that these new stories are a necessary or inevitable means of creating a sense of inclusiveness.

The first issue, the *illusion of neutrality*, is often a holdover from the days when museums saw themselves—and were seen—as objective conveyors of truth. European visitors surveyed by Eunamus expected their national museum to be "'all-inclusive,' presenting a comprehensive picture of the nation/country they belong to" (Bounia et al. 2012, 3). James Wertsch has argued that "collective remembering is better formulated in terms of a site of contestation than a body of structured knowledge" (2009, 235), but museum visitors do not always understand that they are participating in an interpretation of history, and the various outcries over "historical accuracy" that erupt around the world indicate that they do not always appreciate it when they do see the interpretive lens. For museum professionals, by contrast, this notion of objectivity has largely shifted. Sociologist Zygmunt Bauman argued back in 1987 that the Western intellectual was moving from patriarchally "legislating" the grand narrative of a particular history and culture toward more democratically "interpreting" the varieties of history and culture extant in a locality—becoming less curator and more educator. One consequence of the shift to interpretation, however, can be more partisanship, not less, as museums feel freer to present *versions* of history to, and demand critical interpretation from, audiences. Lisa Roberts puts it in linguistic terms: "Language about facts as certainties has been replaced by language about context, meaning, and discourse. . . . Far from eradicating the need for education, however, new views of knowledge have rendered it more acute. Now, the task of education is about not just interpreting objects but also deciphering interpretations" (1997, 3). Visitors are asked to interpret what they see with the helpful guidance of educational tools that encourage more questions, more dialogue—a more contested version of historical data.[1] I said earlier that "history" museums might better be termed "public memory" museums in that they bring present-day values to bear on the selection of past events, but here it is their historicity that encourages critical analysis of that selected past. "Collective memory simplifies," historian Peter Novick explains; it "sees events from a single, committed perspective; it is impatient with ambiguities of any kind, reduces events to mythic archetypes" (1999, 2–3). Public memory may determine what part of the past is selected, but the discipline of history encourages it to be examined critically, from multiple angles—perhaps, as the various public outcries over exhibits suggest, to the chagrin of visitors seeking "the" story.

How to encourage a more ambiguous view of the past? More than mere facts, it is narrative that stimulates the audience to imagine scenes as if it were there reliving the moment in all its complexity. The crafted *ekstasis* of artfully displayed and contextualized artifacts transports viewers into lives and events outside their own experience, and this transport increases the persuasive impact of any accompanying message that seeks to provide interpretive links between the past and present. As the Eunamus final report argues, "National museums often produce narratives and philosophies that adopt a moral position and test the ethical beliefs of visitors. They also seek to develop particular responses, such as empathy, a sense of good and evil, and justice. Visitors can perceive these as intellectual arguments, but they are supported by objects, images and narrative choices that exploit the visitor's emotions" (Aronsson and Knell 2012, 51). They take into account, in other words, what Patrick Hogan calls the necessity of affectivity to promote identity—and like all appeals to pathos, affectivity can be suspect.

"History is being used as an ideological tool," historian Nikita P. Sokolov was quoted as saying in a recent *New York Times* article on the 2014–15 onslaught of revisionist history exhibits in Russian museums. The message of major exhibitions, Sokolov said, was that "Russia is a besieged fortress that needs a strong commander, and anyone trying to democratize Russia and shake the power of the commander is trying to undermine this country." A "wildly popular" historical exhibition at the Manège, for instance, recast Czar Ivan IV "the Terrible" as a Russian leader defamed by the West who fought against foreign sanctions (MacFarquhar and Kishkovsky 2015). "Central themes [of the show] were that Russia has long been under attack, that only in unity had it been able to expel invaders and that numerous legends had grown up about its past," the journalists write. Another exhibition, *Remember*, juxtaposed historical photos of the fight against fascists in World War II with "a distinct nod toward present policy: One soaring lobby wall depicted current right-wing groups in Ukraine"—the rise of which, MacFarquhar and Kishkovsky note, was Russia's justification for annexing Crimea.

For museum professionals, museum narratives are not neutral, they usually do not purport to be neutral, and their use of objects to enhance their message heightens the emotional appeal of their arguments and the resulting affectivity of the national identity they are promoting. As the director of the Museum of Contemporary History in Moscow, Irina Y. Velikanova, put it, "We don't hide the fact that we are interested in forming the patriotic and civic position of Russian youth. Our goal is that when leaving our museum, all Russians would feel proud of their country" (quoted in MacFarquhar and Kiskhovsky 2015). Many visitors, however, still perceive museums as presenting "intellectual arguments" alone—and the inclusion of a more overtly persuasive agenda, as at the Russian museums, is treated as an unhappy aberration.

Like patrons of museums, museum professionals may have a complementary belief about their work that I call the *illusion of inclusivity*. Here, narrative is assumed to be the form that inclusiveness should or does take, perhaps because attention to narrative methods of display has increased during the same decades that attention to greater inclusion of nontraditional voices, artifacts, and nontraditional visitors has grown. This is evident in Max Ross's interpretation of the new museology, a new interpretive stance that he defines as challenging old narratives by including new ones: "There is now no final standard for defining true knowledge and great art. . . . The mission of that earlier period to assert the superiority of modern reason and the inferiority of non-western world views, forms of human life and social organization has been widely abandoned. . . . This circumstance has some notable implications for the role performed by museums, where the old dominant narratives about civilization and progress, science and art, empire, nation, race and class, have become subject to critical scrutiny and revaluation" (2004, 92). The *form* of narrative is often seen as the *means* by which to include new audiences, who bring into the museum alternative narratives that challenge the dominant narrative. Their stories provide the inclusive new narrative that is expected to entice new audiences to the museum, as Sue Glover Frykman writes: "In the 1950s and 1960s, many children experienced museums as dull and boring. Nowadays, museums seem to be much more conscious of their educational role and the need to make their exhibits attractive and interesting. Making use of narratives is one way of achieving this" (2009, 299). But narrative does not inherently translate into inclusivity, if inclusivity means not only that previously excluded groups are included but also that multiple ways of interpreting new stories are presented. In fact, the opposite can often occur, as we have seen—narrative can promote one particular interpretation even more strongly than any previous, diffuse displays of the past do, as it brings to the foreground the formerly obscured deep narrative.

Benedict Anderson points out that these illusions of neutrality and inclusivity are particularly apparent in the museums of former colonies, where the promotion of cultural glue was a conservative response to the pressure for change, a way for the colonial power to become a "guardian of generalized, but also local, Tradition" ripped from its present-day context and musealized (1983, 182–83). As I argued earlier, the very genre of national narrative itself, quite apart from any intention of those in power, pushes toward unifying the diverse diachronic/synchronic threads of the story into a great causality.

However, there are multiple museums around the world that disrupt that unity and provide space for an alternative reconstruction of the national story. Let us turn now to these alternative museums, which call attention to the illusions of neutrality and inclusivity in the state institutions they sit alongside.

Alternative Museums: Filling the Gap

National narratives may respond to the illusions of neutrality and inclusivity in their national museums in a variety of ways. They may *avoid* addressing them openly (the choice of traditional museums), they may work to *mitigate* them through particular attention to polyphony and diversity (the route taken by many progressive museums, and advocated for by the ICOM-affiliated International Institute for the Inclusive Museum), or they may openly *celebrate* their partisanship or niche status with a purposely counterdominant narrative. We have already seen a variety of such niche history museums in this book—in Buenos Aires alone are the National Armaments Museum, the Evita Museum, and the Passion for Boca Juniors Museum, along with its more traditional National Historical Museum. Regional niche museums, like the Newark Earthworks museum and the National Heisey Glass Museum in the town where I live in Ohio, abound wherever there is a particular natural or social phenomenon to be explored. But what I am terming *alternative national museums* do more than the regional and specialty museums that abound throughout the world. Alternative museums celebrate their partisanship and special attachment to a particular story in deliberate contrast to the dominant communal metanarrative of the nation. In many ways, they function as what critical theorist Nancy Fraser, in her critique of Jürgen Habermas's theory of the public sphere of democratic discourse, termed "subaltern counterpublics"—"parallel discursive arenas where members of subordinated social groups invent and circulate counterdiscourses, which in turn permit them to formulate oppositional interpretations of their identities, interests, and needs" (1990, 67).

For example, in Ponca City, Oklahoma, in the United States, and in Alice Springs, Northern Territory, Australia, are two remarkably similar women's museums—the Pioneer Woman Museum and the National Pioneer Women's Hall of Fame—both of which use the dual connotations of "pioneer" to document (1) the nonnative women who were among the early settlers in previously native territories, and (2) women (of all backgrounds) who were outstanding in their fields (see fig. 16). Both museums focus heavily in their displays on the accumulated evidence of photographs and placards to narrate the individual stories of female "pioneers"—both, that is, rely on the persuasive power of evidence-based inductive reasoning to counter gender stereotypes, arguing, in essence, "Look! Here we were!" Both museums, placed in the middle of their respective Great Plains and Outback native-and-cattlemen territories, are more preservationist than radical. Yet both clearly see their portrayal of history as both partisan (the Australian museum's slogan is "History Is Her Story Too")

16 | The Australian and Oklahoman pioneer women's museums feature remarkably similar display concepts.

and oriented to the present (the U.S. museum, when I was there, had a special exhibit on Oklahoma's female pioneers of rock 'n' roll). In other words, both museums preserve overlooked voices of the past because of present-day concerns with women's accomplishments and opportunities—even as these concerns are muted rather than showcased within the museums, which focus their *epideixis* on praise rather than blame.

Despite this focus on the permanence of women's presence alongside men, in both countries, women's museums have faced opposition from establishments worried about change and more willing to establish specialist museums "in which male interests are paramount," as museologists Margaret Anderson and Andrew Reeves write, citing such Australian museums as the Stockman's Hall of Fame and the International Cricket Hall of Fame (1994, 113). In the United States, Senate backers of a proposed National Women's History Museum noted in their 2014 proposal that fewer than 5 percent of the country's twenty-four hundred National Historic Landmarks chronicle women's achievements. In what could be a description of the U.S. situation, Anderson and Reeves write, "It is obvious that the masculine bias inherent in the endorsement of [Australian] museum projects presents major structural difficulties for the public exhibition of women's history" (113). Opponents of the proposed U.S. Women's History Museum "have pressured lawmakers to oppose it because they believe it will reflect a liberal bias" (Huetteman 2014), even as the existing models, the pioneer women's museums, work to counter that perception by including the accomplishments of women of all ideological backgrounds. The realities that alternative museums choose to emphasize, however, by their very existence highlighting the previously ignored, present an inherent challenge to the dominant national identity. By invoking a semiconscious identification with a particular social class (or in this case the gender "women"), they perhaps inevitably raise concerns about their (potentially antithetical) larger agenda, the possibility that their call to identify with a particular group is merely a means to the end of social division and the diminishing of national salience.

In contrast to this view that the alternative museum is disrupting unity, virtually all alternative museums see themselves as filling a perceived gap in the dominant unity, inserting previously unheard voices and thus proving those voices' public existence in the national imaginary. Their alternative stories are often more directive, more partisan, and less tied to the illusion of neutrality, because they are seen as a reaction to what is deflected from the dominant story told by the principal exhibit or the national museum. Stefan Berger and Chris

Lorenz point to historian Jitka Malečková's assertion about history generally (and certainly this holds true for dominant museums as well) that "women were 'added' to the existing national master narratives, rather than new narratives being elaborated, revising the periodisation of national history or including new domains of life" (2008, 4). In contrast to additive history, alternative museums elaborate the new narratives in a way that changes the master narrative. Their presence outside the dominant institutions sparks a conversation, and therefore their presence cannot be understood in isolation from their relation to mainstream museums.

In fact, as I noted in the introduction, it was just such a contrapuntal dialogue between the National Museum and the Museum of Communism in Prague that first inspired me to study the rhetoric of museums. The Museum of Communism—a suite of nondescript rooms next to a casino—is partisan, alternative, and explicitly *not* the official National Museum, but it does promote itself as the only public historical source of the era of Soviet-controlled postwar Czechoslovakia. It clearly feels the pressure of questions about its motives, and its website emphasizes that while "it stands as an authoritative historical narrative relating to this 20th-century phenomenon," it is not attempting to comment on current politics or "be a filter for contemporary political issues in the Czech Republic" (Museum of Communism 2013). Its accompanying guidebook is rather less circumspect, noting that the rise in the number of young Czechs joining the Communist Party once again has made it necessary to tell the story of what happened during past decades of Communist rule (Čarba, Korab, and Borek 2000). The museum relies heavily on large photos and narratives (translated into six languages, unlike the prerenovation National Museum, which had been mostly in Czech, nonnarrative, and object-focused). The Museum of Communism's stories are openly partisan and designed for emotional impact, perhaps nowhere more so than in its concluding film of scenes from the 1989 Velvet Revolution. In the film, as crowds in Wenceslas Square protest and are beaten and protest again, they are accompanied by folksinger Karel Kryl's popular song "Dekuji" (Thank You), the lyrics of which are translated into English onscreen. Kryl thus appears to be talking to the protestors on the screen as he sings, "thank you for the pain . . . the failure . . . humility which teaches me / humility . . . thank you for that clash with / love and animosity." The film ends with a tribute to Jan Palach's self-immolation. "Lambs, thank you, / you did not die in vain," Kryl croons, as many in the audience wipe away tears.

In fact, the Czech National Museum has responded progressively to the gaps in its story that the Museum of Communism reveals. In 2009, it sponsored a special exhibit in its main building on the nation after the Velvet Revolution. It later repurposed a national army memorial in a park overlooking the city to house a long-term exhibit on milestones of twentieth-century history. In 2011, the main building closed for a seven-year renovation that promised to double its exhibition space, which would allow it to update its national history.

Will any new portrayal of the Czech nation be as partisan as that of the alternative Museum of Communism? This seems unlikely. Alternative museums are partisan because they understand their role as addressing a particular, not a universal, audience, which they aim to move through *ekstasis*, appealing to states of mind beyond reason that are more likely to lead to action. In essence, the identification that an alternative museum promotes is a form of means-to-an-end rhetoric, in that it asks visitors to step outside the central national narrative and identify with the margins. It is partly a reflection of the already mentioned increased tendency to partiality of heavily narrative museums—and most niche museums are indeed heavily narrative, in part because telling the story of the underrepresented almost necessarily means speaking of those who have not been collected and catalogued. But, for the most part, alternative museums are not neutral because they do not see the larger conversation as neutral. They recognize that the history they depict has been excluded from the mainstream—indeed, the impetus for their creation is the perception that something has gone unsaid, unexamined in their society. In an earlier article (Weiser 2009), I discussed the implications of this conversation between the dominant narrative of the National Museum of American History and the alternative narrative of the National Museum of the American Indian, and I provide an extended synopsis here as an example of the gap between dominant and alternative.

At the National Museum of the American Indian in Washington, D.C., the story told is very much a "we are still here" story. The curvilinear sand-colored building, with its carefully symbolic landscaping, is one of the most distinctive on the National Mall. Its principal *Map and Guide* opens with neither map nor guide but with a six-page description of Native Americans in the Washington, D.C., region. "The earth is still here. The water is still here. And we are still here," runs a quotation along the top of a page (Volkert, Martin, and Pickworth 2004, 11), and that is the message of the entire section, indeed of the entire museum: the presence of diverse groups of native communities in present-day America. Its message instantiates Anishinaabe scholar Gerald Vizenor's concept of "survivance," which the museum defines for visitors to its exhibit *Our Lives* as "hold-ing onto ancient principles while eagerly embracing change . . . doing what is necessary to keep our cultures alive." Survivance underlines the communal nar-ratives told by each of the twenty-four represented groups. A Lakota curator notes, "We want to let others know that we are still alive as a nation, that we have not been killed off." Blackfoot curators assert, "Our history includes assaults on our lands, our people, our traditions, and our language. These events are very much a part of who we are today. We are the 'continuum of creation.'" The Igloo-lik Inuit assure visitors, "We've been keeping up with the changes in our lives, using what works without changing who we are." The museum wants to assert that there is no single story to tell, that native peoples are diverse and that the representative twenty-four communal stories selected for display demonstrate that "the American Indian story" is that there is no "American Indian story." Yet despite the differences in histories and traditions, the museum stories do in fact have one common theme, and it is survivance—over and over again, the story is that "we have kept our cultures alive."

Survivance is the unifying Native American story in this museum because across the mall, the National Museum of American History so thoroughly erases modern Indians from the American story. In *The Price of Freedom: Americans at War*, American Indians are not only *not* treated as countless diverse peoples; they are also not treated as agents acting on their own behalf but rather as tools used by others for some larger purpose. This lack of agency begins at the opening of the American story as documented in its principal history exhibit, *The Price of Freedom*—a story that actually starts quite late in American history, not with precontact history or even first contact but with the French and Indian War in the mid-1700s. During this and the Revolutionary War, signs explain, Indians fought on both sides—with "both the British and the Americans consider[ing them] unreliable allies, recognizing that Indian nations entered these alliances to protect their own people, territory, and authority." Native interest was not the American interest in life, liberty, and the pursuit of happiness (signposted immediately after this section) but interest in their own autonomy. Americans, meanwhile, during the Revolutionary War, "began a debate about liberty and citizenship that continues today [including the question]: Should the sovereignty of Indians be recognized?" This question is tied to the deep narrative woven throughout the museum: that America is always being forged by debate into "a more perfect union." Thus revolutionary-era debates over "the Indian question" are shown to be one of the first instances of Americans determining what their own story really means—again using Indians as the agency by which to enact that American story, rather than allowing them to be agents in their own right. Any debate among the native tribes themselves about whether to enter the story of the new American nation is either ignored or depicted tragically. The history of Native Americans does not fit into the grand narrative of the assimilation of diverse peoples into one multiethnic nation. Instead, Indians' extermination, their forced migration to unwanted territories, and the Indian Wars of 1865–90 are all depicted as failures by Americans to forge their more perfect union. One final panel briefly depicts the forced assimilation policies of the late 1800s, when children were removed to white boarding schools, as one more historic failure—and with that, the "American Indian story" fades from the scene, the victim of an alternative narrative that does not fit into the deep narrative of diversity becoming unity through successful communal struggle. The native story stands in contrast to that developing unity—perhaps most succinctly represented by a panel image of Sitting Bull, famous for defeating the U.S. cavalry at the Battle of the Little Bighorn in 1876. Beneath the photo is the quotation: "If the white men take my country, where can I go? . . . Let us alone." The deep narrative of inclusion cannot incorporate such an isolationist stance (Weiser 2009).

The excision of native peoples from American history and the American story, then, calls forth the alternative "survivance" narrative of the American Indian Museum, to remind visitors that diverse native peoples live on in the twenty-first century. This survivance narrative, in turn, not only keeps native peoples alive but holds them together. Anthropologist Jonathan Hearn argues that power, or agency, is what binds individuals to a collective identity: "Without the promise of power, of self-determination, or an explanation for one's disempowerment, such identities are hollow" (2002, 764). Along with *emplotment*, the narrative of causality and time, then, we should expect to see *empowerment* within an alternative museum in order for the persuasive power of identification to unite individuals into community. The survivance narrative allows native peoples to tell a different kind of assimilation story, and thus emerge from U.S. history not as diverse failed peoples but as a unified, empowered entity.

In a larger sense, the NMAI demonstrates that a new narrative of identification with a marginalized class does not inevitably have to lead to either overidentifying cultural appropriation or antithetical division. It is an invitation to *dialectical substance*, in which divisions with their audiences are foregrounded along with possible unities. Having survived, native peoples now turn back to the nation at large with a narrative emphasizing inclusion on their own terms. "Welcome to a Native Place," reads the opening to the Museum's *Map and Guide*, and this welcome is repeated in the Welcome Wall just inside the entrance to the building, which projects "welcome" in hundreds of languages indigenous to the Americas. That Native Americans can welcome guests to *their* place in the heart of the national capital is perhaps the ultimate survivance narrative.

The Smithsonian Institution sponsors both the alternative NMAI and the dominant NMAH, as well as the new National Museum of African American History and Culture, opened in 2016 down the mall from the NMAI. As an institution embracing both mainstream and alternative museums, the Smithsonian continues to debate its own role. For instance, a 2012 Smithsonian symposium titled "(Re)Presenting America: The Evolution of Culturally Specific Museums" discussed the possibility of a proliferation of ethnic museums on the mall. Its program pointed specifically to the question of whether it was good for the nation to continue to pursue its current policy of separate museums:

> The National Museum of the American Latino Commission's report recommending the establishment of a Smithsonian National Museum of the American Latino prompts debate concerning the value of "ethnic" or "culturally specific" museums. Thoughtful people ask whether the proliferation of museums dedicated to particular experiences or cultures contributes to the "balkanization" of the United States. Others observe that traditional museums have not represented our country's people and their achievements as fully as they should be. Ethnic/culturally specific museums, they note, provide different portals into what it means to be an American, and their programs provide depth and fullness of perspective, enriching our national narrative. (Smithsonian Institution 2012, 1)

Comparing the two extant alternative museums (American Indian and African American), it is apparent that while both speak to the union/division tension, they take different stances on the dominant conversation. While the American Indian Museum inserts its narrative into a conversation that acknowledges that native peoples have been ignored, the African American Museum must enter the always entangled conversation of race in the United States. The African American Museum, therefore, takes a strong stand on its website for inclusion as its ideal. In this way, it confronts concerns about a possibly divisive agenda in much the same way that women's museums counter claims of liberal-ism with politically balanced exhibits. It highlights inclusion in three of the six paragraphs on its "About the Museum" webpage, as well as in the featured quo-tation from Lonnie Burch, its founding director: "This Museum will tell the American story through the lens of African American history and culture. This is America's Story and this museum is for all Americans" (Smithsonian NMAAHC 2017). By contrast, the corresponding message on the "About the Museum" page of the American Indian Museum projects not conciliation with the majority but a voice for the minority: "The NMAI has been steadfastly com-mitted to bringing Native voices to what the museum writes and presents [and it] . . . is also dedicated to acting as a resource for the hemisphere's Native com-munities and to serving the greater public as an honest and thoughtful conduit to Native cultures—present and past—in all their richness, depth, and diver-sity" (Smithsonian NMAI 2017).

In sum, all alternative museums assert that the nation as a whole is enriched by the inclusion of their stories, but all also negotiate, to varying degrees, the tension of inserting a voice of diversity into that narrative of national unity. Of course, the tensions confronting the Smithsonian would be less fraught if its dominant museum were not named the Museum of *American* History, with its clear if semiconscious identification with a class ("Americans") that is ideally inclusionary but—as the Smithsonian acknowledges in its alternative muse-ums—is increasingly recognized as not so. The fraught Smithsonian names do, though, rather exactly track the role of alternative museums in society, where they always exist in conversation with—and by expanding upon—the domi-nant narrative by reminding those who wish for pure consubstantiality of the dialectical paradox of substance.

Alternative Memorial Museums: Never Again

One kind of alternative museum is particularly dedicated to making sure that voices are not forgotten, and this is the museum that memorializes victims of oppression. The "Red Terror" Martyrs' Memorial Museum in Addis Ababa. The Museum of Memory of Victims of the Repression in Tashkent. The Hector Pieterson Museum in Soweto. Some of these—like Freedom Park in Pretoria, the Memory Park–Monument to the Victims of State Terrorism in Buenos Aires, and the National September 11 Memorial and Museum in New York

City—are museum/memorial hybrids. Others—such as the Kigali Genocide Memorial Centre, the Apartheid Museum, the Jewish Museum, and the Museum of Communism—we have already encountered.

Memorial museums and exhibits on national trauma deal with social devastation large enough to shake the foundation of a cohesive national identity. Sometimes the very nation is threatened, while at other times it is merely challenged by a moment of great change, but always there is something that has caused a rupture in the national identity narrative, and has forced people to question their individual identification with that imagined community of compatriots who make up the nation.

Recall Hogan's two categories of narrative identity—practical identity (what do we or can we do?) and categorial identity (with which groups of people do we share a common label?)—and the multiple categories to which each individual simultaneously belongs. Hogan adds that one of the challenges of nationhood is that the categories of region, religion, ethnicity, and so on interrupt the unity implied by the national label: "discrepancies across non-national categorial identities may disrupt national homogenization and undermine national identification" (2009, 55). A focus on our subnational affiliations as women, Hutus, anti-Senderistas, Afrikaners, or Sunnis can disrupt our sense of self as Americans, Rwandans, Peruvians, South Africans, or Iraqis—a situation that repeatedly and violently plays itself out on the international stage, in armed conflicts in Syria, Nigeria, Somalia, Ukraine, Iraq, Sudan, and Yemen just in the months I spent writing this chapter. Nations, as we have seen, often react to such threats by trying to paper over them or sweep them under the rug. A 1988 exhibit on the Anschluss sponsored by the Vienna Museum, for instance, included a foreword to the exhibition catalogue written by Vienna's then mayor: "For hundreds of thousands of Austrians March 11, 1938 means the beginning of a life of suffering without parallel in the history of our country. . . . Up until April, 1945 hundreds of thousands of Austrians fell as victims of the National Socialist regime: in concentration camps, in death camps, in Gestapo torture cellars, as resistance fighters on the scaffold or in a war willfully begun, which Austrians in foreign uniform were forced to pursue." As rhetorician Alan Gross notes, "This depiction of Austrian victimage is created by a striking omission: Austria's enthusiastic reception of Hitler and Nazism and its active participation in the Holocaust" (2005, 8). The alternative response of memorial museums, then, is to ensure that the victims of any rupture are not forgotten in the (forced or voluntary) push for a return to unity. Memorial museums remind the nation that its alleged healing cannot proceed by covering up the trauma of its victims or the responsibility of its perpetrators.

While memorial museums, like all alternative museums, are open to the charge that they perpetuate division, this is not usually their goal. "Truth" is their watchword. Daniel Jonah Goldhagen, author of a recent book on genocide, explains the growing number of memorial museums, noting, "If you talk to survivors, and I've talked to survivors of many genocides and assaults, they all say the same thing: They want the truth to be known . . . [and they] hope that, by owning up to past sins through a thorough airing of the facts and their meanings, the affected society can move forward without leaving these wounds open to fester" (quoted in Greenblatt 2009, 319). The result, as historian Alan Confino points out, is a quasi-religious "belief that truth can set nations free—or at least [put them] on a path toward repentance and reconciliation" (319). Historian Robert Moeller writes of World War II, "A history of the bombing war . . . in which all the dead have names and faces, might get us closer to the multiple meanings of war" (2006, 125), and names have certainly become synonymous with memorials and—in a digital age—faces are now following (see fig. 17).

As epideictic institutions, museums may provide the space for critical contemplation of uncovered truths absent from other parts of public life. The editors of a recent book on the new Canadian Museum for Human Rights note that "the same government responsible for funding the operating budget of the museum and appointing its board had also cut funding for human rights advocacy and research elsewhere and consistently denied the brutal realities of Canadian settler colonialism" (Busby, Muller, and Woolford 2015, 2). The lack of funding is of course not good for Canadian politics, but the museum's opening is evidence that even in times of deliberative denial, epideictic critique may still be possible. Memorial museums may pay lip service to the need for social action, or—even while seeming to be removed from the political realm—they may play the role of ancient theater, providing critical space that is unavailable outside official institutions.

Rhetoricians have written extensively about the implicit messages in national memorials, but in national memorial *museums*, the message is often quite overt. Their narratives and artifacts are geared toward the rhetorical purpose of educating for action. Both memorials and museums emphasize the commonplace "never again," but in museums the affective response evoked by memorials is combined with the strong educational component characteristic of museums. Thus in museums the collective memory is contextualized and explained, and visitors are often explicitly asked to consider what will happen next and what

17 | The wall of names, as at Memory Park–Monument to the Victims of State Terrorism in Buenos Aires, is a trope repeated in many memorial museums around the world

stance they will take. For instance, the National September 11 Memorial in New York promotes an emotional mission—"Honoring the lives of those who were lost is at the heart of our mission" (National September 11 Memorial and Museum 2014a)—while the accompanying museum tells visitors that it "serves as the country's principal institution concerned with exploring the implications of the events of 9/11, documenting the impact of those events and exploring 9/11's continuing significance" (2014b). The latter is more overtly concerned with both the narrative and the present, educating visitors to make choices today that align with the values presented by its selective narration of the past.

The "truth," anyone's truth, of traumatic events is not easy for nations to either determine or acknowledge, as Sharon Macdonald notes, calling such events in a recent book "difficult heritage." Traumatic truths "require the nation to confront issues, previously submerged in a nation's consciousness, that contradict its sense of itself" as a moral entity, writes Bain Attwood in a recent article with a similar title, "Difficult Histories" (2013, 49). In such circumstances, the modernist desire to let visitors make their own meaning of an exhibit runs up against the significant possibility that these visitors will form a meaning that opposes what the museum intended, "exhibiting not tolerant or egalitarian attri-butes but rather prejudiced (for example, homophobic, racist or sexist) ones," notes Richard Sandell, who asks what museums can do to promote notions of equality. He answers this question with an example of what I described in chap-ter 2 as deep narrative: "Exhibitions, it will be argued here, contain spatial cues, deploy spatial strategies that, while unable to guarantee a given, preordained response in all visitors, can nonetheless privilege certain readings" (2005, 186). Sandell sees these spatial cues as promoting tolerance; as we saw in chapter 2, they can also promote other state-sponsored messages, but his point remains that alternative memorial museums and others devoted to addressing social inequity have a stronger didactic focus than many other museums do. This didactic approach is often necessary because the difficult histories being addressed are still incomplete. For instance, Argentina continues to struggle with memories of its Dirty War (1976–83), on display in the Memory Park–Monument to the Victims of State Terrorism in Buenos Aires. Its central site, the Monument to the Victims, is a zigzagging wall of names of some nine thou-sand civilians and fighters (and counting) killed by the state. It is designed to evoke an open wound. The website explains that "this monument is not trying to close wounds or supplant truth and justice. Nothing will bring real peace to the families" (Memory Park 2014) (my translation).

As at Memory Park, resistance to what is seen as too quick or easy heal-ing—another type of overidentification—is particularly prominent when memorial museums are unofficial or semiofficial. These are often privately funded and founded by survivors who want to bear witness to the truth, even at the possible expense of national reconciliation. As the Argentine memorial puts it, it exists as "a place of memory and witness, because there are the names of those people whom [the state] wanted to erase." At the same time, when such museums (or exhibits) are publicly funded by their governments, there is increased pressure to get past the rupture, to see "never again" as the step that leads less to remembering than to reconciliation—perhaps at the expense of bearing witness to the truth. Such is the tension between unity and division in national memorial museums.

National collectives, clearly, suffer from the same difficulties in healing from past traumas and reidentifying with the "family" that individuals do, and thus I believe that we can productively look at nations' attempted responses through a lens borrowed from psychology—specifically, Stephen Karpman's much-used *drama triangle*, which explores the interrelations that often develop between participants in a traumatic situation. In Karpman's triangle, traumatized indi-

viduals take on the role of victim, persecutor, or rescuer in their internal narrative, slotting others into the remaining roles and reacting accordingly. The victim
is the one who is ashamed or oppressed; the persecutor, the one who blames; the
rescuer, the one who "helps" (Karpman 1968).[2] Simplifying Karpman's complex
theory (developed and used over the course of decades), we might say that the
monovocal narratives of memorial museums necessarily identify with the *victims* of past oppressive acts, with those whose voices need to be heard. Their aim
in telling the spatial story of the past trauma is to persuade visitors to become
rescuers, saving future victims by vowing never again to allow or accept such
atrocities. The museums must therefore deal with past *persecutors*—those who
divide, yet, as in a traumatized family, often remain members of the household.
These identifications, disidentifications, and reidentifications of individuals
with their traumatized nation create the need for the various spatial narratives
that come into play when a museum tells the national story.[3]

In sum, Karpman's drama triangle—which works past victimhood, deals with
persecutors, and promotes continuous rescue—combines with both the continuum of Burke's identification (individual → collective → universal) and its functions (antithetical, semiconscious, or means-to-an-end) on the path to national
healing, as memorial museums maneuver between the need to maintain critical
division (or truth) and desired reunion (or reconciliation) in post-traumatic
nations (see fig. 18). I describe the various combinations in greater detail below.

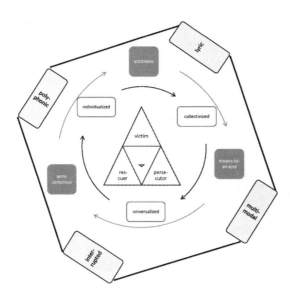

18 | Illustrating in two
dimensions how the multi-
dimensional interaction
between levels and functions
of identification within the
narrative space of the museum
affects the drama triangle.

Identification by Antithesis: Placing the Persecutor Outside

A traumatized nation uses this first type of identification narrative, uniting against a common enemy, because it makes truth and reconciliation particularly easy to resolve, as the oppression has come from outside the nation—foreign invaders have perpetrated a horrible crime against national citizens. Naming the persecutors as outsiders goes hand in hand with strengthening the nation's self-identification in an antithetical relationship. The nation, then, is both the victim of the narrative and—by eventually throwing off the persecutor and telling the truth—the rescuer. Museums that memorialize outside oppression are likely to use a fairly strict univocal narrative to tell the story of the invasion or attack and its aftermath. Thus the website timeline for the National September 11 Memorial and Museum opens with the straightforward statement that "on September 11, 2001, nineteen al Qaeda terrorists hijacked four commercial U.S. jetliners," adding that those killed represent "the single largest loss of life from a foreign attack on American soil" (2014b). A multimodal spatial chronology—using various media and degrees of narrative openness—may allow a museum to tell the same story in different ways throughout the exhibits. In the Czech Museum of Communism, a variety of placards, a space set up as an interrogation room, and a lyrical film all tell pieces of the same story of Soviet oppression of the Czech people.

Placing the persecutors outside allows for the "A and B are united against C" formula of antithetical identification to cause A and B to reconcile rather easily, and thus the motivation to narrate the story this way is strong. Such a narrative is on display in the origin story at the multimodal Kigali Genocide Memorial Centre, where Rwandans tell their history as a "united we" versus an "outsider them" who caused division. "Under the colonial powers," a sign reads, "these [socioeconomic clan] distinctions became racial, particularly with the introduction of the identity card in 1932. . . . We had lived in peace for many centuries, but now the divide between us had begun." The Catholic Church had "conveyed the racist 'Hamitic' ideology" that "portrayed the Tutsis as a superior group," and it was this supposed superiority, taught by outsiders, that led to Tutsi discrimination against the Hutu and eventually to the genocidal backlash of Hutus against Tutsis. In this narrative, then, both Hutus and Tutsis were victims of the outside colonial Catholic persecutors.

Visitors to museums that pursue antithetical identification are invited to identify as patriotic rescuers as they pledge never again to allow the persecutors space in the nation. The Museum of Memory of Victims of the Repression in Tashkent, Uzbekistan—a new structure built in traditional Uzbek (timbered, tiled) style—documents the centuries of Russian involvement in the region, from the 1700s to Uzbek independence in 1991. Its straightforward narrative starts with "the conquest of central Asia (Turkistan) by tsarist Russia and the struggle of the local people against it," although the main focus of the multiroom exhibit is the post-1917 period, the "soviet state's repression policy," and the deportations, deaths, and attempts to erase Uzbek identity through education, language, and the importation of foreign peoples. Uzbek identity, in this telling, is clearly tied to the recovery of language, religion, cultural practices, and history along with "the restoration of the memory of repression victims." Thus, after rooms full of stories of those who resisted and were killed, the narrative takes a multimodal but not unanticipated turn as it shifts from a past narrative of victims to a present narrative of self-rescuers—a narrative that is all about (re) construction. Exhibit cases in the final quarter of the museum focus on the architectural construction of this Uzbek-identified museum itself, along with the nationwide restoration of archaeological sites, mosques, religious literature, and "the main square of our motherland." In this narrative, past generations of Uzbeks yielded up victims who resisted the imposition of Soviet identity, while national visitors today are invited to continue rescuing the nation by participating in the rebuilding of a renewed Uzbek identity that stands in contrast to the imposed Russian one.

Indeed, antithesis is such a powerful determinant of group identification that memorial museums often invoke it even when persecutors are not outsiders at all but members of the national imaginary. This revision of the narrative enables the audience to unite in opposition to an antithetical version of its own past, breaking its old familial ties. Museums may thus employ careful labeling (Burke's "mysteries of social status") to rebrand past compatriot persecutors as outsiders. The *Vienna 1938* exhibit adopted this strategy, where, as Gross points out, "the role of Austrians in the Holocaust [was] minimized by attributing its implementation almost entirely to the invading Germans" (2005, 8). This trope is repeated around the world. In the "Red Terror" Martyrs' Memorial Museum in Addis Ababa, Ethiopia, for instance, visitors learn at the outset that "according to Amnesty International's Report, more than half a million youngsters (male and female), elders, christians, and muslims [*sic*] were indiscriminately slaughtered by the Derg." "The Derg," not fellow Ethiopians, becomes the (external and no longer extant) enemy in this terrible slaughter, even though in fact the Derg takeover (1975–87) was an internal military coup and civil war. So strong is this narrative pull that captions on photos of young men receiving weapons and learning to shoot them label the men not as agents of terror but as its more passive recipients: "The killing machine arming civilians to torture and kill without due process of law." The killing machine is the persecuting agent. Those who resisted the Derg killing machine, meanwhile, are named throughout the museum as actors on behalf of the nation, victims who, as a plaque outside the entryway puts it, were "martyred for their beliefs in the struggle for the Ethiopian peoples' [sic] human and democratic rights."[4] Naming no longer extant groups as persecutors places current visitors in the more reconciling role of rescuers who gain knowledge of the (outsider) persecutors in order to pledge "never again" to let such practices become a part of the social fabric.

A similar process occurs in the Czech Museum of Communism, where a system in which nearly everyone had to be implicated to some extent is narrated with persecutors labeled not "Czechs" (an extant internal category) but the "Communist Party," the "State," and of course the "Soviet Union." "Czechs" take the terminological role of either passive bystander or victim, unless the story is of anticommunist actions—resistance to the regime—that (as in Ethiopia) involve explicitly Czech actors as subjects: the "renowned Czech intellectuals" led by poet Vaclav Havel, who stood up for dissidents during the Prague Spring, and the community itself, described in the museum book as a personified agent: "The Czechoslovak nation was becoming ever more radicalized" (Čarba, Korab, and Borek 2000, 67).

The careful manipulation of persecutor labels allows memorial museums to tell the truth without sacrificing the possibility of reconciliation. After all, the audience may very well include people with real ties to the original persecutors. Manipulation of the labels for these persecutors, then, not only places them outside the union ("the Derg killing machine" versus "the Ethiopian people"); it also allows present-day audiences to dissociate themselves from their possible pasts as persecutors. The Jewish Museum in Berlin introduces its *Axis of the Holocaust* exhibit by noting that "when the National Socialists took power in 1933, the Jewish population in Germany numbered 560,000. Hitler's regime deported and murdered 200,000 Jews from Germany." *National Socialists, Hitler's regime*—these categories, not "Germans" or "neighbors," are the acting agents of the Holocaust in a national museum whose audience includes present-day German neighbors.

Similarly, while outside persecutors can be blamed for the original divisions at the Kigali Genocide Memorial Centre, it is impossible to blame outsiders for the killing itself, and therefore the internal categories *Hutu* and *Tutsi*, both of which continue to be extant groups, require delicate manipulation. As the narrative begins to present the specific chronology of the massacre, victims are called Tutsis (*no Tutsi was exempt*), but persecutors are called not Hutus—an existing identity of visitors today—but "perpetrators" (*the perpetrators had promised an apocalypse*), "murderers" (*the murderers used machetes*), and "genocidaires" (*the genocidaires had been more successful in their evil aims*). The museum then goes further, using language that obscures the agents and depicts the scene of genocide itself as the perpetrator upon a national victim: "Genocide was instant," "Rwanda was dead."

In sum, then, identification by antithesis uses a largely univocal, sometimes multimodal narrative to tell one story in order to reconcile a rescuing nation by encouraging identification with the victims honored in the museum, in terminological contrast to the "outsiders" who persecuted them. Sometimes, however, this terminological "outsider" narrative simply cannot be reconciled with the known truth about national persecutors. In that case, the second function of identification and the emotional persuasion of multimodality are needed.

Semiconscious Identification: Uniting with the Persecutor

When a traumatized nation is faced with a persecutor that is undeniably an internal group, semiconscious identification—the kind that implies that we are already one—strives to unite painful truth and necessary reconciliation by means of symbols and terms so that the audience feels a commonality without being aware of it. This is perhaps nowhere more clear, once again, than at the highly rhetorical Kigali Genocide Memorial Centre. After depicting the genocide, the narrative moves on to the years when the country was stabilized and restructured, and adopts first-person plural pronouns: "It is impossible for *us* to forget the past." "Education has become *our* way forward." "*We* need to learn about the past ... *we* also need to learn from it" (emphasis added). Thus is the power of "that tiny first-person plural pronoun, 'we'" (Burke 1967, 50) displayed—along with the shift from the (divided) past tense to the (unified) present tense in order to show what a united self-rescuing society must do for its future. "We" all become part of the new nation not because "we" are told that we should but because it is already implied that we are united by the use of "we."

Tom Hennes, a designer for the exhibitions at the National September 11 Museum, described at a 2011 conference a similar deliberate shift from antithetical, past-tense "us versus them" language to more present-tense semiconscious "we" language in the move from the original 9/11 Tribute Center (set up by families of the victims) to the national museum. The walls of the original center (in a building overlooking Ground Zero) were covered with memorabilia of the deceased. Even ten years after the tragedy, the visitors' book there was largely still written in present tense: "It's my birthday so I've come to see you," "I'm engaged and I brought my fiancé to show you," etc. It was, Hennes said, as if it were still September 11, 2001, in a room filled with the raw emotion of personal identification with the victims. Numerous scholars have written about the battles over a "proper" commemoration at the 9/11 Museum, and as Paliewicz and Hasian point out, "contests for rhetorical status and for the right to engage in melancholic commemoration were central concerns of many of" the families of victims, who could use their experiential authority to influence design (2016, 142). In contrast, Hennes's purpose for the museum was to help people get through their initial reactions to trauma, make meaning of the event, move it from the constant present into the past, and then celebrate the ongoingness of life choices (Hennes 2011).[5]

At another site Hennes worked on, that inclusive "we" is so powerful that the outsider persecutors have been asking to join. Outside Pretoria, South Africa, a multiacre hilltop complex of museum, gardens, and memorial wall echo the multimodal components of the Kigali Centre's spatial narrative. Freedom Park "inspires reconciliation and nation-building; encourages reflection on our past to improve our present and build our future as a united nation; and, contributes to a better understanding and co-operation among nations and peoples," according to its website (2014). Unlike Argentina's Memory Park, which is partisan in its choice of who can or cannot be termed "victims of the Dirty War," in Freedom Park the wall of names of South African "freedom fighters" is deliberately inclusive, with space for South Africans who were killed in peaceful uprisings like that in Soweto, members of Umkhonto we Sizwe who died in armed struggle against apartheid, all who fought for South Africa in the two world wars, and even those who fought on all sides in the late nineteenth-century South African (Boer) War between British, Afrikaner, and native South African forces. This narrative aims for polyphony, the juxtaposition of differing

voices. That it is not fully polyphonic—that it resists the notion that any narrative can be included in the intentionally reconciling term "freedom fighter"—
became clear in the struggle with the South African Defence Force (SADF).
White SADF soldiers died fighting to extend apartheid into neighboring
Namibia and Angola during the 1970s and '80s. Here, the ambiguity of truth
("we were divided; we all fought for freedom") encounters memory—including
traumatic memory—such that language cannot, ultimately, stretch truth far
enough to reconcile everything and everyone. Fallen SADF veterans are not
listed on the Freedom Park wall—but such is the power of "freedom" that they
wanted to be. As recounted by historian Gary Baines, surviving SADF veterans
staged protests outside the park, demanding that their names be included on
the memorial wall because they followed the orders of their government. Veterans were in fact ignoring the SADF-specific memorial nearby to demand a
place, symbolically, in the new South African narrative (Baines 2009). Ironically,
the SADF memorial is located on the grounds of what had been the primary
spatial symbol of the old South Africa, the massive Voortrekker Monument,
which commemorates in stone dioramas the "Great Trek" of the Boer colonists
into Zulu territory in the 1830s and '40s. For decades, this monument invited
quasi-mystical union among Afrikaners—their own mythic image. Today, however, the SADF-sympathetic South African blogger Allatsea's reaction to the
alternative memorial reflects the lingering bitterness of those who must settle
for it and be refused a place in the new "we" of the changing nation: "Following
the non recognition of members of the SADF by the so-called 'freedom park,' it
was decided that a fitting tribute be made to the members of the SADF that lost
their lives in service" (Allatsea 2014). As historian Laura Hein says of national
histories generally, "With most of these events, there's actually pretty much
agreement on the facts. The fight is then over what symbolic meaning it has for
the society as a whole" (quoted in Greenblatt 2009, 320). And the symbolic
meaning is contested because such a symbol is never truly an act in the past but
a comment "about the priorities, politics, and sensibilities of those who built it"
(Edwin Heathcote, quoted in Balthrop, Blair, and Michel 2010, 195) and those
who experience it today.

Semiconscious identification, in sum, promises reconciliation via a less univocal, more multimodal narrative through its emphasis on the plural "we" and its
shift from the moment of trauma to the feelings of the present day—but its
polyphony is only as inclusive as its audience will allow, which may not always
be sufficient to incorporate persecutors into the reconciling nation. When truth

insists on continuing divisions, a third form of identification is necessary—one that consciously decides to promote unity in the midst of division.

Identification as a Means to an End: Let Us Choose Ongoing Resolution

After a national trauma, an emphasis on unity and reconciliation can, of course, tip the balance too far toward reconciliation, whitewashing the truth of diverse, underrepresented voices. Most memorial museums attempt to resist this outcome through their genre-based attempt to both witness (as memorials) and educate (as museums) on behalf of the victims of past atrocities. As Carole Blair and Neil Michel have argued, "Successful commemoration spaces engage us by asking us to think. Rather than tell us *what* to think, they invite us *to* think, to pose questions, to examine our experiences in relation to the memorial's discourse" (2001, 189). Yet, as we've also seen, the memorial's discourse tends to promote unity. The movement of the ongoing national conversation toward reconciliation is a necessary step if a nation is to remain identified as a collective. In alternative memorial museums, then, the choice to resolve the "drama" of Karpman's drama triangle can be an imperative that requires creative manipulation to break out of the victim-persecutor-rescuer roles. While perpetuating antithetical thinking is one danger that memorial museums must work to overcome, another lies in allowing visitors to be bystanders, passive rescuers who equate experiencing historical injustices in an exhibit with the action of rescuing victims. As rhetorician Wendy Hesford says in *Spectacular Rhetorics*, "'Never again' imagines a progressive narrative of human rights history, which presumes that the more we uncover, witness, and remember, the more just the world will become" (2011, 52). Hesford argues that this narrative too easily equates "seeing" with "rescuing," as individuals are slotted into the passive category "victims," and viewers (or visitors) are allowed to imagine themselves as rescuers by the simple act of their viewing or—as Michael Bernard-Donals (2016) warns—"experiencing" the real trauma of the past inside a museum display.

The use of identification as a means to an end, then, is a conscious attempt to place visitors in a more active, more self-critical stance toward the drama triangle and their own role in the new nation that asserts "never again." To challenge present-day visitors and break out of constrained narratives, museums can use several methods of complicating the roles played in their telling of the drama.

First, victims of past tragedy can be positioned as rescuers themselves, and in this way serve as active exemplars for present-day visitor-rescuers. For instance, the Hector Pieterson Museum in the Soweto district of Johannesburg, South Africa, tells the story of the children killed in the Soweto uprising of 1976. While visitors to the memorial are asked to identify with the ideals of the young martyrs, the museum next door uses much of its exhibit space to chronicle the conditions against which the youth of Soweto protested. Its careful use of grammar in the name of national reconciliation deflects blame from the persecutors and upholds the victims, whom it renames "heroes," narrating their martyrdom as part of the struggle not for their own rights alone but for national reconciliation: "In memory of Hector Pieterson and all other young heroes and heroines of our struggle who laid down their lives for freedom, peace, and democracy." The active agents are not the persecutors who arrested or shot these students but the students themselves, as rescuers of the nation. Visitors to the Hector Pieterson are thus asked to do more than simply learn the victims' story—they are to pick up the students' fallen banner and march on in their stead as a means to the end of eradicating apartheid.

An even more complex resolution of the oppositions represented in the drama triangle can come from disrupting the victim-persecutor dyad that places visitors in the role of rescuer. Victims and persecutors may be shown to inhabit both roles during the course of the drama, so that in order to rescue, visitors must recognize their own potential for both victimhood and persecution, and thus the need for ongoing reconciliation of continually shifting divisions. It is this ambiguity that the polyphonic narrative of the *Yuyanapaq* exhibit at the Museum of the Nation in Peru, discussed in chapter 2, uses to encourage a more critical, less comfortable stance in its visitors. In the exhibit, every sector of Peruvian society is viewed as both victim and persecutor (or passive onlooker) in the "devastating internal violence." In the series of photographs, indigenous women are shown being rescued from Sendero camps, *and* supporting the guerrilla movement in street demonstrations, *and* weeping over their slain men in morgues, *and* hoisting arms in government-sponsored self-defense committees. The military and police heroically defuse a bomb in one photo and rip a man from his screaming family in the photo next to it. The terror of upper-class Lima residents in neighborhoods scarred by bomb explosions is empathetically portrayed, and their protests against the war celebrated, while they are also chastised for ignoring decades of war and its causes in rural areas. There are no completely clean hands in the Peruvian Dirty War. In a way, then, everyone—including the visitor looking at these past events—becomes "we," but this "we" retains the ambiguities of differing experiences. By implicating everyone as victim, persecutor, and potential rescuer, the exhibit moves away from the antithesis function of identification, with its nationalistic opposability, beyond a facile semi-conscious identification with unearned reconciliation, and toward the more self-conscious means-to-an-end function, in which divided people make the conscious choice to seek a common point of ongoing reconciliation. The polyphonic narrative, with its multiple perspectives, asks visitors to make this kind of choice.

Means-to-an-end identification is usually classified as conscious manipulation of another, but a collective body that consciously chooses reconciliation, while acknowledging that tensions and shifting responsibilities can never be fully resolved, is not necessarily a bad thing. As South African journalist Sisonke Msimang put it recently, "We have lived with choreographed unity for long enough to know that we now prefer acrimonious and robust disharmony. We see reconciliation as part of a narrative that was constructed on the basis of anxieties that are no longer relevant: Democracy has taught us that raised voices don't have to lead to war" (2015). For Burke as well, as I wrote in my first book, the messiness of democratic rancor ("parliamentary babel") was preferable to the false unity of a single voice ("that of the dictator") (Weiser 2008, 66–67), but to achieve this parliamentary babel, all parties must recognize the ambiguities inherent in their interactions with one another. The opposite of ambiguity—absolute, dogmatic certainty—is the discourse of the dictator (Burke 1941/1973, 218). In contrast, ambiguity allows for the possibility of dialectical points of commonality between even seemingly opposed positions.

The purpose of means-to-an-end identification with a nation in the process of continuous reconciliation, then, is the same as it is for one of Karpman's couples recovering from a betrayal of trust: not to erase the past but to accept responsibility for a collective trauma that requires ongoing listening, voicing, and identification with a new collective identity in which total reconciliation may never be fully attainable and thus must continuously be chosen.

Like the Argentine memorialists or the betrayed spouse, rhetoricians are often distinctly wary of moves toward reconciliation, which they see as a means of overlooking rather than overcoming the past. Nicole Maurantonio, for instance, criticizes the explicit collective-identity-building agenda that guides visitors' responses in the American Civil War Center in Richmond, Virginia—a museum in the Confederacy's old capital that attempts to narrate the nineteenth-century battle over states' rights and slavery from the perspectives of Unionists, Confederates, and African Americans—for asking visitors "to surrender the [individual] stakes with which they entered the museum for the sake of the collective." This, in Maurantonio's view, "compels a form of participation that translates into shallow engagement with history" (2015, 97–98), rather than an opportunity to contemplate and celebrate polyphonic narratives. Hesford, meanwhile, points out that "the post-Holocaust promise ["never again"] has been broken again and again, as the genocides in Cambodia, Rwanda, Bosnia, northern Iraq, and Darfur confirm" (2011, 52), and she argues that we must turn a critical eye on our own self-narratives. While I agree, I also think that if the nation is to implicate—and therefore rescue—itself, it needs both the division of truth and the underlying union of reconciliation. As anyone involved in a family feud can attest, breaking out of the drama triangle is rarely easy, and it requires more than critique.

In fact, two exhibits related to the *Yuyanapaq* exhibition demonstrate how hard it can be to find this balance between truth and reconciliation. The first is housed in the Museo de la Memoria de ANFASEP,[6] a private alternative memorial museum in the rural Ayacucho region of Peru set up by the relatives of those disappeared or killed in the hardest-hit region in the war. As anthropologist Joseph Feldman points out, the museum sees its purpose as "preserving the memory of the violence, commemorating the lives of the victims of the conflict," describing the work of ANFASEP, and encouraging contemplation of reasons for the war (2012)—clearly the goals of many privately funded memorial museums, where shining a light on the truth understandably outweighs the pursuit of reconciliation. The museum clearly sees the goal of national unity as secondary (at best) to the goal of documenting the state's failure to defend the people of Peru. Thus human rights violations by the army are highlighted and those by Sendero Luminoso are downplayed; "the army" becomes the outside persecutor against categorial victims in an identification by antithesis that leaves visitors with the sole option of siding with the victims against the state.

A second exhibit on the Peruvian Dirty War cast audiences into the same observer-rescuer stance while flipping persecutor, victim, and rescuer roles. Ironically, this exhibit used the same *Yuyanapaq* photos on display at the Museum of the Nation, but in quite a different scene. In 2008, forty of the original two hundred photos were displayed in the United States at the Council on Latin American and Iberian Studies at Yale University's MacMillan Center. The monthlong exhibit narrated a more one-sided history of the Dirty War (which, unlike the version in Lima, it did not refer to in its accompanying catalogue as a "dirty war" but as "unprecedented political violence"). As depicted in the exhibition catalogue, the violence in Peru was a battle between the rescuer state and the perpetrating communist insurgency, with Peruvian civilians the victims—much closer, that is, to a classic drama triangle. According to the catalogue, the violence began when "the Maoist group Shining Path declared war against the State, starting an onslaught of violence and human rights violations that affected hundreds of thousands of Peruvians" (Council on Latin American and Iberian Studies 2008). In Lima, the Museum of the Nation's exhibit, in describing the rural civil defense patrols, or *rondas campesinas*, tells visitors that the *rondas* were most effective at fighting subversion in communities where people supported the armed forces, and that when *rondas* were implemented by force or manipulated by military authorities, they were less effective—and that *rondas* also committed abuses and excesses that are being investigated today. The Yale narrative for the same images of *campesinos* and army helicopters says simply, "After the Chuppac massacre by Shining Path guerrillas . . . the community organizes itself into 'rondas campesinas,' or civil defense patrols to guard themselves with the help of the Army." The Lima exhibit shows police arresting university students (some were disappeared or assassinated), and talks about Shining Path leader Abimael Guzmán's radicalization as a concerned college professor in the impoverished Ayacucho region; the Yale exhibit shows a photo of a classroom covered in communist graffiti as it notes that Shining Path "had a presence in universities" early on, and that "in the mid-1980s the state began sending the police to intervene." When one of the photo captions in the Yale exhibit does discuss an army massacre, it emphasizes the individual nature of the persecutor and illustrates with a photo of scenery, unlike the massacres committed by the other side (always referred to universally as Shining Path and usually illustrated by funerals or close-ups of victims).

Thus, in a substantially altered narrative coupled with selective images, the message of universal responsibility that is the centerpiece of the exhibit in Lima was effectively lost in New Haven. The United States, of course, had no need to reconcile its nation around the Peruvian Dirty War, no need beyond reflexive anticommunism to ostracize Sendero Luminoso/Shining Path as the sole perpetrator of Peruvian atrocities. The United States *was*, however, deeply embroiled in its own "war on terror" in Afghanistan and Iraq in 2008, with reports of human rights abuses from detention centers like Abu Ghraib, civilian deaths, officially sanctioned torture, and other excesses that called into question any ideal of a rescuer state, let alone a "clean war." The complicated Peruvian narrative seems to have succumbed, in this context, to the simplified narrative of terrorist persecutors versus government rescuers fighting over civilian victims. That narrative is less credible in the United States today, after more than sixteen years of war, but not yet in a fundamental way that ruptures national identity—not, that is, in a way that requires the kind of complex retelling evident in Peru. The Yale exhibition catalogue, therefore, seems unintentionally ironic in its closing assertion that "this collection remains a visual legacy for Peruvian society as a whole, with an encouraging assurance: The images don't change, but the eyes that see them do." In fact, the selection and contextualization of the images certainly do change, and the change depends precisely on whose eyes are looking at them.

Rather than present a false identification of universalized victim and complacent rescuer, complicating this dyad can encourage the interplay between victim, rescuer, *and* persecutor and break old patterns of shame and blame, inspiring people to take collective action. Slogans like "giving voice to the voiceless" and "never again" in this way become more than bravado or the simple assertion that "*we* aren't like that here and now"; they become the critical contemplation of the balance between necessary (but not forced) unity and necessary (but not rupturing) division. As the 9/11 Museum designer said, memorial museums are for upholding inspirational choices and critically reflecting on other, less inspiring choices. Their goal is to help both victims and the nation get through the grieving process and to help all of us make meaning for ourselves in the present (Hennes 2011). It is precisely this physical and existential space for contemplation of ambiguous stances that I believe national museums can contribute to our world.

Conclusion: The Museum in the World

Indeed, the very "global" conditions which call for the greater identification of all men with one another have at the same time increased the range of human conflict, the incentives to division. It would require sustained rhetorical effort, backed by the imagery of a richly humane and spontaneous poetry, to make us fully sympathize with people in circumstances greatly different from our own.

—Burke 1950/1969, 34

In this book, I have demonstrated the power of museum narratives to shape meaning for national life stories across the globe. I've discussed the ways in which museums build a continuum of identification between the individual and his or her nation through their stories, their objects, and their architectural spaces. I've analyzed the various forms this national identity can take, and how particularly resonant images and encompassing terms can inspire the affective response necessary for such identification. I've looked at both exclusive and inclusive national identities, and at how museums might carefully walk the line between advocating permanence and promoting change. I've disrupted the unity of overidentification with a look at museums that raise otherwise unheeded voices and insist that identification not be easy.

What good is all this? If national museums, inside their walls, may encourage or inspire visitors to play certain roles and rethink their assumptions, may they also promote, *outside* their walls, an identification that unifies without erasing diversity? In Patrick Hogan's terms, can museum affectivity promote nationalism without external opposability? In Kenneth Burke's, can museums offer a public space that enables a dialectical identification with others that is more critically aware than the scapegoating or boosterism commonly associated with nationalism? Can they truly provide what Eunamus calls "museum diplomacy"? This question is most resonant in nations outside the relative stability of the West.

The National Museum of Iraq in Baghdad, for instance, which was reopened in April 2015 in direct response to Islamic State extremists' destruction of antiquities in Mosul, illustrates both the importance and the difficulty of realizing a museum's potential. In a *New York Times* article that is worth quoting at length, Michael Kimmelman reported:

> A time capsule with yellowing labels and cracked walls, the museum tells a story about Sumerians and Akkadians; Nebuchadnezzar; Hulagu Khan, who destroyed the city in 1258; and Tamerlane, the Mongol warlord who sacked it all over again about 150 years later.
>
> But the museum also speaks about Iraq today: its entrenched corruption, squandered fortunes and the slender thread of heritage by which the very notion of a single reunified country partly hangs.
>
> That is because heritage is intricately bound up with national identity here. . . . Baghdadis are quick to point out that, across sects and tribes, Iraqis share a lifetime of misery and death. But many also say they share a legacy, which the museum enshrines: Iraq as the seedbed of civilization, the source of writing and statehood.
>
> This makes the museum more than just another collection of artifacts, a tourist attraction without tourists. The Islamic State's rampage in Mosul, which horrified countless Iraqis, Sunnis as well as Shiites and Kurds, highlighted the point. It proved that ancient objects like the ones in the museum here still have potent symbolic, spiritual meaning.
>
> . . . Jaffar Darwesh publishes a magazine about Iraqi heritage. He talked about inspiring a new generation to feel pride and kinship because it is Iraq's last, best hope.
>
> "You can't expect Iraqis to protect museums and ancient objects in the ground when they're desperate to protect themselves," is how he put it. "But this shouldn't exempt us from caring about our past. Politics have failed to create a national identity. Religion has failed. The sects have clearly failed. So who are we? That's the question. I think history is partly the answer, it's common ground." (2015)

The Iraqi museum—which, the *Times* noted, is anachronistic, expensive, and largely unvisited—is *still* the holder of the nation's treasures and a reminder of who Iraqis have been and who they are now. It still serves as cultural glue. What would it mean if the museum were also cultural goad, a full participant in the ongoing national identity conversation—if it were, to borrow a fraught phrase, conducting nation building?

The Museum in the World

For many scholars, the notion of a national conversation, nation building, or nationalism itself is often suspect. When radical historians consider the constructed nation, writes Mark Bevir, they are drawn to a nonnational history: "Their narratives of transnational flows disperse the nation, highlighting the movement of ideas, customs, and norms across borders. Their narratives of difference fragment the nation, exhibiting some of the plural groups within it. Their narratives of discontinuity interrupt the nation, revealing ruptures and transformations through time" (2007, 317). Bevir asks whether this "denaturalised, dispersed, fragmented, and interrupted nation" can in fact be called a nation at all. Scholars of the public sphere, as well, question the legitimacy of a national public. Nancy Fraser argues that any so-called national citizenry in fact includes immigrants, dual citizens, members of indigenous groups, and noncitizens. "In all these cases, it is difficult to recognize the sort of (national) literary cultural formation seen by Habermas (and by Anderson, 1991) as underpinning the subjective stance of public sphere interlocutors," she writes. "On the contrary, insofar as public spheres require the cultural support of shared social imaginaries, rooted in national literary cultures, it is hard to see them functioning effectively today" (2007, 19)—particular as the institutions they must address are so often transnational.

I was most struck by this embrace of the transnational sphere in western Europe, where colleagues routinely equated national identity with nationalistic identity of the opposable, antithetical variety. It is certainly true that in Europe the competitive proximity among nations that led to the first national museums also led to centuries of bloodshed that has rendered nationalism particularly suspect. It is also possible that western Europe is our era's first region to fully recognize that globalization makes all nationalisms too close for competition. Perhaps the Eunamus vision of transnational "museum diplomacy" is therefore needed everywhere. What might that look like? The House of European History in Brussels, perhaps the world's first continent-wide museum, is scheduled to open in May 2017 as "a cultural institution for debate on European history," according to its sponsor, the European Parliament (2015). In its exhibits (which focus on the twentieth and twenty-first centuries), it "aims to convey a transnational overview of European history, taking into account its diverse nature and its many interpretations and perceptions," with the goal of facilitating "debate about Europe and the European integration process." Indeed, these aims are laid out clearly on the European Parliament's webpage about the museum, where the word "debate" occurs four times and "diverse/diversity" and their synonyms another fourteen. While it promises that "internationally renowned historians and museologists will guarantee the academic accuracy and relevance of the content and the story," there is probably no way to present the history of so many and such proximate nations without allowing for debate over the interpretations of that story. However, whether that debate will lead to greater European affectivity, greater feelings of identification with the ideal of "Europe," is an open question. Certainly, those involved in its construction hope so: Answering the question "why this museum?" on the website, the Parliament notes that the generation that forged the European Union out of the ruins of war is dying off, and with it the impetus for union. "Now is the time, therefore, to record their stories and memories to allow future generations to understand how and why today's Union developed as and when it did. In times of crisis, it is particularly important to articulate the crucial role of culture and heritage and to remember that peaceful cooperation is not to be taken for granted" (2015).

Though many in the European Union feel keenly the desire for transnational unity (against growing antithetical nationalism in response), history suggests that the museum may face an uphill battle, particularly as it is pulled by member nations to put greater emphasis on differences in historical interpretation than on collective identification. Conversely, some feel that the positive story of transnationalism overpowers critical voices, leaving them out of "European history." After all, scholars of nationalism such as Hogan and Anderson take as a given that national, not international, identity is the highest form of imagined community, and surveys of individuals seem to bear them out. Sociologist Tim Phillips has demonstrated how individuals simultaneously identify with multiple imagined communities but rarely with extranational ones. Asking Australians with which community they identified *first* and then *second* (their town, state/region, Australia, Asia, or the world), he found that the most common identity combination was "the local-looking nationalist," someone with affinity for nation first and then town (Phillips 2002, 606). While Phillips's point is that people are more than *only* nationalist in their identity, this "more" is rarely directed toward the world beyond national boundaries. Eunamus surveys reveal that even in Europe, where researchers might find the national-looking localist alongside Australia's local-looking nationalist, only rarely does the gaze extend beyond the nation, even after several decades of Eurocentric marketing (Bounia et al. 2012).

Beyond Europe, moreover, it is rare to see the same level of concern about national identity. In fact, national identity is often praised as an alternative to internecine battles or old internal divisions. In New Zealand, the new Kiwi is asked to be proud of her unique multicultural island nation. The changing Australian protests when his sense of national pride is too greatly undercut in the original narrative of his national museum. During my visits to Argentina and the Czech Republic, outmoded and ignored national museums were being revamped and updated to increase their relevance to the national dialogue, while China's recent multimillion-dollar renovation features a particularly heroic retelling of its modern history. In newly emerging or reconstituting nations like Uzbekistan, South Africa, and Rwanda, the self-conscious promotion of national identity is clearly a means to an end, promoting, for instance, the shared history of "Our Rwanda" at the Kigali Genocide Memorial Centre. Are these nation-aware museums "less mature," as one Western museum professional put it to me? Is our role as scholars simply to "announce the implications" of a critical museum master narrative that "remains a powerful source in shaping public memory, constructing cultural authority, and enabling public forgetting" (Mancino 2015, 266)? Or might we move outside our paradigms to search for ways in which "museum diplomacy" can take place at both the international and the intranational levels?

South African English studies scholar Duncan Brown argues that the Western liberal "retreat from nationalism into multiplicity and difference can be immensely disabling in certain contexts, such as the South African one, in which the rebuilding of society requires a common commitment" (2001, 757). Yet he readily agrees that it is not enough merely to assert that a country is a "rainbow nation" or "united in diversity"—or worse, to deny difference altogether. These overidentifications come too close to replicating the old nationalist hierarchies in a new context. At the same time, abandoning national identity for individualistic subdivisions can be equally dangerous. Brown argues for a version of identity that is "united around a shared problematic: a mutual implication in a history of difference" within interwoven communities (757). His idea is akin to the presentation of intertwining responsibilities in the Peruvian *Yuyanapaq* exhibit. Brown writes, "If we are to replace 'common national feeling' with 'common citizenship'—without of course falling back on mythology or fiction—the basis which we propose for belonging must run, in emotional, spiritual and intellectual ways, through every aspect of our society" (764). Citizenship, in other words, must be seen not as a stable, permanent noun but as an active, changing verb, fully operative only when it is *chosen* and *enacted* by all. As I have argued throughout this book, one safe place in which to explore and discuss the "shared problematic" that could lead to enacted citizenship is the national museum that displays a "mutual implication in the history of difference," or the identification/division dialectic we've been exploring. Such a museum could be more transparent than traditional national museums, less "polished" from its very conception as a public space. It would be constructed around "a history which exposes the social contexts, relations and practices through which architecture is produced; a view of the space of the museum as contradictory and encapsulating many, sometimes oppositional, values and beliefs; and an understanding of (museum) architecture as a complex and contested activity, far from the pure ideal of architecture that has dominated our thinking for so long," as Suzanne MacLeod says of her vision for museum spaces that are more communally tied, accessible, and relevant (2005b, 21–22). And that dialectical perspective on the space would carry over into planning for collections, education, and public events as well.

If the House of European History celebrates consciously chosen unity as well as rightful diversity, if it provides space to debate not only the facts of a century of entanglement but also the competing responsibilities of citizenship in both nation and transnational union, then perhaps its museum diplomacy stands a chance. Alan Gross points out that the Belgian rhetorician Chaim Perelman, writing just after the devastation of World War II, insisted that rationality did not mean winning arguments but the dialectical interaction of opposing views: "In dialectical argumentation, it is conceptions considered as generally accepted that are confronted and contrasted with each other. Because of that, the dialectical method is the method par excellence of any philosophy which realizes the social, imperfect and incomplete aspect of philosophical knowledge, instead of relying upon intuitions and self-evident truths considered as irrefragable" (quoted in Gross 2005, 18–19). Critical (including self-critical) debate among peers is a necessity of shared civil society, yet how infrequently it seems

19 | A sign in the Nordic Museum's *Sápmi* exhibit invites Stockholm visitors to reconsider their relationship to Sweden's indigenous people as they learn more about them.

to be accepted in our overly certain world, and therefore how badly we need it in the places we entrust with our public memory (see fig. 19). As Mancino concludes, "Communication scholars"—and I would expand this term to include all who study contemporary museums as sites of social glue and goad—"offer a perspective attentive to the power of museum rhetoric in the shaping of public memory and shared identities" (2015, 269).

Educational theorist Gert Biesta calls this growth into dialectical citizenship the process of people's "coming into the world" neither as templates nor as blank slates but as individuals who are allowed to grow in diversity while being subjected to ongoing communal judgment (2011, 9). He takes his inspiration from the political theorist Hannah Arendt, whose philosophy insisted on plurality in order for action to occur. "As soon as we erase plurality—as soon as we erase the otherness of others by attempting to control how they respond to our initiatives—we deprive others of their actions and their freedom, and as a result deprive *ourselves* of the possibility to act, and hence of our freedom," Biesta asserts (11). For Burke, as we have seen, this freedom to act, to engage in dialogue with others who must be persuaded of the ambiguous connection between identification and division, constitutes the "characteristic invitation to rhetoric" (1950/1969, 25). The invitation is not open-ended: Biesta envisions individuals growing in diversity *as they are subjected to ongoing communal judgment.* Any resulting national identity is therefore always in the process of moving toward a unity that recognizes that part of its identity will always include division, and therefore engagement. Rhetoricians Melanie Loehwing and Jeff Motter caution us not to overlook the dialectical democracy inherent in both rhetoric and the public sphere. In an era of counterpublic critiques, they note that Habermas's public "posits the necessity of an always negotiated and renegotiated ecology between liberalism's injunction to protect individual rights and needs and democracy's promise of self-rule and popular sovereignty" (2009, 236). This is the essence of Burke's dialectic substance, an acknowledgment of the paradox of unity and division. Without this dialectic, "the very commendable concern of counterpublic scholarship to specify strategies for fighting political exclusion may nonetheless deny a key resource in Burke's grounding of rhetoric in identification *and* division," Loehwing and Motter write (237). Belgian educators Rutten, Mottart, and Soetaert address this tension in democratic identity as they discuss how to teach about "us" when, as in Belgium, there is no longer one clear "us." They emphasize the *process* of narrating the past rather than the *product* of unchanging facts. The question "why are we telling this story in this way?" (2010, 778) allows for both the glue, the experience of one common historical version of a story, and the goad, the discussion of other possible versions. This type of critical rhetorical education teaches people to recognize how symbols shape their views of reality and encourages them, as Burke puts it, to "meditate upon the tangle of symbolism in which all men are by their nature caught" (quoted in ibid., 782).

Aesthetic *Epideixis* for Engaged Citizenship

But with all this talk of critical contemplation and respect for pluralism, I wonder whether we intellectuals, hoping to avoid the extremes of overidentification, on the one hand, and hegemonic unity, on the other, are downplaying the importance not only of a *cerebration* but of a *celebration* of the shared problematic. At the risk of oversimplification, I could say that the geopolitical world lives in division and seeks unity at the cost of hegemony, while the aesthetic world of artists, intellectuals, and humanists live in counterbalancing diversity at the cost of unified fellowship with those outside our bubble. How can we bring the two worlds closer together in citizenship? I am reminded of Greg Clark's sense that it is the experience of social democracy in civic displays that allows individuals to identify fully with their fellow citizens. The emotion that makes the slogan *Wir sind ein Volk* not only a dispassionate description of fact but a celebratory expression of unity at the Brandenburg Gate is both the danger and the power of nationalism. The challenge lies not in avoiding its affectivity but in channeling that affectivity away from simple jingoism. Sandra Dudley advocates "a gentle, twenty-first century revolution in which the object is once more at the heart of the museum, this time as a material focus of experience and opportunity, a subtle and nuanced, constructed, shifting thing, but also physical, ever-present, beating pulse of potential, quickening the institution and all that it is and could be" (2012a, 5). She argues that objects not only intertwine with their museum narratives; they also intertwine with us "because of the ability of the sensible, material characteristics of objects to trigger our particular sensory experience" (6). Debra Hawhee wrote recently that incorporating the sensorium—the "sensing package that incorporates our participation in the world"—back into rhetoric can help us to deal with the divide between individual and collective without erasing the individual. "If rhetorical theorists were to take seriously the participatory dimension of the sensorium," she notes, "we might find more specific ways to think about political feeling that does not simply stall with the emotion/affect distinction." We might then better appreciate philosopher David Hume's insight that "we feel more through the public exposure to others' emotions than through an interior circuit of sensation"—a link between what Hawhee calls emotion and being-with-others (2015, 12–13). Both of these scholars envision individual engagement with the world in not only more sensory but also more feminist, less bifurcated terms; they both, I would say, reenvision Burke's ultimate identification, the mystical union of self and world that celebrates conscious togetherness.

That identification of self and world is what inspires action, and it is what makes museums relevant in the civic space outside their doors. Museums, after all, are epideictic institutions that celebrate shared values, and their "epidictic [*sic*] oratory . . . strengthens the disposition toward action by increasing adherence to the values it lauds," note Perelman and Olbrechts-Tyteca (1969/1991, 50). "Increasing adherence" is necessary if we want people to *do* anything—first, because agreement to a proposition may conflict with other propositions that they value more highly (51), and second, because agreement is only the halfway point "between a disposition to take action and the action itself" (49). To build a nation, people must not only agree to build, and agree to build rather than do something else, but must actually roll up their sleeves and *build*—and this takes attitude, both as mental emotive reaction and as physical action or orientation.

In a place with a deep narrative of unity and potentially multiple displays of diversity in time and space, then, the museum aesthetic can encourage an identification that is not monological but dialogical, celebrating a transformed civic identity that engages with others "coming into the world." The kind of transformative vision imagined here has always been the realm of literature, the essence of the epiphany—that moment of ambiguous realization when life is seen in the dawn of a new light. The literary epiphany, what we might call the narrated epideictic space, by its nature invites its audience to entertain new perceptions and alternative viewpoints, to join in a collective identity that is not monolithic but the reverse: unified in a diversity of multitudinous epiphanies. As Sheona Thomson sees it, poetic epiphanies are critical outside the page as well:

> In conjuring up such space in imagination, the writer or poet is apparently able to delve much farther than the architect into space's poetical, mystical, and mythical substance. In imagination the unconscious residues of experience and the metaphorical potential of architecture are sounded. The writer thus transforms the physical experience of architecture into an imaginary, even fantastic one. A physical reality becomes an imaginative, literary idea. The poet (and writer) "creates imaginary figments which, in a way, are more real than the physical reality itself" [Thomson is quoting Giambattista Vico here]. . . . Our individual interpretation of space and place is endlessly dynamic and subjectively charged with our own perceptions. A writer can offer us another experience of space—another point of view, no less subjective, but outside our own, and charged with a different perception. (2004, 321–22)

Dialectical exhibits and critical debates can indeed promote engagement with multiple perspectives, but such debates have a better chance of promoting adherence if they are joined with epideictic celebrations of the values that bind those perspectives together—of the values that citizens determine *need* to bind them together for the benefit of civic life. Without dialogue, the celebration is mere propaganda; without celebration, the dialogue is mere words.

The World in the Museum

Identification and division: while Burkean scholars have argued back and forth about which is the foundational state and which the ultimate goal in Burke's philosophy, James Kastely recently presented a strong argument for both positions. "Given Burke's commitment to the human as *Homo Dialecticus*," he writes, "he cannot embrace a single term as primary and definitive for rhetoric. The logic of dialectic requires him to posit a pair of terms as foundational for rhetoric. And if the two always present and always impossible goals for rhetoric are unity and division, then the two ultimate motives for rhetoric must be love and strife, with love as the fundamental drive to unity and strife as the fundamental drive toward division" (2013, 192). The ongoing, necessary tension between these two poles explains why ambiguity rather than certainty is the clearest lens through which to examine human motives—because life itself is never fully resolved. We have seen throughout this book attempts to overcome the uneasiness that ambiguity creates: museums that have attempted to overcome division with one clear, unchallenged message. We have likewise seen attempts to overcome the hegemony of that one unchallenged message by presenting equally relevant messages "resting side by side," without the risk of confrontation. We have also seen occasional glimpses of a third way, in museums striving to live within the unresolved tension between unity and division.

They are far from perfect. But there are few public spaces outside museums where the parliamentary babel of real dialogue between engaged visionaries can be sustained by more than the privileged few. Universities face the troublesome competition of rankings and assessments that interfere with critical contemplation. The political arena is even more fraught with competitive clamor, and with the need to deliberate and decide *now*. The public square has ceded its soapbox to the individual niches of blogging communities writing to themselves. National museums are, or can be, an "idea in debate," to return to Aronsson's phrase; they are Hawhee's "sensorium" and Thomson's "space in imagination": the aesthetic space inserting itself into the existential narrative, celebrating poetic ambiguity and thus allowing people to experience the epiphanic pleasure of critical contemplation together.

This visionary contemplation of the dance of unity and diversity—this epideictic celebration of values that may not always be in harmony, and of an imagined, shared past that may have more than one interpretation—is what makes national museums such a rich resource for the world. To return to our original questions, then, what rhetoric contributes to museum studies is the recognition that symbols are always acting—and acting in particular and necessarily ambiguous ways—on their audiences, while what museum studies contributes to rhetoric is the recognition that the audience is made not of words or theories but of sensing people walking individually but collectively through carefully crafted spaces. What both disciplines recognize, and what they contribute to broader scholarship, is that inviting these people to identify with the values enacted inside that museum can have real consequences for shared life outside its doors.

Appendix: Museums Examined for This Study

Argentina
  Evita Museum
  Memory Park–Monument to the Victims of State Terrorism
  National Armaments Museum
  National Historical Museum
  Passion for Boca Juniors Museum

Australia
  Australian Museum
  National Museum of Australia
  National Pioneer Women's Hall of Fame
  Uluru-Kata Tjuta Cultural Centre

Belgium
  BELvue Museum

China
  Capital Museum
  National Museum

Czech Republic
  Museum of Communism
  National Museum

Egypt
  Museum of Egyptian Antiquities

Ethiopia
  Ethnological Museum
  National Museum of Ethiopia
  "Red Terror" Martyrs' Memorial Museum

Germany
  Bundeswehr Military History Museum
  DDR Museum
  German Historical Museum
  Jewish Museum

Greece
  National Archaeological Museum

India
  Indian Museum
  National Gandhi Museum
  National Museum

Italy
   Museum of Rome
   National Roman Museum
   Vatican Museums

Mexico
   National History Museum
   National Museum of Anthropology

The Netherlands
   Amsterdam Museum

New Zealand
   Museum of New Zealand Te Papa Tongarewa
   Museum of Wellington City and Sea

Peru
   Inca Museum
   Museum of Machu Picchu
   Museum of the Nation
   National Museum of Archaeology, Anthropology, and History
   Qorikancha Site Museum

Rwanda
   Kigali Genocide Memorial Centre

South Africa
   Apartheid Museum
   Freedom Park
   Hector Pieterson Museum
   Voortrekker Monument

Sweden
   Museum of Work
   Nordic Museum

Thailand
   Museum of Siam
   National Museum

Tunisia
   Bardo National Museum

Turkey
   Anıtkabir
   Ethnography Museum
   Istanbul Military Museum
   Museum of Anatolian Civilizations
   Panorama 1453 Historical Museum
   Topkapı Palace Museum
   Turkish and Islamic Arts Museum

United Kingdom
   British Museum
   Imperial War Museum North

Museum of London
New Walk Museum
People's History Museum
Sir John Soane's Museum

United States
National Museum of American History
National Museum of the American Indian
National Museum of the United States Air Force
National September 11 Memorial and Museum
National Underground Railroad Freedom Center
Newark Earthworks
Pioneer Woman Museum
United States Holocaust Memorial Museum
The Works: Ohio Center for History, Art, and Technology

Uzbekistan
Museum of History and Art of the Uzbek People
Museum of Memory of Victims of the Repression
State Museum of History
State Museum of Temurids History (Amir Temur Museum)

Notes

Introduction

1. Museums, exhibits, and guides are as I found them during my visits, and all photos were taken by the author.

2. Excellent examples of this gap can be seen in Izumi's 2014 rhetoric article "Museums as Our New Epic Theatre" and Soares's 2016 museology chapter (based on his 2014 paper) "Experiencing Dialogue Behind the Curtains of Museum Performance." Both pieces insightfully explore the implications of the museum as a theatrical performance that reflects its audience so as to engage it in social discourse, and both cite nearly a score of references to enhance their conversations—but there is no overlap at all between their sources.

3. I use "citizen" and "citizenship" throughout this book for want of better terms to indicate people who consider themselves members of a nation. I do not mean to imply any sense of legal status. As rhetorician Ekaterina Haskins writes, "I regard [citizenship] as a relationship among strangers that is modeled by discourses of public culture and embodied through performance" (2015, 2).

4. Communication scholars Melissa Johnson and Larissa Carneiro (2014) extend the scope of museums' representations to museum websites as well, in their analysis of identity depictions in the websites of forty-three U.S. ethnic museums.

5. Throughout this book, for simplicity's sake, I give agency to "museums" with the understanding that, of course, decisions about what and how history is presented are the product of many discussions among staff members responding to the contingencies of space, timing, personnel, funding, political pressures, audience desires, and other considerations. All of these contingencies, uniquely specific to each museum, are necessarily simplified, for this study of the rhetorical *effect* of those decisions, into the agent "the museum."

Chapter 1

The epigraph to this chapter derives from Kimmelman 2015.

1. Throughout the book, texts quoted are from the English translations provided by the museums unless otherwise noted.

Chapter 2

The epigraph to this chapter derives from Blair 2006, 57.

1. Of course, a continuation narrative not only reincorporates indigenous culture into Peruvian history; it also exonerates the Spanish, denying their culpability for any destruction. I explore this theme of deliberate reconciliation with a perpetrator further in chapter 6. Communication scholar Miranda Brady also examines museum-mediated indigenous voices in several articles, including Brady 2011.

2. Architect Mark Jarzombek (2004) has a fascinating critique of the imperfect dialectic between narrative and materiality in the rebuilding of the city of Dresden itself, arguing that the official story of the rebuilt city is about all that is new healing the trauma of all that is old, whereas the reality wants to juxtapose and overlap messily these various ruptures inherent in civic life. I discuss similar questions of rupture and healing in chapter 6.

3. David Gruber's examination of an exhibit on loan from China in the Hong Kong Museum of History (2014) comes to similar conclusions about its use of affective immersion techniques such as music and visitor participation to promote a unification narrative.

Chapter 3

The epigraphs to this chapter derive from Perelman and Olbrechts-Tyteca 1969/1991, 116–17, and Berger 1972, 9.

1. For an analysis of how visitors and objects interact in the modern science museum, see Herman 2014.

2. Communication scholar Brian Kaylor (2009) makes a similar point about how the placement and interpretation of museum objects involves a process of "decontextualizing" and "recontextualizing" meaning.

3. Head scarves had never been banned from the Anıtkabir, but they appeared to be much more common in 2012 than in 2000.

4. An August 2016 analysis, in fact, questions whether President Erdoğan isn't using the unity engendered by a failed military coup "as a chance to supplant Atatürk" in the national mythology, noting that "for years, Mr. Erdogan, an Islamist, has celebrated great moments of the Ottoman past . . . and played down Turkey's secular history established by Ataturk. With last month's failed coup, he now has his own story, and he has wasted little time propagating his own set of events and symbols to cement the narrative in the national consciousness" (Arango 2016).

Chapter 4

The epigraph to this chapter derives from Burke 1950/1969, 22.

1. Susan Pearce tells an interesting story of a similar "pious" object in a different context: the sample of moon rock on display at the National Air and Space Museum in Washington, D.C. She quotes archaeologist David J. Meltzer, who says that "it is a rather standard piece of volcanic basalt some 4 million years old. Yet, unlike many other old rocks, this one comes displayed in an altar-like structure, set in glass. . . . There is a sign above it which reads, 'You may touch it with care.' *Everyone touches it*" (Pearce 2012, 24).

2. This sense of the translated importance to the nation of an individual's decision to vote helps to explain two aspects of U.S. political life: (1) why the United States worries so much about low voter turnout and voting fraud yet refuses to mandate voting as a legal obligation—we need to be allowed (not forced) to "create" the U.S. identity if that identity is to be the one we imagine; and (2) why recent presidential campaigns' reliance on delegate counts (2016) and Supreme Court decisions (2000) rather than popular votes—a system that has always been there, albeit more invisible—seems like cheating to so many, as the actual system calls into question the collective identity invoked by individual acts of voting.

3. To counter this possible lack of action, another permanent exhibit at the Freedom Center calls explicitly for visitors to acknowledge, identify with, and then act to end modern-day slavery.

4. As is typical of Burke, his depictions of the functions of identification are scattered throughout his work. I am therefore using the three functions as summarized by Foss, Foss, and Trapp in their chapter on Burke in *Contemporary Perspectives on Rhetoric* (2002, 192–93), but modifying their "unconscious" function into what seems to me a more accurate term, "semiconscious."

Chapter 5

The epigraph to this chapter derives from Knell 2011, 26.

1. Of course, Shome and others would rightly argue that the fourth choice of nations is to declare those Others "outsiders," to exclude them physically, economically, politically, and psychically from the nation, "conceived as a deep, horizontal comradeship." Modern history is awash with examples of such a choice—but it is not a choice that museums generally make.

2. This practical division was on display in the split vote in Scotland's 2014 referendum on independence, as well as in disagreements over holding another such referendum after the UK's own identity crisis with "Brexit," the vote in 2016 to leave the European Union.

3. Such a question becomes even murkier when the two spaces are inhabited simultaneously, as with Israel and Palestine.

4. For a fine analysis of a similar exhibit, see Hubbard and Hasian 1998.

5. That the potential for Western appropriation of indigenous identity is a long-standing and global possibility is evident in Olson 2014, an examination of nineteenth-century Ecuadoran rhetorical appropriation.

Chapter 6

The epigraph to this chapter derives from Bevir 2007, 317.

1. I am grateful to my former student Miria Katelyn Waldrop for her contributions to this line of reasoning.

2. I am thankful to psychologist Joseph Horak for the genesis of this idea, with apologies for simplifying it in the application to museums.

3. Of course, many visitors to memorial museums are tourists, outsiders to the nation. As the Czech Museum of Communism notes, its dual purpose is to help Czechs avoid "distanc[ing] their thoughts from the past" and to help tourists "learn about the history of this small nation other than through a beer glass" (Čarba, Korab, and Borek 2000, 9). These tourists are outsiders to the drama triangle, and thus the museum's aim is to persuade them of the victim-persecutor dyad and encourage them to identify with a (prescribed) rescuer role. I will touch on this "outside rescuer," but mostly I am interested in how the nation speaks to *itself* through its triangulated identifications.

4. I am very grateful to Jennifer Hodbod for her photos of this museum.

5. Donofrio 2010 analyzes the controversy between designers like Hennes and 9/11 families who wanted to insist on a univocal past-centered narrative for the new museum/memorial complex and deemed any hint of polyphony too political. Paliewicz and Hasian's follow-up indicates that Hennes's intention was not fully actualized, as visitors instead focus on "melancholic commemorative acts" of loss at "this haunted place of remembrance" (2016, 142).

6. ANFASEP is the Asociación Nacional de Familiares de Secuestrados, Detenidos y Desaparecidos del Perú, or National Association of Families of the Kidnapped, Detained, and Disappeared of Peru.

References

Aden, Roger C., Min Wha Han, Stephanie Norander, Michael Pfahl, Timothy Pollack Jr., and Stephanie Young. 2009. "Re-collection: A Proposal for Refining the Study of Collective Memory and Its Places." *Communication Theory* 19:311–36.

Ahmed, Sara. 2004. *The Cultural Politics of Emotion.* New York: Routledge.

airepal. 2011. "Istanbul 1453 Panorama Museum." YouTube video, 5:22, posted July 6. http://www.youtube.com/watch?v=1fbmYIZ92Uo.

Allatsea. 2014. "South African Defence Force Wall of Remembrance: Voortrekker Monument." February 7. http://allatsea.co.za/blog/south-african-defence-force-wall-of-remembrance-voortrekker-monument/.

Anderson, Benedict. 1983. *Imagined Communities: Reflections on the Origin and Spread of Nationalism.* London: Verso.

Anderson, Margaret, and Andrew Reeves. 1994. "Contested Identities: Museums and the Nation in Australia." In *Museums and the Making of Ourselves: The Role of Objects in National Identity*, edited by Flora E. S. Kaplan, 79–124. London: Leicester University Press.

Anderson, Robert. 2003. "Introduction." In *Enlightening the British: Knowledge, Discovery, and the Museum in the Eighteenth Century*, edited by R. G. W. Anderson, M. L. Caygill, A. C. MacGregor, and L. Syson, 1–4. London: British Museum.

Aoki, Eric, Greg Dickinson, and Brian L. Ott. 2013. "Memory and the West: Reflections on Place, Practice, and Performance." *Cultural Studies—Critical Methodologies* 13 (1): 3–5.

Apartheid Museum. 2013. "Home." Accessed February 21. http://www.apartheidmuseum.org/.

Arango, Tim. 2016. "Erdogan Seizes Failed Coup in Turkey as a Chance to Supplant Ataturk." *New York Times*, August 7. http://www.nytimes.com/2016/08/08/world/europe/turkey-erdogan-coup-ataturk.html.

Aristotle. 1991. *Rhetoric.* Translated by George A. Kennedy. New York: Oxford University Press.

Armada, Bernard. 1998. "Memorial Agon: An Interpretive Tour of the National Civil Rights Museum." *Southern Communication Journal* 63:235–43.

Arnold, David. 2007. "Contesting History: The Evolution of the Australian National Museum." *Screen Education* 46:42–56.

Aronsson, Peter. 2008. "Comparing National Museums: Methodological Reflections." In *Comparing: National Museums, Territories, Nation-Building, and Change*, edited by Peter Aronsson, 5–20. Linköping: Linköping University Electronic Press.

———. 2012. Keynote address delivered at "Eunamus Final Conference: The Cultural Force of National Museums," Budapest, Hungary, December 12.

Aronsson, Peter, Arne Bugge Amundsen, and Simon Knell, eds. 2011. *National Museums: New Studies from Around the World.* London: Routledge.

Aronsson, Peter, and Simon Knell, coordinators. 2012. *European National Museums Making Histories in a Diverse Europe.* Linköping: Linköping University Electronic Press.

Attwood, Bain. 2013. "Difficult Histories: The Museum of New Zealand Te Papa Tongarewa and the Treaty of Waitangi Exhibit." *Public Historian* 35 (3): 46–71.

Atwater, Deborah F., and Sandra L. Herndon. 2003. "Cultural Space and Race: The National Civil Rights Museum and MuseumAfrica." *Howard Journal of Communications* 14 (1): 15–28.

Baines, Gary. 2009. "South Africa's Forgotten War." *History Today* 59 (4). http://www.history today.com/gary-baines/south-africa%E2%80%99s-forgotten-war.

Balthrop, William, Carole Blair, and Neil Michel. 2010. "The Presence of the Present: Hijacking 'The Good War'?" *Western Journal of Communication* 74 (2): 170–207.

Bangkok National Museum. 2012. "Dharmarājādhirāja: Righteous King of Kings." Bangkok: National Museum.

Bastéa, Eleni. 2004a. "Introduction." In Bastéa 2004b, 1–22.

———, ed. 2004b. *Memory and Architecture.* Albuquerque: University of New Mexico Press.

———. 2004c. "Storied Cities: Literary Memories of Thessaloniki and Istanbul." In Bastéa 2004b, 191–210.

Bauman, Zygmunt. 1987. *Legislators and Interpreters: On Modernity, Postmodernity, and the Intellectuals.* Oxford: Polity Press.

BBC News. 2015. "Tunis Bardo Museum: Nine Suspects Arrested for Links to Attack." March 20. http://www.bbc.com/news/world-africa-31960926.

Belova, Olga. 2012. "The Event of Seeing: A Phenomenological Perspective on Visual Sense-Making." In Dudley 2012b, 116–33.

Bennett, Gwen. 2012. "National History and Identity Narratives in China: Cultural Heritage Interpretation in Xinjiang." In *The Archaeology of Power and Politics in Eurasia: Regimes and Revolutions,* edited by Charles Hartley, Bike Yazıcıoğlu, and Adam Smith, 37–57. Cambridge: Cambridge University Press.

Berdichevsky, Hernán, and Gustavo Stecher. 2007. *Idarg: Identidad Argentina.* Buenos Aires: STF Ediciones.

Berger, John. 1972. *Ways of Seeing.* London: British Broadcasting Corporation.

Berger, Stefan. 2010. "Narrating the Nation in Modern Europe—Some Reflections on the Formation of National Master Narratives." Paper presented at the "Mapping and Framing National Museums" conference, Stockholm, Sweden, April 28.

Berger, Stefan, and Chris Lorenz, eds. 2008. *The Contested Nation: Ethnicity, Class, Religion, and Gender in National Histories.* Houndmills, Basingstoke: Palgrave Macmillan.

Berggren, Erik, and Kosta Economou. 2012. "The Political Is Collective—Factions." Norrköping: Museet för Glömska.

Bernard-Donals, Michael. 2012. "Synecdochic Memory at the United States Holocaust Memorial Museum." *College English* 74 (5): 417–36.

———. 2016. *Figures of Memory: The Rhetoric of Displacement at the United States Holocaust Memorial Museum.* Albany: State University of New York Press.

Bersuit Vergarabat. 2004. *La Argentinidad al Palo.* Universal Latino B0001WJNHS, compact disc.

Bevir, Mark. 2007. "National Histories: Prospects for Critique and Narrative." *Journal of the Philosophy of History* 1 (3): 293–317.

Biesta, Gert. 2011. "Philosophy, Exposure, and Children: How to Resist the Instrumentalisation of Philosophy in Education." *Journal of Philosophy of Education* 45 (2): 1–15.

Bilefsky, Dan. 2012. "As If the Ottoman Period Never Ended." *New York Times,* October 29. http://www.nytimes.com/2012/10/30/movies/in-turkey-ottoman-nostalgia-returns .html?_r=0.

Blair, Carole. 1999. "Contemporary US Memorial Sites as Exemplars of Rhetoric's Materiality." In *Rhetorical Bodies,* edited by Jack Selzer and Sharon Crowley, 6–57. Milwaukee: University of Wisconsin Press.

———. 2006. "Communication as Collective Memory." In *Communication as . . . Perspectives on Theory*, edited by Gregory J. Shepherd, Jeffrey St. John, and Ted Striphas, 51–59. Thousand Oaks, Calif.: Sage Publications.

Blair, Carole, Greg Dickinson, and Brian L. Ott. 2010. "Introduction." In Dickinson, Blair, and Ott 2010, 1–54.

Blair, Carole, Marsha S. Jeppeson, and Enrico Pucci Jr. 1991. "Public Memorializing in Postmodernity: The Vietnam Veterans Memorial as Prototype." *Quarterly Journal of Speech* 77 (3): 263–88.

Blair, Carole, and Neil Michel. 2001. "Designing Memories . . . of What? Reading the Landscape at the Astronauts Memorial." In *Places of Commemoration: Search for Identity and Landscape Design*, edited by Joachim Wolschke-Buhlman, 185–214. Washington, D.C.: Dumbarton Oaks.

Bodnar, John. 1992. *Remaking America: Public Memory, Commemoration, and Patriotism in the Twentieth Century*. Princeton: Princeton University Press.

Bounia, Alexandra, Niki Nikonanou, Alexandra Nikiforidou, and Ntigran Matossian. 2012. *Voices from the Museum: Survey Research in Europe's National Museums*. Linköping: Linköping University Electronic Press.

Brady, Miranda. 2011. "Mediating Indigenous Voice in the Museum: Narratives of Place, Land, and Environment in New Exhibition Practice." *Environmental Communication* 5 (2): 202–20.

British Museum. 2016. "Enlightenment (Room 1)." Accessed May 24. http://www.britishmuseum.org/visiting/galleries/themes/room_1_enlightenment/natural_world.aspx.

Brown, Duncan. 2001. "National Belonging and Cultural Difference: South Africa and the Global Imaginary." *Journal of South African Studies* 27 (4): 757–69.

Brummett, Barry. 1991. *Rhetorical Dimensions of Popular Culture*. Tuscaloosa: University of Alabama Press.

Burke, Kenneth. 1935/1984. *Permanence and Change: An Anatomy of Purpose*. 3rd rev. ed., 1984. Berkeley: University of California Press.

———. 1937/1984. *Attitudes Toward History*. 3rd rev. ed., 1984. Berkeley: University of California Press.

———. 1941/1973. *The Philosophy of Literary Form*. Berkeley: University of California Press.

———. 1943a. "The Problem of the Intrinsic." *Accent* 3:80–94.

———. 1943b. "Tactics of Motivation." *Chimera* 1 (4): 21–33.

———. 1945/1969. *A Grammar of Motives*. Berkeley: University of California Press.

———. 1950/1969. *A Rhetoric of Motives*. Berkeley: University of California Press.

———. 1953/1968. *Counter-Statement*. 2nd ed. Berkeley: University of California Press.

———. 1966. *Language as Symbolic Action*. Berkeley: University of California Press.

———. 1967. "Responsibilities of National Greatness." *Nation*, July 17, 46–50.

Busby, Karen, Adam Muller, and Andrew John Woolford. 2015. *The Idea of a Human Rights Museum*. Manitoba: University of Manitoba Press.

Caplan, Harry, trans. 1954. *Rhetorica ad Herennium*. Cambridge: Harvard University Press.

Čarba, Tomas, Alexander Korab, and David Borek. 2000. *Legacy*. Translated by Lily Cisarovska. Prague: Jana Kappelerova.

Casey, Dawn. 2002. "Battleground of Ideas and Histories." In Reed 2002, 18–27.

Clark, Gregory. 2004. *Rhetorical Landscapes in America: Variations on a Theme from Kenneth Burke*. Columbia: University of South Carolina Press.

———. 2010. "Rhetorical Experience and the National Jazz Museum in Harlem." In Dickinson, Blair, and Ott 2010, 13–35.

Commonwealth of Australia. 2003. *Review of the National Museum of Australia: Its Exhibitions and Public Programs—A Report to the Council of the National Museum of Australia*. July.

Canberra: Commonwealth of Australia. http://www.nma.gov.au/__data/assets/pdf_file/0017/2492/ReviewReport20030715.pdf.

Conn, Steven. 2000. *Museums and American Intellectual Life, 1876–1920*. Chicago: University of Chicago Press.

Council on Latin American and Iberian Studies. 2008. *Yuyanapaq: To Remember, October 15–November 16*. New Haven: Yale University MacMillan Center. Exhibition catalogue. http://www.yale.edu/macmillan/lais/YuyaExhibitBook.pdf.

Crable, Bryan. 2009. "Distance as Ultimate Motive: A Dialectical Interpretation of *A Rhetoric of Motives*." *Rhetoric Society Quarterly* 39 (3): 213–39.

Crane, Susan, ed. 2000. *Museums and Memory*. Stanford: Stanford University Press.

Dadabaev, Timur. 2010. "Power, Social Life, and Public Memory in Uzbekistan and Kyrgyzstan." *Inner Asia* 12 (1): 25–48.

Davis, Ann. 2016. "Empowering the Visitors: Process and Problems." In Davis and Smeds 2016, 89–103.

Davis, Ann, and Kerstin Smeds, eds. 2016. *Visiting the Visitor: An Enquiry into the Visitor Business in Museums*. Bielefeld: Transcript-Verlag.

Demo, Anne, and Bradford Vivian. 2012. *Rhetoric, Remembrance, and Visual Form: Sighting Memory*. New York: Routledge.

De Quincey, Thomas. 1848. "The Literature of Knowledge and the Literature of Power." *North British Review* (August). http://supervert.com/elibrary/thomas_de_quincey/the_literature_of_knowledge_and_the_literature_of_power.

Desvallées, André, and François Mairesse, eds. 2010. *Key Concepts in Museology*. Paris: Armand Colin.

Dickinson, Greg, Carole Blair, and Brian L. Ott, eds. 2010. *Places of Public Memory*. Tuscaloosa: University of Alabama Press.

Dickinson, Greg, Brian L. Ott, and Eric Aoki. 2006. "Spaces of Remembering and Forgetting: The Reverent Eye/I at the Plains Indian Museum." *Communication and Critical/Cultural Studies* 3 (1): 27–47.

Donofrio, Theresa Ann. 2010. "Ground Zero and Place-Making Authority." *Western Journal of Communications* 74 (2): 150–69.

Dudley, Sandra H. 2012a. "Encountering a Chinese Horse: Engaging with the Thingness of Things." In Dudley 2012b, 1–16.

———, ed. 2012b. *Museum Objects: Experiencing the Properties of Things*. New York: Routledge.

———. 2012c. "Preface." In Dudley 2012b, xxvii–xxix.

Egypt Independent. 2012. "Film Screening in Egyptian Museum Cancelled Due to Sudden Exorbitant Fee." July 27. http://www.egyptindependent.com/news/film-screening-egyptian-museum-cancelled-due-sudden-exorbitant-fee.

European Parliament. 2015. "House of European History." Accessed May 2. http://www.europarl.europa.eu/visiting/en/visits/historyhouse.html.

Evans, Fred, and Leonard Lawler. 2000. *Chiasms: Merleau-Ponty's Notion of Flesh*. Albany: State University of New York Press.

Falk, John. 2009. *Identity and the Museum Visitor Experience*. Walnut Creek, Calif.: Left Coast Press.

Feldman, Joseph. 2012. "Exhibiting Conflict: History and Politics at the Museo de la Memoria de ANFASEP in Ayacucho, Peru." *Anthropological Quarterly* 85 (2): 487–518.

Fivush, Robyn, and Catherine A. Haden. 2003. "Introduction: Autobiographical Memory, Narrative, and Self." In *Autobiographical Memory and the Construction of a Narrative Self: Developmental and Cultural Perspectives*, edited by Robyn Fivush and Catherine A. Haden, vii–xiii. Mahwah, N.J.: Lawrence Erlbaum.

Fleming, David. 2005. "Creative Space." In MacLeod 2005a, 53–61.

Foss, Sandra, Karen Foss, and Robert Trapp. 2002. *Contemporary Perspectives on Rhetoric*. 3rd ed. Long Grove, Ill.: Waveland Press.

Fradkin, Hillel, and Lewis Libby. 2013. "Erdogan's War on Ataturk's Legacy." Hudson Institute, June 25. http://www.hudson.org/research/9638-erdogan-s-war-on-ataturk-s-legacy.

Fraser, Nancy. 1990. "Rethinking the Public Sphere: A Contribution to the Critique of Actually Existing Democracy." *Social Text* 25–26:56–80.

———. 2007. "Transnationalizing the Public Sphere: On the Legitimacy and Efficacy of Public Opinion in a Post-Westphalian World." *Theory, Culture, and Society* 24 (4): 7–30.

Freedom Park. 2014. "About Us." Accessed May 19. http://www.freedompark.co.za/about-us/overview.

Freud, Sigmund. 1955. "Group Psychology and the Analysis of the Ego." In *The Standard Edition of the Complete Psychological Works of Sigmund Freud*, edited by James Strachey, 18:69–92. London: Hogarth Press.

Fried, Amy. 2006. "The Personalization of Collective Memory: The Smithsonian's September 11 Exhibit." *Political Communication* 23 (4): 387–405.

Frykman, Sue Glover. 2009. "Stories to Tell? Narrative Tools in Museum Education Texts." *Educational Research* 51 (3): 299–319.

Geisbusch, Jan. 2012. "For Your Eyes Only? The Magic Touch of Relics." In Dudley 2012b, 202–13.

George, Ann, Elizabeth Weiser, and Janet Zepernick. 2013. "Introduction." In *Women and Rhetoric Between the Wars*, edited by Ann George, Elizabeth Weiser, and Janet Zepernick, 1–17. Carbondale: Southern Illinois University Press.

Golding, Viv. 2012. *Learning at the Museum Frontiers: Identity, Race, and Power*. London: Routledge.

Governmental Portal of the Republic of Uzbekistan. 2011. "Temurids History Museum Marks 15 Years." October 19. Accessed January 15, 2013. https://www.gov.uz/en.

Greenberg, Stephen. 2005. "The Vital Museum." In MacLeod 2005a, 226–37.

Greenblatt, Alan. 2009. "Rewriting History: Can Nations Come to Terms with Their Own Legacies?" *CQ Global Researcher* 3 (12): 311–36.

Gross, Alan G. 2005. "Presence as Argument in the Public Sphere." *Rhetoric Society Quarterly* 35 (2): 5–21.

Gruber, David R. 2014. "The (Digital) Majesty of All Under Heaven: Affective Constitutive Rhetoric at the Hong Kong Museum of History's Multi-Media Exhibition of Terracotta Warriors." *Rhetoric Society Quarterly* 44 (2): 148–67.

Gurian, Elaine Heumann. 2005. "Threshold Fear." In MacLeod 2005a, 203–14.

———. 2006. "Choosing Among the Options: An Opinion About Museum Definitions." In *Civilizing the Museum: The Collected Writings of Elaine Heumann Gurian*, 48–56. New York: Routledge.

Harris, Jennifer. 2016. "Affect-Based Exhibition." In Davis and Smeds 2016, 15–38.

Hasian, Marouf A., Jr. 2004. "Remembering and Forgetting the 'Final Solution': A Rhetorical Pilgrimage Through the U.S. Holocaust Memorial Museum." *Critical Studies in Media Communication* 21 (1): 64–92.

Haskins, Ekaterina. 2015. *Popular Memories: Commemoration, Participatory Culture, and Democratic Citizenship*. Columbia: University of South Carolina Press.

Hauser, Gerard. 1999a. "Aristotle on Epideictic: The Formation of Public Morality." *Rhetoric Society Quarterly* 29 (1): 5–23.

————. 1999b. *Vernacular Voices: The Rhetoric of Publics and Public Spheres.* Columbia: University of South Carolina Press.

Hawhee, Debra. 2006. "Rhetorics, Bodies, and Everyday Life." *Rhetoric Society Quarterly* 36 (2): 155–64.

————. 2009. *Moving Bodies: Kenneth Burke at the Edges of Language.* Columbia: University of South Carolina Press.

————. 2015. "Rhetoric's Sensorium." *Quarterly Journal of Speech* 101 (1): 2–17.

Hawhee, Debra, and Bradford Vivian. 2009. "Review Essay: On the Language of Forgetting." *Quarterly Journal of Speech* 95 (1): 89–104.

Hearn, Jonathan. 2002. "Narrative, Agency, and Mood: On the Social Construction of National History in Scotland." *Society for Comparative Study of Society and History* 2:745–69.

Hennes, Tom. 2011. Plenary speech delivered at the International Conference on the Inclusive Museum, Johannesburg, South Africa, July 1.

Herman, Jennifer Linda. 2014. "Effecting Science in Affective Places: The Rhetoric of Science in American Science and Technology Centers." Ph.D. diss., Ohio State University.

Herzog, Marc. 2012. *Anit Kabir—Battleground over the Nation.* FPC Briefing. London: Foreign Policy Centre.

Hesford, Wendy. 2011. *Spectacular Rhetorics: Human Rights Visions, Recognitions, Feminisms.* Durham: Duke University Press.

Hogan, Patrick Colm. 2009. *Understanding Nationalism: On Narrative, Cognitive Science, and Identity.* Columbus: Ohio State University Press.

Hooper-Greenhill, Eilean. 1992. *Museums and the Shaping of Knowledge.* London: Routledge.

Hubbard, Bryan, and Marouf A. Hasian Jr. 1998. "Atomic Memories of the Enola Gay: Strategies of Remembrance at the National Air and Space Museum." *Rhetoric and Public Affairs* 1 (3): 363–85.

Huetteman, Emmarie. 2014. "House Approves Panel to Study Building Women's Museum." *New York Times,* May 7. http://www.nytimes.com/2014/05/08/us/politics/house-approves-panel-to-study-building-womens-museum.html.

Hume, Janice. 2010. "Memory Matters: The Evolution of Scholarship in Collective Memory and Mass Communication." *Review of Communication* 10 (3): 181–96.

Imperial War Museum North. 2013. "About IWM North." Accessed April 25. http://www.iwm.org.uk/visits/iwm-north/about.

Izumi, Mariko. 2014. "Museums as Our New Epic Theatre." *Poroi* 10 (2). http://dx.doi.org/10.13008/2151-2957.1200.

Jarzombek, Mark. 2004. "Disguised Visibilities." In Bastéa 2004b, 49–78.

Jencks, Charles. 2002. "Constructing a National Identity." In Reed 2002, 58–75.

Joffe, Alex. 2011. "Egypt's Antiquities Fall Victim to the Mob." *Wall Street Journal,* February 1. http://www.wsj.com/articles/SB10001424052748703833204576114580200904212.

Johnson, Ian. 2011. "At China's New Museum, History Toes Party Line." *New York Times,* April 3. http://www.nytimes.com/2011/04/04/world/asia/04museum.html.

Johnson, Melissa A., and Larissa Carneiro. 2014. "Communicating Visual Identities on Ethnic Museum Websites." *Visual Communication* 13 (3): 357–72.

Kaplan, Flora E. S. 1994. "Introduction." In *Museums and the Making of Ourselves: The Role of Objects in National Identity,* edited by Flora E. S. Kaplan, 1–15. London: Leicester University Press.

Karpman, Stephen. 1968. "Fairy Tales and Script Drama Analysis." *Transactional Analysis Bulletin* 7 (26): 39–43.

Kastely, James. 2013. "Love and Strife: Ultimate Motives in Burke's *A Rhetoric of Motives*." *Rhetorica* 31 (2): 172–98.

Kaylor, Brian T. 2009. "The Holy Land Experience: Proposing a Typology for Studying Museum Communication." *Florida Communication Journal* 37 (2): 11–22.

Keith, Michael. 2010. *Te Papa: Your Essential Guide*. Wellington: Te Papa Press.

Kelly, Casey Ryan, and Kristen E. Hoerl. 2012. "Genesis in Hyperreality: Legitimizing Disingenuous Controversy at the Creation Museum." *Argumentation and Advocacy* 48 (3): 123–41.

Kendrick, Kathleen, and Peter Liebhold. 2006. *Smithsonian Treasures of American History*. Washington, D.C.: Smithsonian Institution.

Kimmelman, Michael. 2011. "'Cultural Revolt' over Sarkozy's Museum Plans." *New York Times*, March 8. http://www.nytimes.com/2011/03/09/arts/design/sarkozy-wants-his-history-museum-in-paris.html.

———. 2015. "A Struggle to Secure Iraq's Shared Past, and Perhaps Its Future." *New York Times*, April 9. http://www.nytimes.com/2015/04/10/world/middleeast/a-struggle-to-secure-iraqs-shared-past-and-perhaps-its-future.html.

Klumpp, James. 2010. Review of *Moving Bodies: Kenneth Burke at the Edges of Language*, by Debra Hawhee. *Quarterly Journal of Speech* 96 (4): 469–72.

Knell, Simon J. 2011. "National Museums and the National Imagination." In Aronsson, Amundsen, and Knell 2011, 3–28.

———. 2012. "The Intangibility of Things." In Dudley 2012b, 324–35.

Knell, Simon J., Bodil Axelsson, Lill Eilertsen, and Eleni Myrivili. 2012. *Crossing Borders: Connecting European Identities in Museums and Online*. Linköping: Linköping University Electronic Press.

Landsberg, Alison. 2004. *Prosthetic Memory: The Transformation of American Remembrance in the Age of Mass Culture*. New York: Columbia University Press.

Levin, Amy K. 2007. *Defining Memory: Local Museums and the Construction of History in America's Changing Communities*. Lanham, Md.: AltaMira Press.

Loehwing, Melanie, and Jeff Motter. 2009. "Publics, Counterpublics, and the Promise of Democracy." *Philosophy and Rhetoric* 42 (3): 220–41.

Lynch, John. 2013. "'Prepare to Believe': The Creation Museum as Embodied Conversion Narrative." *Rhetoric and Public Affairs* 16 (1): 1–27.

Macdonald, Sharon J. 2003. "Museums, National, Postnational, and Transcultural Identities." *Museum and Society* 1:1–16.

MacFarquhar, Neil, and Sophia Kishkovsky. 2015. "Russian History Receives a Makeover That Starts with Ivan the Terrible." *New York Times*, March 30. http://www.nytimes.com/2015/03/31/world/europe/russian-museum-seeks-a-warmer-adjective-for-ivan-the-terrible.html.

MacLeod, Suzanne, ed. 2005a. *Reshaping Museum Space: Architecture, Design, Exhibitions*. New York: Routledge.

———. 2005b. "Rethinking Museum Architecture: Towards a Site-Specific History of Production and Use." In MacLeod 2005a, 9–25.

Mancino, Susan. 2015. "A Communicative Review of Museums." *Review of Communication* 15 (3): 258–73.

Mason, Rhiannon, Christopher Whitehead, and Helen Graham. 2013. "One Voice to Many Voices? Displaying Polyvocality in an Art Gallery." In *Museums and Communities: Curators, Collections, and Collaboration*, edited by Viv Golding and Wayne Modest, 163–77. London: Bloomsbury Academic.

Maurantonio, Nicole. 2015. "Material Rhetoric, Public Memory, and the Post-It Note." *Southern Communication Journal* 80 (2): 83–101.

McAdams, Dan P. 2003. "Identity and the Life Story." In *Autobiographical Memory and the Construction of a Narrative Self: Developmental and Cultural Perspectives,* edited by Robyn Fivush and Catherine A. Haden, 187–207. Mahwah, N.J.: Lawrence Erlbaum.

Memory Park–Monument to the Victims of State Terrorism. 2014. "A Project to Not Forget." [In Spanish.] Accessed May 19. http://www.parquedelamemoria.org.ar/.

Miller, Carolyn. 1984. "Genre as Social Action." *Quarterly Journal of Speech* 70 (2): 151–67.

Miller, Robert. 2012. *The Development of European Identity/European Identities: Policy and Research Issues.* Brussels: European Commission.

Moeller, Robert. 2006. "On the History of Man-Made Destruction: Loss, Death, Memory, and Germany in the Bombing War." *History Workshop Journal* 61:103–34.

Msimang, Sisonke. 2015. "The End of the Rainbow Nation Myth." *New York Times,* April 12. http://www.nytimes.com/2015/04/13/opinion/the-end-of-the-rainbow-nation-myth.html.

Museet för Glömska. 2017. "About the Museum of Forgetting." Accessed March 15. http://www.museetforglomska.se/About-The-Museum-of-Forgetting.

Museum of Communism. 2013. "About the Museum." Accessed February 25. http://muzeumkomunismu.cz/.

Museum of London. N.d. *Museum of London.* London: Museum of London.

Museum of New Zealand Te Papa Tongarewa. 2016. *Te Pūrongo ā Tau Annual Report.* Wellington: Te Papa Press.

———. N.d. *Te Papa Explorer.* Wellington: Te Papa Press.

National Museum of Anthropology. 2013a. "Pasado y Presente." Accessed April 2. http://www.mna.inah.gob.mx.

———. 2013b. "Salas de Arqueología." Accessed April 2. http://www.mna.inah.gob.mx.

National Museum of Australia. 2001. *Yesterday Tomorrow: The National Museum of Australia.* Canberra: National Museum of Australia Press.

———. 2004. *Land, Nation, People: Stories from the National Museum of Australia.* Canberra: National Museum of Australia Press.

———. 2013. "About Landmarks." Accessed June 3. http://www.nma.gov.au/exhibitions/landmarks/about_landmarks.

National September 11 Memorial and Museum. 2014a. "Memorial." Accessed June 15. https://www.911memorial.org/memorial.

———. 2014b. "Museum." Accessed June 15. https://www.911memorial.org/museum.

Nora, Pierre. 1996. *Realms of Memory: Rethinking the French Past.* Vol. 1, *Conflicts and Divisions.* Translated by Arthur Goldhammer. New York: Columbia University Press.

Novick, Peter. 1999. *The Holocaust in American Life.* Boston: Houghton Mifflin.

Noy, Chaim. 2015. "Writing in Museums: Toward a Rhetoric of Participation." *Written Communication* 32 (2): 195–219.

Obermark, Lauren. 2013. "Revising Rhetorical Education: Museums and Pedagogy." Ph.D. diss., Ohio State University.

Oechsner, Mathilde. 2015. "The Belvue Museum Gets a Youthful Makeover." Press release, BELvue Museum, Brussels, February 24. http://www.belvue.be/sites/default/files/press-file/pdf/20150224-belvue2016-press_release_0.pdf.

Olson, Christa. 2014. *Constitutive Visions: Indigeneity and Commonplaces of National Identity in Republican Ecuador.* University Park: Pennsylvania State University Press.

Ott, Brian L., Eric Aoki, and Greg Dickinson. 2011. "Ways of (Not) Seeing Guns: Presence and Absence at the Cody Firearms Museum." *Communication and Critical/Cultural Studies* 8 (3): 215–39.

Paliewicz, Nicholas S., and Marouf A. Hasian Jr. 2016. "Mourning Absences, Melancholic Commemoration, and the Contested Public Memories of the National September 11 Memorial and Museum." *Western Journal of Communication* 80 (2): 140–62.

Parks Australia. 2016. "Uluṟu-Kata Tjuṯa Cultural Centre." Accessed February 7. http://www.parksaustralia.gov.au/uluru/do/cultural-centre.html.

Pearce, Susan M. 2012. "Museum Objects." In Dudley 2012b, 23–25.

Penuel, William R., and James V. Wertsch. 1995. "Vygotsky and Identity Formation: A Socio-cultural Approach." *Educational Psychology* 30 (2): 83–92.

People's History Museum. 2013. "Main Galleries." Accessed April 1. http://www.phm.org.uk/whats-on/main-galleries/.

Perelman, Chaim, and Lucie Olbrechts-Tyteca. 1969/1991. *The New Rhetoric: A Treatise on Argumentation.* Notre Dame: University of Notre Dame Press.

Phelan, James. 2006. "Narrative Theory, 1966–2006: A Narrative." In *The Nature of Narrative,* edited by James Phelan, Robert Kellogg, and Robert Scholes, 283–336. New York: Oxford University Press.

Phillips, Kendall R. 2010. "The Failure of Memory: Reflections on Rhetoric and Public Remembrance." *Western Journal of Communication* 74 (2): 208–23.

Phillips, Kendall R., and G. Mitchell Reyes, eds. 2011. *Global Memoryscapes: Contesting Remembrance in a Transnational Age.* Tuscaloosa: University of Alabama Press.

Phillips, Tim. 2002. "Imagined Communities and Self-Identity: An Exploratory Quantitative Analysis." *Sociology* 36 (3): 597–617.

Poirot, Kristan, and Shevaun E. Watson. 2015. "Memories of Freedom and White Resilience: Place, Tourism, and Urban Slavery." *Rhetoric Society Quarterly* 45 (2): 91–116.

Poulot, Dominique. 2012. "Preface: Uses of the Past—Historical Narratives and the Museum." In *Great Narratives of the Past: Traditions and Revisions in National Muse-ums,* edited by Dominique Poulot, Felicity Bodenstein, and José María Lanzarote, 1–8. Linköping: Linköping University Electronic Press.

Preziosi, Donald. 2011. "Myths of Nationality." In Aronsson, Amundsen, and Knell 2011, 55–66.

Psarra, Sophia. 2005. "Spatial Culture, Way-Finding, and the Educational Message." In MacLeod 2005a, 78–94.

Raposo, Luís. 2012. Response delivered at "Eunamus Final Conference: The Cultural Force of National Museums," Budapest, Hungary, December 12.

Ratcliffe, Krista. 2005. *Rhetorical Listening: Identification, Gender, Whiteness.* Carbondale: Southern Illinois University Press.

Reed, Dimity, ed. 2002. *Tangled Destinies: National Museum of Australia.* Victoria: Images Publishing Group.

Reeves, Joshua. 2013. "Suspended Identification: Atopos and the Work of Public Memory." *Philosophy and Rhetoric* 46 (3): 306–27.

Renan, Ernst. 1882/1992. "What Is a Nation?" Translated by Ethan Rundell. Paris: Presses-Pocket. http://ucparis.fr/files/9313/6549/9943/What_is_a_Nation.pdf.

Reyes, G. Mitchell. 2010. "Memory and Alterity: The Case for an Analytic of Difference." *Philosophy and Rhetoric* 43 (3): 222–52.

Roberts, Lisa C. 1997. *From Knowledge to Narrative: Educators and the Changing Museum.* Washington, D.C.: Smithsonian Institution Press.

Ross, Max. 2004. "Interpreting the New Museology." *Museum and Society* 2 (2): 84–103.

Rounds, Jay. 2006. "Doing Identity Work in Museums." *Curator* 49 (2): 133–50.

Rowe, Shawn, James Wertsch, and Tatyana Kosyaeva. 2002. "Linking Little Narratives to Big Ones: Narrative and Public Memory in History Museums." *Culture and Psychology* 8 (1): 96–112.

Rutten, Kris, André Mottart, and Ronald Soetaert. 2010. "The Rhetorical Construction of the Nation in Education: The Case of Flanders." *Journal of Curriculum Studies* 42 (6): 775–90.

Sadiki, Larbi. 2015. "A Turning Point in Tunisia." *Al Jazeera*, March 19. http://www.aljazeera.com/indepth/opinion/2015/03/museum-attack-tunisia-150319055014149.html.

Sandell, Richard. 2005. "Constructing and Communicating Equality: The Social Agency of Museums." In MacLeod 2005a, 185–200.

Sandweiss, Eric. 2004. "Framing Urban Memory." In Bastéa 2004b, 25–47.

Schudson, Michael. 1995. "Dynamics of Distortion in Collective Memory." In *Memory Distortion: How Minds, Brains, and Societies Reconstruct the Past*, edited by D. L. Schacter, 346–64. Cambridge: Harvard University Press.

Schwartz, Barry. 1991. "Social Change and Collective Memory: The Democratization of George Washington." *American Sociological Review* 56:221–36.

Scott, David W. 2014. "Dinosaurs on Noah's Ark? Multi-Media Narratives and Natural Science Museum Discourse at the Creation Museum in Kentucky." *Journal of Media and Religion* 13 (4): 226–43.

Sheard, Cynthia Miecznikowski. 1996. "The Public Value of Epideictic Rhetoric." *College English* 58 (7): 765–94.

Shome, Raka. 2003. "Space Matters: The Power and Practice of Space." *Communication Theory* 13 (1): 39–56.

Siegel, Jonah, ed. 2008. *The Emergence of the Modern Museum: An Anthology of Nineteenth-Century Sources*. Oxford: Oxford University Press.

Smith, Anthony D. 1995. "Gastronomy or Geology? The Role of Nationalism in the Reconstruction of Nations." *Nations and Nationalism* 1 (1): 3–23.

Smithsonian Institution. 2012. "(Re)Presenting America: The Evolution of Culturally Specific Museums." Smithsonian Institution special symposium, Washington, D.C., April 25. http://nmai.si.edu/sites/1/files/pdf/seminars-symposia/(Re)PresentingAmerica_Program.pdf.

Smithsonian National Museum of African American History and Culture. 2017. "About the Museum." Accessed March 15. http://nmaahc.si.edu/about.

Smithsonian National Museum of American History. 2008. *The Star-Spangled Banner: A National Treasure*. Washington, D.C.: Smithsonian: National Museum of American History. Exhibition catalogue.

———. 2013a. "The Flag in the Sixties." Accessed December 31. http://amhistory.si.edu/starspangledbanner/the-flag-in-the-sixties.aspx.

———. 2013b. "Symbols of a New Nation." Accessed July 17. http://amhistory.si.edu/starspangledbanner/symbols-of-a-new-nation.aspx.

Smithsonian National Museum of the American Indian. 2017. "About the Museum." Accessed March 16. http://www.nmai.si.edu/about/.

Soares, Bruno Brulon. 2016. "Experiencing Dialogue Behind the Curtains of Museum Performance." In Davis and Smeds 2016, 127–38.

Steves, Rick. 2014. *Rick Steves' Great Britain*. Berkeley: Avalon Travel.

Story, Inc. and Pico Thailand. 2013. "Museum of Siam." Accessed April 24. http://www.museumofsiamproject.com.

Studio Libeskind. 2014. "Military History Museum." Accessed June 10. http://libeskind.com/work/military-history-museum/.

Sturken, Marita. 1997. *Tangled Memories: The Vietnam War, the AIDS Epidemic, and the Politics of Remembering*. Berkeley: University of California Press.

Thomson, Sheona. 2004. "Places Within and Without: Memory, the Literary Imagination, and the Project in the Design Studio." In Bastéa 2004b, 317–29.

Trustees of the British Museum. 2012. *The Parthenon Sculptures*. London: British Museum. Exhibition catalogue.

U.S. Holocaust Memorial Museum. 2013. "About the Museum." Accessed February 21. https://www.ushmm.org/information/about-the-museum.

van Hasselt, Gwenny. 2011. "The Dutch National Historical Museum: A Museum for the Twenty-First Century." In Aronsson, Amundsen, and Knell 2011, 313–24.

Vivian, Bradford. 2010. *Public Forgetting: The Rhetoric and Politics of Beginning Again*. University Park: Pennsylvania State University Press.

Volkert, James, Linda Martin, and Amy Pickworth. 2004. *National Museum of the American Indian Map and Guide*. Washington, D.C.: Smithsonian Institution.

Walker, Jeffrey. 2000. *Rhetoric and Poetics in Antiquity*. New York: Oxford University Press.

Watson, Sheila. 2012. "Museums and the Origins of Nations." In *Great Narratives of the Past: Traditions and Revisions in National Museums*, edited by Dominique Poulot, Felicity Bodenstein, and José María Lanzarote, 545–65. Linköping: Linköping University Electronic Press.

Weiser, M. Elizabeth. 2008. *Burke, War, Words: Rhetoricizing Dramatism*. Columbia: University of South Carolina Press.

———. 2009. "Who Are We? Museums Telling the Nation's Story." *International Journal of the Inclusive Museum* 2 (2): 29–38.

———. 2012. "Past as Future: Narrative Identities in Communal History Museums." *International Journal of the Inclusive Museum* 4:73–84.

Wertsch, James V. 2009. "Collective Remembering." *Semiotica* 1 (4): 233–47.

Wittlin, Alma Stephanie. 1949. *The Museum: Its History and Its Tasks in Education*. London: Routledge.

Wyatt, Jean. 2012. *Risking Difference: Identification, Race, and Community in Contemporary Fiction and Feminism*. Albany: State University of New York Press.

Yates, Frances A. 1966. *The Art of Memory*. Chicago: University of Chicago Press.

Zagacki, Kenneth, and Victoria Gallagher. 2009. "Rhetoric and Materiality in the Museum Park at the North Carolina Museum of Art." *Quarterly Journal of Speech* 95 (2): 171–91.

Index

Page numbers in *italics* refer to illustrations.